The Happy Lawyer

NANCY LEVIT & DOUGLAS O. LINDER

The Happy Lawyer

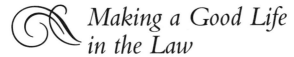 *Making a Good Life in the Law*

OXFORD
UNIVERSITY PRESS

2010

OXFORD
UNIVERSITY PRESS

Oxford University Press, Inc., publishes works that further
Oxford University's objective of excellence
in research, scholarship, and education.

Oxford   New York
Auckland   Cape Town   Dar es Salaam   Hong Kong   Karachi
Kuala Lumpur   Madrid   Melbourne   Mexico City   Nairobi
New Delhi   Shanghai   Taipei   Toronto

With offices in
Argentina   Austria   Brazil   Chile   Czech Republic   France   Greece
Guatemala   Hungary   Italy   Japan   Poland   Portugal   Singapore
South Korea   Switzerland   Thailand   Turkey   Ukraine   Vietnam

Published by Oxford University Press, Inc.
198 Madison Avenue, New York, New York 10016

www.oup.com

Oxford is a registered trademark of Oxford University Press

Library of Congress Cataloging-in-Publication Data
Levit, Nancy.
The happy lawyer : making a good life in the law / Nancy Levit
and Douglas O. Linder.
p. cm.
Includes bibliographical references and index.
ISBN 978-0-19-539232-6
1. Practice of law—United States—Psychological aspects.
2. Lawyers—Job satisfaction—United States.   I. Linder, Douglas O., 1951–
II. Title.
KF300.L485 2010
340.023'73—dc22   2009047527

9 8 7 6 5 4 3 2 1

Printed in the United States of America
on acid-free paper

For Tim, Dylan, and Aaron
NEL

For Cheryl, Kari, and Ann
DOL

The logic of the rebel is to want to serve justice so as not to add to the injustice of the human condition, to insist on plain language so as not to increase the universal falsehood, and to wager, in spite of human misery, for happiness.

—Albert Camus

Contents

Foreword

WE LIVE IN A NATION FOUNDED BY LAWYERS. THIRTY-four of the fifty-five men who gathered in Philadelphia in 1787 to draft our Constitution were lawyers, including the document's principal architect, James Madison. Lawyer Thomas Jefferson authored the Declaration of Independence (with the help of John Adams, another lawyer).

Among the inalienable rights Jefferson listed in his famous document of 1776, along with the rights to life and to liberty, was the right "to the pursuit of Happiness." "Happiness" is not a word you expect to find in a formal document drafted and debated by sober eighteenth-century politicians. But there it is on parchment, one of the three most important rights of a free people.

Of course, Jefferson couldn't promise we would find happiness, only that we had a right to pursue it. And pursue it we have, and still do—with ever more intensity—today. A quick Google search or perusal of the self-help section at your local bookstore will reveal the depth of our current interest in happiness. A whole movement in modern psychology called "positive psychology" has sprung up to help improve our odds of finding a greater measure of happiness.

For all our efforts, Americans are no happier today than we were a half century ago—and, by most measures, we're less happy. We're richer than ever before, have more leisure time, and are awash in happiness literature, but we still cannot seem to get more satisfaction.

For lawyers, the picture is even bleaker. Many lawyers, as many as 70 percent in one poll, say they would not choose a legal career if they had to do it all over again.[1] Half of all lawyers would discourage their kids from becoming lawyers.[2] Over one-third of big firm associates leave their firms within three years of being hired.[3] Students at Stanford Law School, dissatisfied with the nature of large firm practice, have launched a movement to change the way law is practiced.

It is an exaggeration, however, to describe law as a profession in crisis. We do not see headlines announcing: "Lawyers leaving profession in droves." The number of law school applicants remains consistent, and the number of law schools is increasing. Despite the odd story of a lawyer leaving practice to start a vineyard or become a hot air balloonist, most in the practice say they intend to stick it out. Moreover, many say they are at least reasonably happy, even while admitting they'd like to be more so.

The story of the emotional state of American lawyers today is complicated and nuanced. Lawyers are smart people; they expect complications and appreciate nuance. If lawyers are not as happy as they'd like to be, there are many possible explanations for that. People generally don't become lawyers because they wake up one day and say, "By God, I love the law!" They might become lawyers because as college seniors they simply wanted to keep their options open and law school seemed a better place to do that than, say, dental school. Moreover, it might well be that the sort of person best suited to the practice of law is more likely to have a personality type somewhat prone to unhappiness. In law, unlike in many other fields, it often helps to be an anxious, pessimistic person who worries about all the things that can go wrong if, for example, a contract isn't written just so. If lawyers are slightly unhappier than the typical American, it may be because unhappy people are more likely to become lawyers rather than that the practice of law has made them unhappy.

Sorting out this complex story is one of the goals of this book. But we don't stop there. While recognizing the limits of self-help, we offer "a happiness toolbox" that we believe can lead to happiness boosts for lawyers who follow our suggestions. There are multiple paths to happiness, and a tool that works well for you might not for the lawyer in the next-door office. We also will offer tips for law firms and law schools that wish to improve levels of satisfaction among their ranks. Along the way, we'll share stories of both unhappy lawyers and happy lawyers, learning what we can from the insights they've garnered along their diverse professional trails.

Now seems like the right time for a book about finding satisfaction in a law career. The past couple of decades have produced a torrent of research on happiness from the fields of neuroscience and positive psychology. Some of the research results suggest happiness boosts that are largely to be found outside the office, through activities ranging from playing tennis to meditating to eating chocolate. But many other of these research findings have important implications for the way law is practiced, if happiness really matters to lawyers—and it obviously does. Perhaps more critically, such research also contributes to the better design of happiness strategies: we know, for example, that liking and trusting your co-workers contributes more to your long run satisfaction than snagging the corner office or a six-figure bonus.

In addition to the explosion of research on happiness, the practice of law has changed in a way that makes career satisfaction much more relevant to law schools than used to be the case. Law schools that previously told entering students, "Look to your left and look to your right; one of the three of you won't be here at the end of the year" now realize they have a stake in convincing prospective students that they can best help them achieve that satisfying law career they're looking for—happy alumni are more likely to be generous and supportive alumni. This generation of students, more than any previous generation, ranks life satisfaction highest among their goals. Schools that can credibly promise a better shot at career happiness are in a better position to recruit the best and brightest students.

Law firms also have a growing interest in making associates happy. The old system that welcomed many to the firm but retained few of them (the "up or out" system) has given way to a process that places a premium on careful selection and retention. Firms have come to recognize the high costs of associate attrition. They now understand that demoralization among associates affects the quality of their work product as well as the law firms' bottom line. There is a growing consensus that trends adversely affecting happiness—such as ever-increasing billable hour requirements and declining civility in the profession—no longer can be ignored if firms hope to continue to attract the members of a new generation that places personal happiness on the top of life's wish list. Moreover, many older lawyers are coming to the same conclusion as a lot of newer ones: "If I'm not happy doing what I'm doing, what's the point?"

In short, lawyers, law schools, and law firms have a greater interest than ever in happiness. In the pages to come, we will provide tips and techniques, shaped by the new research, for all who have an interest in increasing satisfaction with the practice of law.

Of course, as wise people have told us, happiness isn't everything. It's a very important thing, but so are other values that matter. There is even something to be said for melancholy—and we will say it. Without unhappiness from time to time, would happiness lose its meaning? Would society lose an important source of creative inspiration, and would we lose a springboard to personal growth? We'll explore those questions.

Mainly, though, this is a book about forging a path to a better life for law students and lawyers. We cannot offer any promises—lawyers, of all people, should understand that—but it is our hope that the words that follow will help make your life as a lawyer more satisfying, fulfilling, and, well, happy.

The Happy Lawyer

CHAPTER I

Are Lawyers Unhappy?

Lawyers have never made more money and never been so unhappy.
—Cordell Parvin, "Career Happiness," September 24, 2008

ARE WE HAPPY BEING LAWYERS? BEING LAWYERS, WE tend to answer that question with other questions: What do you mean by "happy"? On a scale that runs from having root canals to a night of fine wines and sex on a tropical island, where does "unhappiness" turn into "happiness"? Do you mean "happy" right now as I write footnote 17 on this brief for Acme Investments or "happy" during the course of my ten-year legal career? If I'm happy one-quarter of the time, miserable one-quarter of the time, and somewhere in between half the time, how do I answer your question? Also, is anyone else going to know the answer that I give you?—because if they do I'm going to inflate my happiness quotient.

Those are all good questions and just the sort that bedevil happiness researchers. The fact is that happiness to one person might not mean the same thing as happiness to another person, yet that doesn't stop researchers from asking people whether or not they are happy. Nor are researchers stymied by the fact that happiness, when it happens, is a temporary state and your two-o'clock giggles might turn into three-o'clock tears. And then there is the "Lake Wobegon problem"—just like the children in the mythical Minnesota town, nearly everyone—in just about every category that matters (including happiness)—considers themselves above average. *Well* above average. When a researcher synthesized 916 surveys on happiness, conducted in forty-five countries and including more than one million respondents, he found that people, on average, ranked their own happiness as about a seven on a one-to-ten scale.[1] A reviewer, summarizing recent literature on happiness research, concluded that "claiming to be happy...appears to be nearly universal, as long as you're not living in a war zone, on the street, or in extreme emotional or physical pain."[2]

So, once again, are lawyers happy? Given that most humans are—or say they are—happy, it is not surprising that most of the 1.2 million of us (one of every 250 people in the United States), say we are.[3] Yet it is revealing that lawyers, as a group, are decidedly less happy than are members of many other professions. Members of the clergy, travel agents, architects, scientists, engineers, airline pilots, physicians, financial planners, and detectives are all happier than lawyers. Even repair persons, housekeepers, and butlers report higher levels of happiness than do members of the legal profession. Still, it could be worse: lawyers do report more career satisfaction than either roofers or gas station attendants. Overall, 43 percent of American lawyers say they are "very happy these days"—a statistic that is hardly alarming, but also suggests plenty of room for improvement.[4] Not all lawyers are miserable, but neither is it a cheery profession.

You probably don't need convincing that the question whether lawyers are satisfied with their careers is an important one. Consider that you probably spend about one-third of your life and one-half of your waking hours on the job.[5] How good can a whole life be if one-third of it is miserable?

In this chapter, we examine both empirical and anecdotal information about lawyers' happinesses and dissatisfactions. A wealth of research exists, but it seems conflicted: "There are two literatures on lawyer satisfaction, and their findings differ so starkly that one might wonder whether they are studying the same phenomenon."[6] We'll attempt to make sense of the seemingly contradictory data. We'll also look at who in the legal profession is happy and who's not, which may in turn shed more light on the lawyer happiness surveys.

MAKING SENSE OF LAWYER HAPPINESS DATA

Survey data, of course, depend on the nature of the question asked. The 43 percent of lawyers in the survey by the National Opinion Research Center at the University of Chicago who said they were "very happy" with their lives might make you think that there is a large contingent of happy lawyers. But when survey questions focus on *career*, as opposed to *life*, satisfaction, there is only about a coin-flip chance of being content. Results from an American Bar Association (ABA) survey revealed that only 55 percent of the lawyers responding said that they were satisfied with their job.[7] A 2001 ABA survey of two thousand members of its Young Lawyers Division showed similar job satisfaction levels, with a majority of those responding saying that they were "at least somewhat satisfied with both their current position and the practice of law generally."[8] Yes, more than half reporting satisfaction is good—but remember, seven on a one-to-ten scale is just par on the happiness course. Turning from satisfied lawyers to those who are dissatisfied (ignoring for now those who report neutral feelings about their careers), we find that career dissatisfaction numbers have remained fairly steady across two decades, according to several empirical studies conducted by the ABA Young Lawyers Division. In surveys conducted in 1984, 1990, and 1995, between 20 and 27 percent of lawyers stated that they were either "dissatisfied or very dissatisfied with their work."[9] Most of the young lawyers reporting dissatisfaction didn't hate their jobs: fewer than seven percent of respondents "expressed *great* dissatisfaction with either their career or the practice of law."[10] The Young Lawyer Division's survey, sampling a population of joiners (who tend to be a disproportionately happy group), probably suggests more satisfaction with the practice than there really is.[11]

Grimmer is the 1992 *California Lawyer* poll reporting that seven out of ten respondents would select a career other than law if they could make the decision over.[12] A 1998 survey of Michigan lawyers echoed the California results, with 60 percent of lawyers saying "they would not choose to become lawyers again if they had the chance to start their careers again."[13] These studies of wishful do-over rates should be viewed with some skepticism. When surveys depend on voluntary participation from a wide swath of attorneys, ask about job dissatisfaction, and have a low response rate, they probably overstate dissatisfaction levels. Disgruntled lawyers are likely to be vastly overrepresented, as they are the lawyers most likely to take the trouble to respond to such a poll. For instance, the *California Lawyer* survey—which showed so many lawyers to be miserable with their careers—was sent to potential respondents by fax; and it suffers from possible data collection flaws:

> Because this survey does not use a random sample of lawyers, but instead relies on the voluntary participation of the magazine's readership, it is highly unlikely to provide a representative picture of the target population. Selection bias occurs in at least two ways: first, the readers of this magazine may not be representative of all California lawyers, and second (and more important), lawyers with an axe to grind may be much more likely to participate in a poll about job satisfaction. The magazine does not even report the total number of respondents to the poll, further diminishing its value as a measure of the attitudes of its target population.[14]

On the other hand, a recent twenty-year longitudinal study of the University of Virginia (UVA) Law School class of 1987, in which 81 percent of the respondents said they were "satisfied with their decision to become a lawyer, and 86 percent satisfied with their lives more broadly"[15] might overstate lawyer happiness. Perhaps Virginia law alumni are just a satisfied bunch, of course, but it is also possible that respondents to a poll sponsored by their alma mater might feel subtle pressure to help those who dedicated their lives to educating UVA law grads feel good about the effort they put in: "See, you did well: I'm pretty happy being a lawyer."

The Virginia findings, however, are generally supported by a 2007 study of lawyers in firms of varying sizes from across the country. The study showed satisfaction levels only slightly below those of the UVA law graduates, with the vast majority of respondents either "extremely satisfied" (35 percent) or "moderately satisfied" (44 percent) with their decisions to become a lawyer.[16] Happy and *proud*, it seems. Eighty percent of those responding to a recent ABA survey were proud to be attorneys, and an equal percentage found legal practice to be intellectually stimulating.[17]

When lawyers are asked about their decision to become a lawyer—reflecting on all the profession has meant and could mean to them in the future—it is probably reasonable to expect a somewhat higher rate of satisfaction than when they are asked about how satisfied they are with their present law job, which might call to mind memories of long work hours, uncivil lawyers, and inadequate compensation—especially when compared to the chum next door. It is not a stretch to say that while lawyers are only about as satisfied with their jobs as random workers off the street, they still tend to feel, deep down, that law is a career worth pursuing.

Generic surveys of lawyer happiness lump all lawyers together, obscuring the fact that some populations of lawyers are happier than others. In large law firms, for example, dissatisfaction runs high. Firms across the nation report high rates of attorney attrition—"a whopping 37 percent of associates at big law firms, defined by the study as those employing more than 500 lawyers, quit their firms by the end of their third years of practice."[18] Firms are hemorrhaging their newer lawyers: in any single year, law firms will lose almost one-fifth of their associates, although most enter other jobs in law.[19] A focus on large firm turmoil has led many to conclude that state of the profession is worse than it probably is. Law professor Douglas Litowitz capsulizes the state of despair: "Lawyers are pathologically unhappy."[20] A much-cited article in the *Cardozo Law Review*, "Why Lawyers Are Unhappy," notes what the authors call "pervasive disenchantment" in the legal profession.[21] Robert Kurson, a 1990 Harvard Law School graduate, bemoaned the state of practice in an article in *Esquire* entitled "Who's Killing the Great Lawyers of Harvard?" Kurson describes classmates either moving out of law firms or anxious to do so: "One after another, those who have left law, especially law firms, seem happy. Those who have not are suffering, or worse, resigned. They talk about losing themselves.... More vow to leave the law with the next infusion of cash or gumption."[22]

Top law firms aren't begging law grads to apply. Associates are not abandoning jobs in droves and applying to art schools. Rarely do lawyers leap out of seventeenth-story windows. It is clear that portrayals of a profession in crisis are somewhat exaggerated.

Still, there are other indications that all is not well within the profession. Lawyers suffer exceptionally high rates of depression, alcoholism, and suicide. Studies reveal that lawyers have the highest rate of depression among all occupational categories, with incidents of major depressive disorders at 3.6 times the rates for nonlawyers with similar sociodemographic characteristics. A Johns Hopkins University study of twelve thousand workers in 104 occupations found that while only 3 to 5 percent of the general population suffers from major depressive disorders, more than 10 percent of people in three job categories (secretaries, prekindergarten and special education teachers, and attorneys) suffer major depression. Lawyers also experience higher rates of drug and alcohol abuse than both the general population and other professionals. A survey of lawyers in the state of Washington estimated that one in five lawyers suffers substance abuse problems, a rate almost twice the national average.[23]

The high rates of depression and suicide among lawyers is indisputable, but it is unclear what this tells us about satisfaction in the legal career generally. Depression is a qualitatively different state than merely being unhappy. Depressed and suicidal people are unhappy, to be sure, but clinical depression can be attributable to genetics, biochemistry, personality traits, and medical conditions, as well as situational or environmental factors, such as what is happening at work. Unhappiness rates and depression rates do not correlate precisely. Finland, a nation with one of the happiest populations on the planet according to surveys, also reports one of the highest suicide rates. Artists are, as a group, extremely happy with their chosen career, yet have one of the highest suicide rates among all occupations.[24] (The same artist who cannot imagine being anything else might turn to alcohol or internal demons for inspiration.) Law might attract some seriously depressed people—more so than primary education, let's say—so we can hardly blame the practice when surveys later show that people who were depressed when they became lawyers are still depressed years later.[25] At the least, however, the high rates of depression and alcoholism should be a caution. The practice of law—with its accompanying time pressures, high stakes, adversarial positions, and win-loss outcomes—doesn't seem to be a great cure for depression.[26]

WHERE WE STAND

What should we make of this decidedly mixed bag of data? Professor Kathleen Hull, a sociologist who specializes in qualitative methods, concludes that "the most valid, well-designed research has produced little, if any support for the notion that lawyers are unhappy in their work."[27] We come down a little differently. When we look at the cumulative picture painted by all of the studies, the results are mixed, but we are inclined to conclude that most lawyers fall somewhere near the middle of the happiness continuum. The more recent studies, and those with better sampling techniques and more sophisticated methodologies—such as the emerging longitudinal research—do indicate that the majority of lawyers are happy with their decision to become an attorney and generally satisfied with their lives.[28] Nevertheless, even among lawyers who are pleased that they chose law, dissatisfaction, sometimes deep, exists regarding certain aspects of their jobs.

For most lawyers, things could be better. We believe lawyers could become happier with their work. Some lawyers are in the wrong type of practice—their work does not align with their values, strengths, or interests. Law students often flounder, don't know what they want to do with their law degree, and surrender to traditional career paths or other people's expectations for them. Law schools could do a much better job of steering their students toward satisfying careers. But we will talk with you about all of those issues in the remaining chapters.

Whether lawyers are happy is a question with an answer more complicated than "yes" or "no." Some lawyers are happy; some are not. Let's see who is which category. In the next section, we also will consider what characteristics—of both individuals and their jobs—are more likely to lead to a lawyer's satisfaction.

WHO'S HAPPY AND WHO'S NOT

Good news! If you are an attorney who is over fifty years old and work at a smaller firm, or work in-house or for the government, or work part-time, chances are you are among the happiest of lawyers. If you work part-time for a small branch of government, you could be in lawyer nirvana. On the other hand, if you are a mid-level associate at a large firm who is stuck in a library with fourteen crates of discovery documents, then you have been thinking about jumping ship, haven't you?

Probing deeper into the data on reported career satisfaction, job happiness among attorneys is dependent in part on a number of variables: age, race, sex, firm size, and type of practice.

What Do Lawyers Do?

74% are in private practice.

8% work in government.

8% work in private industry.

5% are retired or inactive.

3% are in the judiciary.

2% are in academic, consulting or accounting jobs.

1% work in legal aid or public defender offices.[29]

Type of Practice

More than two-thirds (68 percent) of attorneys who work in the public sector report being satisfied with their career, the appreciation they receive, and their work-life balance. The least happy (although wealthiest) lawyers are those in large law firms, with only 44 percent reporting that they are satisfied.[30] In between those two extremes fall solo practitioners and small firm lawyers, who generally report that their work autonomy results in greater career satisfaction. Lawyers who engage in routine or repetitive types of practice with little room for creativity, autonomy, or innovation—and especially those who wear the straightjacket of billable hours—are more likely to experience discontent. Attorneys working part-time report greater job satisfaction than those working full-time.[31]

Age

Lawyers over the age of fifty are happier than younger lawyers. This comports with a study of more than two million subjects in eighty countries on happiness levels in the general population, which showed a somewhat U-shaped curve: young people and people over the age of fifty are generally happier than those in-between, with a slight trough of unhappiness for women around age forty and men around fifty.[32] Somewhat related to age is a person's position or status in a firm. Much of the anecdotal evidence relates to disgruntled associates rather than partners. A survey of lawyers in practice between six and nine years showed that four out of ten were satisfied with their careers, compared to six out of ten who had been in practice for more than a decade. The reported increase in happiness as a career progresses may also have something to do with those who are least happy in law taking another job after several years of practice or finding their niche or gaining more control in their job over time.[33]

INCOME

Money matters, but maybe not in the way you'd think. You might assume that because law is a generally well-compensated occupation, its practitioners would not have economic dissatisfactions. But it isn't the absolute income levels that matter to lawyer happiness: far more important for lawyers is how their salaries compare to people they perceive as peers, as well as the pressure and uncertainty attached to keeping a steady flow of income. In 2006 the median earnings of all lawyers was $102,470, although salaries varied by geographic region, sphere of work (public or private), practice size, and area of practice.[34] Interestingly, the salaries of most lawyers are well above the amounts where research shows income matters much to happiness. While the difference in happiness levels between the wealthy and those below the poverty line is significant,[35] studies show only a weak link between income and life satisfaction, particularly if the wage earner makes more than $50,000. "Those with incomes over $90,000 were nearly twice as likely to report being 'very happy' as those with incomes below $20,000, although there is hardly any difference between the highest income group and those in the $50,000 to $89,999 bracket."[36] So, if you earn more than, say, $70,000 (the midpoint of the $50,000 to $89,999 bracket), your absolute salary level should not matter much to your general life satisfaction—you will be earning enough to live comfortably.

But, as we will discuss in chapter 4, relative income matters to people—maybe even especially to lawyers, being the competitive bunch that we are. And, of course, lawyers just starting out and shouldering law school debt will have economic worries. Even for the well paid, uncertainty makes people unhappy,[37] and uncertainty attaches to the pressures of keeping a steady flow of business coming in the door.

SEX

During the past thirty-five years, women have become less happy, both in absolute measures and in relation to men. Across all education levels and in most industrialized countries, whether women are young or old, single or married, working or staying at home, they report less happiness than women did three decades ago. One speculation is that work-family pressures have intensified for women, with women shouldering more economic responsibilities and no fewer family responsibilities. Another possible explanation is that increases in opportunities to succeed come with increased pressures to do so.[38]

Female lawyers have distinctive patterns of happiness and dissatisfactions with the practice of law.[39] Women are leaving the profession much more rapidly than their male counterparts. Attrition from private law firms is almost twice as high among female associates than among comparable male associates.[40] Women do not leave law because they are dissatisfied with the substance of their work; in fact, female attorneys are generally happier than male attorneys with the type of work that they do.[41] Rather, the problems women have with the practice of law relate to a lack of opportunities for professional development, concerns about their work environment, and the difficulties of juggling careers and families. A study of Massachusetts lawyers who worked at the one hundred largest firms in the state showed that for women who were leaving firms but not leaving the workforce, the reason most often cited was "difficulty integrating work and family/personal life."[42] A twenty-year longitudinal study of University of Virginia law graduates showed two major differences between male and female lawyers. Males were more satisfied with their work-life balance than female lawyers, while women "were far more likely than men to interrupt or forego full time employment (39% v. 1%), mainly in order to care for children, and were also more likely to have a spouse or partner employed full-time outside the home (77% v. 24%)."[43]

Professors Kenneth Dau-Schmidt, Marc Galanter, Kaushik Mukhopadhaya, and Kathleen Hull evaluated surveys from 12,000 University of Michigan Law School alumni spanning more than a quarter of a century,[44] looking for the impact of gender on legal careers; what they found was that taking time away from law practice to care for children, more than gender, altered lawyers' career paths and affected their satisfaction. As Galanter explains: "'The big dividing line in terms of the experience attorneys have in private practice is not between men and women . . . It is between women with children and everybody else.'"[45] While the major differences in the aggregate appear between mothers and others, fathers who assume primary caretaking roles (a smaller group) suffer greater career setbacks. Attorneys who take time off from paid work for childcare, whether male or female, will experience reduced earnings and a reduced chance of partnership later in their careers, and "male attorneys who perform childcare fare even worse than female attorneys who do the same."[46] Despite the career costs, however, taking time away from work to do childcare turns out to be the right call for most lawyers: "Both the men and women who take time away from paid work to do childcare, and who work fewer hours, are significantly happier with the balance of work and family in their lives as compared with any of the other groups."[47]

Although almost one-third of attorneys are female,[48] and women have comprised 40 percent or more of law school graduates since 1985, women account for only 17 percent of "partnership positions in law firms, despite graduating from law school and obtaining junior associate positions at an equal rate as men for the last twenty years."[49] But not all partnerships are created equal. Almost three-quarters of larger law firms (defined as those employing more than seventy-five lawyers) have several tiers of partnership; women hold nonequity partner positions in disproportionate shares and collect smaller income shares upon attaining partnership status.[50] In addition to the glass ceiling, female lawyers report several frustrations: a lack of networking opportunities, less desirable assignments, an absence of mentors, and instances of bias in the courtroom.[51] Of course, men are not immune from discrimination, as law firms are much less hospitable to paternity leave than maternity leave.

RACE

African Americans, Hispanics, Asian Americans, and Native Americans collectively constitute just less than 10 percent of all lawyers in this country, significantly below their representation in the population.[52] An American Bar Foundation survey of law school graduates who had been in practice for three years or less found that Blacks expressed the highest level of satisfaction with their decision to become a lawyer, as well as the highest level of satisfaction—among all racial groups—with the substance of their work. Satisfaction levels regarding career choice were almost as high among Hispanics. More than 80 percent of Blacks and just less than 80 percent of Hispanics reported that they were either moderately or extremely satisfied with the decision to enter law.[53] These reported rates of satisfaction may have to do with practice setting—Black and Hispanic lawyers were much more likely to be working in nonprofit or government jobs. Interestingly, their satisfaction levels were higher despite having lower median salaries.

Asians reported the lowest satisfaction levels for the substance of their work; but Asians and Whites expressed the highest satisfaction averages with their job setting. Both of those groups were more likely than members of other races to be working in business settings or at larger law firms. Yet members of the three largest minority groups (Blacks, Asians, and Hispanics), while satisfied with their decisions to become lawyers, "were all more likely than their white peers to report that they were already looking for another position or intended to remain in their current position for less than a year."[54] For Asians, the dissatisfactions may relate to the conditions at large law firms; Hispanics and Blacks expressed concerns about the absence of power track opportunities.

At the intersection of race, sex, and practice area, the unhappiest lawyers working for the nation's top firms are mid-level females of color. Thus, although Blacks and Hispanics may be happier than other races with their decisions to become lawyers, when all races are combined and the cohort is lawyers in practice at large firms, women of color are distinctly unhappy. In 2005, eight out of ten minority women associates left their jobs within five years.[55] In one study conducted by the ABA, almost half of all women reported that they were subjected to demeaning remarks or harassment. Respondents in large firms gave negative report cards in areas such as the quality of work, the number of interesting projects, and the quality of professional development: "white male lawyers graded their career satisfaction A, white women and minority men B and minority women B minus to a C plus."[56]

OTHER FACTORS

Various personal and demographic factors enter into lawyer happiness. Graduates of lower-ranked law schools report higher levels of happiness than graduates of top-ranked law schools. In one study, only 27 percent of graduates of the top-ten law schools reported that they were extremely satisfied with their career choice, compared to 43 percent of graduates from fourth-tier law schools. Six out of ten graduates of top-tier law schools intended to leave their employer within two years, while only four out of ten graduates from fourth-tier law schools reported any intent to move. Researchers considered the possibility that top-tier law school graduates were more likely to be working at large corporate firms and, therefore, might be dissatisfied simply by the nature of their practice. But when researchers controlled for that possibility by only comparing responses from lawyers working at the one hundred largest law firms, the differences became even more pronounced: "26 percent of elites report extreme satisfaction, compared with almost half (49 percent) of those in the fourth tier."[57]

Individual traits and circumstances can combine with firm policies or practices to produce unhappiness. Gay and lesbian lawyers at firms that afford no benefits to their partners may chafe at the arbitrariness. Lawyers whose religion recognizes Sabbath on Saturday may feel that they don't fit the culture of law firms in which attorneys are expected to show up for face time on Saturdays. Unattractive or obese lawyers may receive fewer assignments that involve public or court appearances. One law firm back in the 1960s did not hire men less than six feet tall because the firm thought that smaller men would not have a commanding presence in the courtroom. Life isn't always fair, and neither are the powers-that-be in law firms. When you feel that you have been the victim of discrimination, your happiness is bound to take a nose-dive.

THERE'S NO SORTING HAT

At the Hogwarts of J. K. Rowling's imagination, the Sorting Hat magically assesses the character and talents of first-year students and assigns them to the house—Hufflepuff, Ravenclaw, Slytherin, or Gryffindor—that best matches their individual strengths. Every student ends up where he or she belongs and stands the best chance of thriving.

In the muggle world—our world—there is no Sorting Hat. Choosing a career path requires doing our own assessments of our abilities, interests, and desires. Every year some 48,000 Americans perform that assessment, however imperfectly, and set down a path that they hope will lead to a satisfying career of practicing law. The fact that so many of them, perhaps 20,000 or so, will end up disappointed has many, varied causes. Some of the disappointed were never meant to be lawyers, their talents and passions pointing elsewhere—perhaps in the direction of winemaking, printmaking, or teaching.

Other unsatisfied lawyers embarked on their careers with unrealistic expectations about law practice. They considered themselves the best and the brightest, excelling in college and graduating from top law schools, and they believed their hard work entitled them to fulfilling and happy careers. High expectations and feelings of entitlement to great jobs might account for the higher levels of dissatisfaction among graduates of the nation's highest-ranked schools compared to those lower on the pecking order. People who go into sanitation work do not expect to be made deliriously happy by their jobs. They haven't dreamed since junior high of joining the sanitation force. "It's a job isn't it?" they might say, and they are pleased to have one. Once at work, however, they find some things about the job they like—the camaraderie, the work in the sunshine, the sense that they are serving their community—and, you know, they begin to feel pretty good about their job. When reality fails to match high expectations, however, as it probably does for many lawyers, the result can be a gnawing sense that a better career choice could have been made.

Finally, one other point should be made about the surveys that place lawyers somewhere in the middle of the career satisfaction continuum. What it means to be, say, "fairly satisfied" with a job might be very different for different types of lawyers. For the trial lawyer, whose career is marked with the emotional peaks and valleys that result from our adversarial process, "fairly satisfied" might in fact reflect a perceived ratio of quite high highs and quite low lows. Trial work is a "high amplitude" career. On the other hand, a "fairly satisfied" transactional lawyer might be one who finds modest pleasures in the daily practice of law but keeps wishing for a bit more of an emotional charge. One person's "fairly happy" is not the same as another person's "fairly happy."

The fact that more lawyers are happy with their decision to choose law than they are with their specific jobs suggests a sense among lawyers that careers could be better, either if they found another firm, found a new area of practice, or discovered better ways of coping with the frustrations of their existing work situations. We believe that they are right—most law careers *could* be better—and that's really what this book is all about.

Next, however, we turn to the question of what happiness really is, not just in one's career, but in one's life more generally. To become a happy lawyer it helps first to understand what makes a happy person. The answer turns out to be pretty complicated, involving a mix of genetics, circumstances, and our own choices.

CHAPTER 2

Happiness: A Primer

IT'S EASIER TO BECOME A HAPPY LAWYER IF YOU ARE already a happy person. We're not all that lucky, and you might be wondering why. Before exploring how to achieve happiness and meaning in a career, we consider in this chapter how to achieve a happy and meaningful life. We offer a brief survey of the scientific literature on the general question of happiness, leaving for the rest of the book the question of finding happiness within the practice of law.

The literature on happiness is voluminous and often contradictory, with more than 4,000 books published on the subject in 2008 alone,[1] and runs the gamut from first-rate science to garden-variety self-help vacuity. We've done the hard work for you and read at least the best of it. Here's what we think you should know about happiness.

THREE MEANINGS OF HAPPINESS

"Happiness" is one of those chameleon words whose color depends upon where you find it. It has a bright hue for the lawyer on the golf course, dance floor, neighborhood tavern, or ice cream shop. It has a different tone, somewhat paler usually, in a law office. You might be happy, yes, but the feeling is less intensely positive. Finally, "happiness" looks altogether different to the lawyer looking back at a career—the happy times and not-so happy times merge in memory and, in the well-spent life, become a sort of soft glow. As a concept, "happiness" really does triple duty and thus confuses our quest to achieve it. The fact is that maximizing one type of happiness, the giggles and pleasures of the present, might make it more difficult to achieve another type of happiness, the sense of satisfaction that comes later in life with a feeling that however hard life has been at times, you've come close to realizing your potential. In between these two types of happiness, short-term joy and the well-lived life, is an intermediate sort of happiness— a variety we might also call contentment or satisfaction—that is probably the type most relevant to you.

Although intermediate-term happiness might be our primary goal, none among us would wish a life without its moments of pure joy (and maybe even a dash of ecstasy). Indeed, a life bereft of joyful moments hardly seems a strong candidate for satisfaction or contentment either. In this chapter, we lay out what researchers really know about achieving happiness in general before turning to what they can tell us about short-term pleasure and intermediate-term satisfaction. We leave for a later chapter some reflections on self-realization, or what it means to have lived life well.

SUDDENLY, STUDYING HAPPINESS IS IN

Good lawyers understand the importance of facts. In the end, you cannot get around them. As John Adams said during his defense of British soldiers in the Boston Massacre trial, "Facts are stubborn things." The facts about happiness—and some of them are especially stubborn—determine and limit our abilities to achieve greater satisfaction in our legal careers.

And there are a great many facts. More pile up each day, with researchers competing for space in *The Journal of Happiness Studies* or sending abstracts off to the Netherlands, home of the *World Database of Happiness*.[2] Serious students of happiness are busy adding new bookshelves to their libraries or are seeking positions at the University of Pennsylvania's Authentic Happiness Center. It didn't always used to be this way.

A couple of decades ago, this chapter on the science of happiness would have been briefer because, until recently, scientists generally ignored the subject. They considered it nearly impossible to evaluate and resistant to scientific methods. Definitional issues ("What exactly is happiness anyway?") and a sense that the whole subject, despite its obvious interest to nearly everyone, was unworthy of serious study added to the reluctance of scientific community to take up the cause. Until recently, the people talking about happiness were mostly pastors and self-help speakers, such as Reverend Rick Warren (*The Purpose Driven Life*) and Norman Vincent Peale (*The Power of Positive Thinking*).

When the misgivings of researchers gave way, they really gave way. Now we are inundated with studies from numerous fields exploring this or that aspect of happiness. Happiness studies in the psychological and biological sciences generally are coming from three different, but related, fields.[3] Neuroscientists, using new technology, study brain chemistry and evaluate how various firing patterns of brain cells are associated with happiness or other emotional states. Evolutionary psychologists develop and promote their theories as to how the reproductive advantages and disadvantages of different emotional reactions to events molded the brains of early humans and shaped the patterns of happiness and unhappiness we see today. Finally, members of the fast-growing field of "positive psychology" (encompassing cognitive and social psychology) use surveys and other research tools to explore everything from the genetics of happiness to what role geography, relationships, or careers play in determining happiness levels. Taken together, the lessons offered from these three fields of research give us a rich understanding of what happiness is, and what it takes to get there.

TRANSIENT HAPPINESS

Neuroscientists and evolutionary psychologists generally have focused their research on transient states of happiness ranging from pleasure to exhilaration to euphoria. For neuroscientists, the reason is obvious: it's a lot easier to measure and observe brain changes in reaction to specific stimuli than it is to track changes in brain patterns over long periods of time and then try to explain them in anything resembling scientific terms. A neuroscientist can see what waving a one hundred dollar bill in front of our eyes does to our brains, but cannot conclude much about what ten years of practicing corporate law does for our happiness. Similarly, theories of evolutionary psychology offer little in the way of explanations for longer term satisfaction but instead provide insights into why sex or competitive success brings us pleasure.

What Evolutionary Psychology Teaches Us

Evolutionary psychology tells us why we have emotions in the first place, as well as why we have the ones we do. As evolutionary psychologist David Buss explains it, "Mechanisms of the mind are end products of a selective process, a sieve through which features passed that contributed to reproductive success."[4]

Nature cares not for our happiness. From an evolutionary standpoint, being in a persistent state of contentment would not be a recipe for reproductive success; that is, it is more important to have a brain that sends out the message "Danger!" than to have one that says "Be happy." Early humans who ignored poisonous snakes and saber-toothed tigers weren't around long enough to pass their genes on to future generations. As a result, nature has programmed us to better recognize the negative than the positive. When we see our mate sneaking off into a cave with another member of our tribe, we're designed to feel jealous or angry, not content. Humans whose genes might have predisposed them to stop and smell the roses when they should have been gathering berries and firewood for the harsh winter ahead left us little of their genetic heritage.

Of course, it is also true that any early human who never took the time to eat or have sex would make no contribution to the gene pool, so it should come as no surprise that two of the activities most likely to cause our brains to send the "okay, you're happy now" message are eating and having sex. Evolutionary calculations are all about mate-finding and survival, not about achieving bliss or contentment. Most of what modern humans do with the bulk of their time has little to do with evolutionary biology. Drafting contracts just wasn't part of everyday life on the ancestral savannah, and nothing in our genetic programming is designed to turn on a happy button when we spend our time fine-tuning paragraph 17 on page 4 of a brief.

Reproductive success has been facilitated by having a variety of emotional responses, some positive but many negative. The ability to experience fright kept our ancestors from being eaten by lions or battered by invaders. The ability to experience envy or jealousy or sadness kept them searching for positions in their social group that would provide food, sex, and shelter. Pleasure had its place in primitive times, but it was only one of many emotions adapted to be triggered only under certain conditions. Evolution has made it impossible for us to maintain a constant state of happiness—the best we can hope for is to grab more of it than we presently do.

WHAT NEUROSCIENCE TEACHES US ABOUT OUR THREE BRAINS

Evolution has left humans with three brains. The most primitive part of our brain is the brainstem, sometimes called the "reptilian brain" because its origins trace back that far in our evolutionary history. The brainstem controls heartbeat, respiration, body temperature, and other essential functions. The next part of our brain to develop was the limbic system, sometimes called the "mammalian brain" because it emerged more than one hundred million years ago at the beginning of the mammalian era and is something we share with other mammals, from rats to hippopotamuses. The limbic brain includes three main structures: the amygdala, the hippocampus, and the hypothalamus. The limbic brain is the source of our basic emotions, including love, fear, rage, jealousy, and—yes—happiness (at least of the transient variety). Our unconscious value judgments also are primarily the limbic brain's doing. Finally, the arrival of primates resulted in the construction on top of the brain stem and limbic system of a "third brain": the neocortex, where intellect and logic reside. The highly flexible neocortex, divided into a left and a right hemisphere, is the source of language, abstract thought, imagination, and consciousness. All three brains co-inhabit our skulls and, in the well-balanced individual, work in a sort of rough harmony with help from neural pathways that connect the limbic system to the neocortex.

The amygdala, part of our ancient limbic brain, plays a critical role in our emotional lives. When, for example, the amygdala is sending out "be scared" messages or "be jealous" messages, it is impossible to be happy. Many more neural circuits run from this manager of emotions to the prefrontal cortex, the section of the brain in charge of planning and reasoning, than run toward it. Without the amygdala and its constant emotional reporting to the prefrontal cortex, we would be unable to make decisions. The prefrontal cortex, confronted with an overload of information, ultimately relies on the amygdala to move us from inaction to action. We are, at bottom, and to the disappointment of some, still much more emotional creatures than we are intellectual creatures. Eduardo Punset, a Spanish lawyer, professor of neuroscience, and author of *The Happiness Trip: A Scientific Journey*, bluntly describes the challenge presented by our evolutionary legacy: "the problem with the search for happiness" is "despite our ardent wishes, we are anchored in a world of genetics and volatile, preset emotions."[5]

With CAT scans and other brain-imaging and monitoring tools, neuroscientists have begun to learn what is going on inside brains that are experiencing transient states of happiness. A study of the brains of dogs being shown food, for example, revealed firing in the hypothalamus, which might be called the "seeking circuit" of the brain. Interestingly, researchers observed, the hypothalamus ceases firing as soon as a dog begins eating the food.[6] (This probably comes as no revelation to many dog owners, who might have noticed that dogs wag their tails when they are expecting food but not during the act of eating itself.) This study suggests that happiness might often lie more in anticipation of events than in the actual event itself. Or, as Punset says, "Happiness is hidden in the waiting room for happiness."[7]

Research reveals that positive emotions are associated with high levels of brain activity in the left frontal cortex, while negative emotions are associated with active firing in the right frontal cortex. If the "blue bird of happiness" has a favorite roosting place, it is in the left prefrontal cortex.[8] When subjects experience high levels of anger, depression, or anxiety, the area of the right prefrontal cortex (just behind the forehead) goes into overdrive. Watching an amusing movie clip produces enhanced brain activity in the left frontal cortex of test subjects, while a sad movie caused increased activity in the right.[9] Interestingly, this is even true for babies.

Of course, researchers peering into our brains are not actually *seeing* happiness, which is a feeling and therefore lacks physical attributes. Neuroscientists cannot be confident that the same brain scan pattern produces the same *intensity* of happiness in all subjects. Harvard University psychologist Jerome Kagan reminds us that a brain scan "is no more equivalent to an emotion than a picture of an apple represents the texture and taste of the fruit."[10]

Ultimately, all claims of happiness come from the closed closet of an individual's point of view.

THE SCIENCE OF PLEASURE: A CHEMISTRY LESSON

Understanding transient emotions turns out to be a chemistry lesson as much as anything. Although the number of brain chemicals having effects on emotions is large, four in particular are worth mentioning here.

Cortisol, to oversimplify, is the stress chemical. When this hormone is coursing through the brain in significant quantities, we can't be happy. We are, instead, frightened or angry or jealous, just as we were designed to be in frightening or anger- or jealousy-inducing situations. Cortisol might not make us happy, but it has adaptive benefits, and even if we could somehow drain it from our systems entirely, we'd be better advised not to. Nonetheless, according to Richard Davidson of the University of Washington, the brain of a generally happy person is one with an "adaptive pattern of cortisol release" that allows effective regulation of the negative emotions we all experience from time to time.[11] Davidson's research shows that cortisol levels are naturally lower at night than in the morning and that happier people tend to have lower nighttime levels of cortisol than do less happy people.

If cortisol causes stress, is there another substance in our brains that might be a "happy juice"? Things aren't quite so simple, it turns out. Various chemicals, including the neurotransmitters dopamine, oxytocin, and serotonin, play roles in producing good feelings, but each does many other things as well, and not all of those things make us happy.

Dopamine is the compact molecule, made of twenty-two atoms, that gets the most attention from researchers—and deservedly so. When we anticipate a pleasurable event, dopamine flows along a specialized circuit of neurons above the brain. It is the *expectation* of pleasure, not the pleasure itself, triggering the flow.

Dopamine is a key component of the motivation system that nature has built in to reward us for searching for the food and sex critical to our reproductive success and survival as a species. It's also been called the brain's "get-a-load-of-this device," the source of our attraction to the novel.[12]

Dopamine is critical for our survival as a species, and it has the side benefit of producing boosts in moods and alertness. To call it a source of happiness, however, is misleading. The neurotransmitter is really all about survival, and dopamine neurons fire just as hard at the sight of an object we fear (a snake) as one that excites us in a positive way (a naked lover). Dopamine's goal is to keep us alive and produce offspring, and that means making us pay attention to threats as well as getting us to enjoy food highs and good sex.

Dopamine also is blamed for our addictions. As complex as the causes of addiction are, one aspect that they all share is dopamine. Addictions, from drugs to pornography to gambling, can be tied to this "craving" neurochemical. Dopamine, in effect, tells us to pay attention to whatever promises us short-term pleasure and to ignore whether our behavior might lead to longer term problems. Call it a design flaw, but our limbic systems are just not built to alert us when we're experiencing too much of a good thing.

Dopamine, as we said, is associated with sex—and sex is an activity associated with happiness. Most people would rather not be asked as the moment of sexual climax approaches, but if they were, they would almost universally report being happy. In fact, sex is the activity that produces the highest average ratings of happiness among all activities measured in a recent survey. (Respondents gave sex an average ranking of 4.7 on a 5.0 scale, compared to a 3.8 for eating and a 2.7 for working.[13]) So what is going on in our brains when we engage in sexual activity? In anticipation of sex, dopamine levels soar. Orgasm has been described as "the biggest blast of dopamine (legally) available to us."[14] Brain scans of people experiencing orgasm closely resemble scans of people experiencing heroin rushes. Alas, the happiness from sex is short-lived. After climax, dopamine levels drop off dramatically and the levels of neurochemical prolactin (telling us "Whoa!" and then asking us whether it's time for sleep) rise. Stimulants also produce happiness boosts because they increase dopamine levels. Cocaine and amphetamines, for example, provide short-term pleasure by essentially hijacking the neural system for a joyride that evolution never intended. Cocaine works by blocking the dopamine transporter, "a kind of janitor that picks up the used dopamine molecules and sweeps them back into the cells where they were born."[15] With the transporter blocked, dopamine keeps banging its signals. Caffeine has a similar, if much milder, effect. That morning cup of joe increases dopamine flow and produces a short-term mood boost, but heavy caffeine consumption can also cause increased levels of aggression, anxiety, and sleep loss.

Music can make us happy—even euphoric. Is the reason, as with sex and drugs, linked to dopamine levels in some way? The answer turns out to be "yes." Neuroscientists have discovered that music increases dopamine flow (as well as levels of endorphins and oxytocin) and creates activity in the amygdala and prefrontal cortex. Harvard University psychologist Steven Pinker describes "the direct effect of music" as "simply, the generation of meaningless pleasure."[16]

Sex, drugs, and rock and roll are three happiness-producing activities associated with dopamine flows—and the list could be made much longer. More generally, dopamine accounts for the pleasure we derive from new and stimulating environments. If variety is the spice of life, dopamine explains why.

Practicing law generally is not associated with increased dopamine levels, but practice areas with surprises and novelty provide more frequent boosts than jobs where one day at the office is virtually the same as any other. Almost all lawyers, however, have the opportunity to inject a bit of variety into their days—perhaps by checking out that new restaurant down the street or striking up a conversation with the new associate down the hall—to perhaps get the dopamine flowing a bit. Laughter can have the same effect—getting to know your office comedian can have its benefits.

Dopamine is responsible for our highest highs, but it is serotonin—or rather, the lack thereof—that is associated with our lowest lows. Research shows a clear link between low levels of serotonin and elevated rates of serious depression and anxiety disorders. Prozac, Zoloft, and other antidepressants work by steeping neurons longer in what little serotonin a depressed individual is able to produce, thus improving mood. When our levels of the critical neurotransmitter go up, we feel (depending on the situation) more empathetic, insightful, and uninhibited. For these reasons, serotonin is sometimes called "the happy chemical"—a simplistic view that has been undermined by recent research showing that increased serotonin activity and pleasurable feelings do not always go hand in hand.

There are ways, both legal and illegal, to raise your serotonin levels. Falling in love does the trick. So does enjoying an intimate conversation with a good friend. Natural sunlight also increases serotonin turnover and, if you're stuck in Seattle in January, bright light therapy has the same effect. If you're more desperate, acupuncture seems also to increase serotonin. And if you're more desperate still for a serotonin rush, and won't let the law stand in your way, there's the recreational drug Ecstasy (MDMA). (While Ecstasy typically produces a relaxed and empathetic state, unfortunately for users of the party drug, the rapid deployment of serotonin results in a depletion of serotonin levels once the drug wears off, tumbling the user into a short-term depressed state.)

Finally, to complete our brief survey of the brain's emotion-regulating chemistry set, a word about the hormone oxytocin. Oxytocin is sometimes called "the bonding chemical" because it is closely associated with the deep connections of lovers or of mothers and babies. During sex, the hormone is released by both men and women, explaining the deep bonding often associated with that experience. Oxytocin is also released during childbirth and flows in a mother at the sound or sight of her young baby, triggering the release of breast milk. When the release of oxytocin is blocked, bad things happen. Experiments show, for example, that sheep and rats will reject their own young. (On the other hand, injecting oxytocin into a female rat causes her to bond with whatever other female rat's young might be nearby, protecting them just as if they were her own.)

Recent evidence, however, indicates that oxytocin plays a far more extensive role than previously thought. According to Dr. C. Sue Carter of the University of Illinois, the hormone is suddenly "very hot." Scientists have demonstrated, as Natalie Angier concludes in a recent summary of the research in the *New York Times*, that oxytocin does nothing less than underlie "the twin emotional pillars of civilized life, our capacity to feel empathy and trust."[17] She cites a Swiss study finding that subjects given a nasal squirt of oxytocin were far more likely to trust strangers with their money than were subjects given a squirt of a placebo solution. A second study compared two groups of people, one group with a genetic code that made their oxytocin receptors more responsive to the effects of the hormone, and one group without that genetic variant. The study found that having the gene that increased responsiveness to oxytocin resulted in an improved ability to read faces, feel distress at another's hardship, and identify with characters in a novel. The enhanced receptor also made people less stress-prone. The results of the study left Dr. Sarina Rodriquez of the University of Oregon "floored."

Does understanding the chemistry behind transient happiness make us better equipped to find it? We cannot change the chemistry sets our brains came equipped with, but if we know what activities and substances produce brain responses associated with pleasure, we are better able to obtain happiness boosts when we really need them. While some of the lessons of neuroscience reach beyond pleasure to what we've called satisfaction or contentment, the scientific research suggests that happiness is more easily achieved for the short-term than the longer term. There is no magic bean for contentment.

THE SCIENCE OF SATISFACTION: TWO THINGS THAT WORK

While temporarily increasing or decreasing the flow of various brain chemicals can bring about moments of pleasure, it does little to increase our intermediate-term happiness. To achieve happiness that stays with us for weeks rather than minutes or hours, it's not a simple matter of turning on this or that neurotransmitter faucet. Rather, the structures and the pathways of the brain need to be reshaped. An impressive body of growing evidence suggests two ways that can be done and produce long-lasting improvements in mood.

The first proven technique for increasing activity in the left prefrontal cortex is meditation. If you are inclined to dismiss mindfulness meditation as some sort of New Age mumbo-jumbo, you will have to ignore a number of studies that show meditation programs of eight-weeks or less reduce anxiety and depression, while increasing well-being and immune system responses. Most persons practicing regular meditation also report an enhanced ability to experience the present moment. Neuroscientists confirm that meditation and bio-feedback techniques can reprogram brains and re-direct brain activity from the right to left prefrontal cortex. As neuroscientist Richard Davidson puts it, happiness can be thought of "as a skill, not fundamentally different than learning to play the violin or learning to play golf."[18]

Our second recommendation for improving moods over the longer term is to exercise. It's even a good idea if you're a rat. Princeton scientists recently discovered that rats that exercise create new brain cells that respond much better to stress than the brain cells of slothful rats. Exercise does nothing less than reshape your brain, making it more stress-resistant. Michael Hopkins, affiliated with Dartmouth's Neurobiology of Learning and Memory Laboratory concludes, "It looks more and more like the positive stress of exercise prepares structures and pathways within the brain so that they're more equipped to handle stress in other forms."[19] Hopkins calls the translation from the realm of the physical to the psychological "pretty amazing, really." Don't expect, however, that thirty minutes on the treadmill will wipe away your problems. According to researchers at the University of Colorado, it seems to take at least three to six weeks of regular exercise to reap the psychological benefits.

THE SLOPPY BUSINESS OF MEASURING SATISFACTION

While researchers interested in the transient type of happiness can peer into brains or speculate about adaptation in early humans, they lack a tool that can objectively measure and compare the pleasure of one person to another. There is no "hedonometer" that can accurately measure how many "hedons" of happiness you are experiencing at the present moment and show for certain that it is more or less than the person sitting next to you. For a measure of how much pleasure a person is presently experiencing, researchers have to rely on self-reports of subjects ("How happy are you feeling right now—very happy, happy, indifferent, unhappy, or very unhappy?").

Studies of (the ultimately more important) intermediate-term happiness, such as measures of career or marital satisfaction, generally depend on self-reporting. Self-reporting is subject to variation over time and culture. For example, most studies suggest that the Japanese are generally less happy than Americans, but there is some reason to question that finding.[20] It is difficult to determine how much the difference in reports of satisfaction might be attributable to the greater emphasis Western culture places on happiness. Because of that emphasis, it is possible that Americans might feel psychologically compelled to report higher happiness levels than do residents of Japan, who place a higher value on harmony and obligations. This could explain why moment-by-moment reporting (our make-do hedonometer) indicates that Asians and Americans have similar overall levels of transient happiness.

The vast majority of people (about 85 percent) claim above average satisfaction with their lives.[21] "Claiming that you're happy—that is to an interviewer who is asking you to rate your life satisfaction on a scale from zero to ten—appears to be nearly universal, as long as you're not living in a war zone, on the street, or in extreme emotional or physical pain."[22] Are people really as happy as they say they are? Probably not. More likely, reported levels of satisfaction are skewed by the desire of people to "manage impressions."[23] An admission of unhappiness could be perceived today by many Americans as a sense of failure.

Any measure of happiness is imperfect. Yet that is no reason not to study it, nor to draw lessons from those that have. As political scientist Alan Wolfe noted, "The proper question...is which of the many imperfect measures of happiness we ought to rely on."[24]

THE THREE COMPONENTS OF SATISFACTION

Satisfaction, or intermediate-term happiness, is determined by three things: genetics, circumstances, and our own internal decisions and actions. Our focus for most of this book will be on the third factor, those choices you can make to increase your own job and life satisfaction regardless of your genes or specific circumstances. Yet it is important to understand that happiness is not completely within your control. Understanding and accepting limitations on your satisfaction may actually prove helpful to your efforts to boost your own happiness. We are reminded of the wise words of theologian Reinhold Niebuhr's "Serenity Prayer":

> God grant me the serenity
> to accept the things I cannot change;
> courage to change the things I can;
> and wisdom to know the difference.

Genetics: The Stubborn Reality of Happiness Set Points

The most important insight about the nature of happiness that science has given to us is that, to a surprisingly large extent, our happiness levels are genetically determined. Genetics isn't fate— how genes express themselves is not inevitable—but genes provide strong behavioral momentum. Estimates as to the genetic contribution to happiness levels vary considerably (from about 40 percent to 80 percent),[25] but nearly everyone recognizes the contribution to be substantial. The seminal study was a twin study conducted by David Lykken and Auke Tellegen. The two researchers asked pairs of identical twins to report on their happiness levels on two occasions nine years apart. They found that happiness levels reported on the first occasion predicted, to a large degree, happiness levels reported nine years later. In other words, they found happiness levels to be remarkably consistent over time. Second, and even more surprising, Lykken and Tellegen discovered that the happiness level of one twin could predict the happiness level of the other twin nine years later just as well as that twin's *own* earlier happiness level. This turned out to be true even if the identical twins were separated at birth and raised in very different circumstances.[26] The researchers concluded that inherited factors play large roles in shaping our perceived levels of happiness, much larger than the environments in which we live. The label that has been given to this genetic component of our happiness level is our happiness "set point."

Your happiness set point is the baseline level of happiness to which you *tend* to return after periods of either unusual positive (falling in love, enjoying a dream vacation) or negative (getting fired, breaking a leg) emotion. We all know people who seem to keep a smile on their face even when circumstances would suggest otherwise. We know others for whom almost every day seems like a bleak Monday in November. When it comes to happiness, the genetic lottery produces both winners and losers. Happiness researcher Sonja Lyubomirsky puts it this way: "[L]ike genes for intelligence or cholesterol, the magnitude of innate set points—that is, whether it is high (a six on a seven-point scale) or low (a two) or in between (a four)—governs to a large extent how happy we will be over the course of our lives."[27] Lyubomirsky estimates that happiness levels are 50 percent determined by genetics, putting her squarely in the mainstream of happiness researchers. Regardless of your set point, as we discuss later, you still have a great deal of control over your own feelings of happiness.

Various personality traits have been linked to higher or lower happiness set points. People who are extroverted, optimistic, and take risks, for example, tend to be relatively happy. On the other hand, introverted, pessimistic, risk-averse people tend to be relatively unhappy. The least happy people of all, unsurprisingly, tend to be people who take worry and anxiety to a whole different level: neurotics.

The traits associated with higher or lower set points are not truly independent. Extroverts, for example, in addition to being sociable tend to take more risks, whether the risks involves sports such as downhill skiing, or behaviors such as excessive drinking and having multiple sex partners. In general, extroverts find more shops enticing than do introverts as both groups meander through the bazaar that is life.

Although extroverts outnumber introverts by a three-to-one margin in the general U.S. population, there are more introverted than extroverted lawyers. According to a study of more than 3,000 lawyers, introverts outnumber extroverts by a 57 percent to 43 percent margin.[28] The difference in ratios between the general population and population of lawyers is dramatic and suggests two things. First, the practice of law is a career that disproportionately appeals to introverts. As Michael Melcher notes in *The Creative Lawyer*: "Introvert characteristics are more apt to be accepted and appreciated in the field of law than in the rest of the world."[29] The work environments of lawyers are typically quiet, private, and place a premium on contemplation, preparation, and writing skills. (Trial lawyers, of course, rely more heavily on skills better suited for extroverts, such as face-to-face meetings and courtroom speech-making.)

The American Bar Association survey results suggest that when it comes to achieving happiness, most lawyers have one strike against them, their introversion, and other research suggests a second strike: pessimism. Psychologist Martin Seligman describes pessimism as "a well-documented...major risk factor for unhappiness," and notes there is "a surprising correlation between pessimism and success in law school."[30] This correlation appears to be because a pessimist finds it much easier to conjure up the worst-case scenarios that it is a lawyer's job to guard against, whether in writing contracts or defending a client in court. Pessimism, in short, has a positive dimension that we often refer to as "prudence." By spotting pitfalls ahead, the prudent lawyer brings clients safely into a happy harbor when a more optimistic sort might have left the client marooned by an unanticipated disaster. As helpful as this honed pessimism might be in the actual practice of law, it doesn't make for a happy worker in the office.

Circumstances: The 10 Percent Determinant of Happiness Levels

> Happiness depends, as Nature shows,
> Less on exterior things than most suppose.
>
> —William Cowper (1782)

When asked to imagine a happy person, most people immediately put that person in fortunate circumstances. They imagine a person cruising around the Mediterranean on a yacht with her lover. They picture a fabulously wealthy person with power and fame to spare. Always, the persons imagined are healthy, good-looking, and well-short of old age. The reality of happy people is much different.

As we hope our discussion of set points has convinced you, circumstances have a lot less to do with our happiness levels than most people think. What is most surprising, however, is how little circumstances affect happiness at all. Millionaires are not much happier than middle-income folks. People in their twenties are no happier than people in their sixties. Men are about as happy as women, although women have a wider emotional range.[31] Achieving fame barely moves the happiness register. In general, circumstances as a whole account for only about 10 percent of the difference in happiness levels.[32]

Nor is well-being significantly affected by where you live in the United States. When the Centers for Disease Control (CDC) asked 1.3 million Americans between 2005 and 2008, "In general, how satisfied are you with your life?," it turned out that residents in the happiest and least happy states differed by only one-tenth of a point on a 4-point happiness scale.[33] Nonetheless, the CDC study provided plenty of fodder for researchers who offered their interpretations of the tiny differences. While the data suggested that residents of western states are, on the whole, slightly happier than residents of other states (the merriest five, in order, were Utah, Hawaii, Wyoming, Colorado, and Minnesota),[34] when two researchers controlled for factors such as income, marital status, and age, they found that residents of southern states came out on top. In their study reported in the December 2009 issue of *Science* online, economists Andrew J. Oswald of the University of Warwick and Stephen Wu of Hamilton College in New York concluded that the states that made people happiest were actually (generally poorer) southern states, with Louisiana, Hawaii, Florida, Tennessee, and Arizona ranking best using their methodology.[35] Mississippians, for example, who ranked 48th in satisfaction in the raw averages, came in at an impressive number 7 on the satisfaction scale after Oswald and Wu made their statistical adjustments. Typically, the media overplays rankings of these sorts and readers are rarely informed as to how very modest the state-by-state differences actually are.[36]

Nonetheless, there are a few circumstances that account for significant differences in reported levels of happiness. One of these is belonging to a church. People who describe themselves as "very religious" or "religious" are happier than those who don't.[37] Why religious people are happier than their more secular brethren is somewhat of an open question. One theory is that religion gives the believer a sense of purpose and optimism about the future. A second possibility is that members within religious communities often develop deep bonds, and it is these relationships rather than the religious beliefs that account for the happiness boost. Finally, it is possible that the type of people who gravitate to religions tend to be happier people in the first place, rather than the religion making them happier. A secular person could say on Tuesday, "I'll become religious as of today and get happier," but that is not a leap of faith most people could make even if they wanted to. (Interestingly, Ruut Veenhoven, director of the World Database of Happiness, reports that hedonists appear to be somewhat happier than nonhedonists.[38] What this says about the higher levels of happiness reported by churchgoers is not clear. At the very least Veenhoven's finding suggests abstinence is not the answer to everything.)

Enjoying a number of close relationships also makes people happier. This is one of those happiness determinants with both a circumstantial and intentional aspect to it, so it's hard to know exactly how to categorize it. We are social animals and interaction with others usually (we all have personal knowledge of many exceptions) makes us happy. Measured on a 5-point scale, with 5 being ecstatically happy, people report average happiness levels of 3.7 when they are interacting with friends, 3.3 to 3.4 when they are interacting with spouses or children, and 2.8 at times when they are interacting with clients or co-workers. By comparison, hanging out alone produces an average happiness rating of 2.7, although that's still better than time with the boss, which comes in at only 2.4.[39]

While married people are only slightly happier than single people, it is clear that ending a close relationship can have devastating short-term consequences for happiness levels. People going through a divorce are generally unhappy. Over time, most people get over the loss and move back toward their set points. Having intimate relationships appears to be a basic human need, and people who lack them rarely are as happy as those who have them. Moreover, the more such close friendships a person has, the happier he or she will be.

Our social nature is reflected in recent studies that show happiness is contagious. In a study of nearly 5,000 residents of a Boston suburb, researchers examined how a sense of happiness moved through various social networks to which the study subjects belonged, including friends, family, neighbors, and co-workers.[40] The study showed that happy people tend to cluster together and that happy people occupied the center of social networks. By contrast, researchers found unhappy people stranded on the periphery of networks, plugged into the center by only a few social lines. Neither of these results should surprise anyone. More interesting, however, was the conclusion that happiness is transmitted though social networks, weakening as it spreads out over the chain of relationships. For example, if Ann becomes happy and is a friend of Barb, then Barb is about 15 percent more likely to become happy herself; if Barb is a friend with Carol, Carol is about 10 percent more likely to benefit from spillover happiness that starts with Ann. Friends, the study suggested, are better transmitters of happiness than family, and family better transmitters than co-workers. The study found geographical distance key to the effectiveness of the transmission, with transmission most effective for friends living less than a half mile apart.

Wealth is the most overrated of all factors in people's guesses as to what will improve their happiness. Asked what single thing would be most likely to make them happier, a majority of Americans answer "more money." Almost three-quarters of college freshmen in a recent survey said it was important to be "very well off financially."[41] Harvard University psychology professor Daniel Gilbert sums up the situation this way: "'[W]e think money will bring lots of happiness for a long time, and it actually brings a little happiness for a short time.'"[42]

What is true is that rich people are somewhat happier than poor people. About 45 percent of the wealthiest quarter of Americans describes themselves as "very happy" compared to 33 percent of the poorest quarter of Americans who describe themselves that way. (Still, 86 percent of the poorest Americans call themselves at least "quite happy.")[43] Beyond lower-middle-income levels, however, increases in wealth give only the tiniest of happiness boosts. Some satisfaction seems to come from belonging to a higher social class, probably because membership in the higher class correlates with an increased likelihood of feeling of having "control over life."

Although geography makes little difference in happiness levels among Americans, it is worth noting that significant differences do appear when comparing citizens of different countries. Many factors, including standard of living and degree of individual freedom, seem to affect happiness differences among nations, yet no factor plays a bigger role than the level of trust people have in their government institutions and fellow citizens. Citizens of Denmark, a country where residents have a very high level of trust in their government, are much happier than citizens of Moldova, who think very poorly of their government. A map of world happiness shows high rates of happiness in the most democratic of nations, from Western Europe through the United States and Canada to Australia and New Zealand. On the other hand, the most autocratic of the old Soviet bloc countries, such as Belarus and Ukraine, as well as the governmentally challenged nations of Africa, tend to be home to the least happy of citizens.[44]

Trust in general seems a key component of happiness. The relationships that provide the biggest happiness boost are ones that are built on trust. Communities where residents trust each other are far happier than communities where they don't. Researchers dropped wallets on the streets of cities around the world. The wallets contained the name and address of a supposed owner. The nations with the highest return rate of wallets, such as Scandinavian countries, also turned out to be at the top of the happiness charts. The study showed a high correlation between return rates, a plausible measure of trust within a society, and happiness.[45]

Ultimately, the circumstances that have the biggest effects on happiness are family relationships, employment status, health, and quality of government. Of these, the biggest drags on happiness are being recently separated (which makes a person less happy than either being divorced or never married), losing a job (almost, but not quite, as bad as separation), being in seriously bad health,[46] and having the misfortune of growing up in a country such as Moldova. For people in these circumstances, their situation is a serious impediment to happiness. But for most people, all these situational differences hardly amount to a hill of beans on the hike up happy mountain.

Adaptation: Life on the Hedonic Treadmill

Even if circumstances matter little, a sudden change in circumstances might affect happiness levels—at least for a brief time. When it comes to measuring our happiness, one thing we all know is that it's not a flat line. Some days (or moments) we're feeling relatively up, and then the next day (or moment), we're down in the dumps. Happiness set points don't determine our day-to-day levels of happiness; rather they are a measure of the happiness level we tend to gravitate back to over time. Our day-to-day, moment-to-moment happiness levels are strongly influenced by our circumstances and intentional activity, as we'll discuss below.

The tendency of our happiness levels to drift back toward our set points from our fluctuating highs and lows is called *adaptation*, or life on "the hedonic treadmill." If we get that hoped-for promotion, marry our sweetheart, or win the lottery, we will undoubtedly become happier in the short-term, but at some point in the future (be it days or months) we'll start moving back toward our set point. The same goes for negative experiences. If we get fired, end a relationship, or lose our fortune in a bear market, we'll undoubtedly experience some short-term unhappiness (or even depression), but the vast majority of us will see our happiness levels rise back in the long-term to near the point that they were before our misfortune. In general, events that we think will make us happy forever and ever (as the fairy tales suggest) rarely do, and even the most devastating of life's blows seldom leave us emotionally crippled for life. That is not to say, however, that there are not some circumstances to which we will never fully adapt. For example, chronic pain, life-threatening danger, and high ambient noise levels are all circumstances associated with long-term lower levels of reported happiness. Paraplegics are not as happy as other people. We adapt over time, but sometimes not completely back to where we started. Interestingly, we adapt less to minor annoyances and small pleasures than to more significant events. That too-long wait at work for the elevator grates every day because the negative experience is insufficient to trigger a response from "our psychological immune system." Because adaptation is not well understood, you are likely to overestimate the amount of happiness that a positive events will bring you—just as you underestimate your own ability to recover from one of life's many setbacks.

As it happens, people also generally do a rather poor job of predicting future levels of happiness. Most people (although not so much lawyers) have a bias toward optimism that causes them to overestimate future levels of happiness. Asked to predict how happy they will be five years from now, almost three-quarters of people surveyed expect to be happier and only about 5 percent predict that they will be less happy.[47] In fact the best prediction of how happy you will be in five or ten years is precisely how happy you now are. Our mistake? Usually it is in thinking that the future will be more like the present than it actually will be. In our imagined futures, we continue to value the same experiences we do today, and we then adjust our happiness upward based on a few anticipated events, such as having kids, moving into a new home, or landing a sought-after promotion. The reality is that how we value various experiences continues to change over time and that life, almost always, pushes us in unexpected directions.

Internal Factors: The 40 Percent Determinant of Happiness Levels That Is within Your Control

With genetics accounting for 50 percent of our happiness, and those circumstances that are largely out of our control a paltry 10 percent, that leaves 40 percent within the power of our own actions and ways of thinking to determine.[48] In other words, well-chosen happiness strategies can boost happiness levels four times more than if somehow the circumstances of life that are largely beyond our control magically were to swing to the ideal. Of course, there is no single silver-bullet solution to improving happiness levels by 40 percent. Rather, the 40 percent figure represents the upper limit of the possible if you adopt all the approaches to improving happiness that happen to be best suited for your own circumstances and personality.

What *are* these happiness strategies that can give our happiness levels powerful boosts? They are many and they are varied.

GETTING MORE SATISFACTION

The "forty-percent solution" to happiness,[49] focusing on those two-fifths of our overall happiness that we can control, is really the only solution we have. You cannot change the genes you've been dealt, and most of what we've labeled "circumstances" are either unchangeable (such as your age or health) or very difficult to change. The potential 40 percent gain in happiness from intentional strategies represents a ceiling, and one that is difficult to reach. Getting a full 40-percent boost might be as unrealistic as going from the ten push-ups you can do now to the hundred you'd like to do. It will involve a lot of focus and even then you might not make it. But if it isn't worth trying to get happier, then what *is* worth trying?

We will discuss specific steps lawyers can take to increase career satisfaction in chapter 4, but the rest of your life matters too, so here we offer some strategies that can help boost overall life satisfaction. A happier person is usually also a happier lawyer, so adopting some of these strategies will probably make you feel better about your career, even though careers are not the focus of these strategies.

For the most part, the strategies we suggest are aimed at increasing satisfaction, not the more transient variety of happiness. Need we remind you, however, that the passing pleasures of life make a contribution to overall life satisfaction? So, in addition to trying out the strategies below, don't forget to treat yourself to life's pleasures. Once in a while, go for that double-fudge ice cream, grab the skis and head for the slopes, or indulge yourself with a Swedish massage.

And don't forget the activities known to promote satisfaction, and not just short-term happiness. These activities include exercise, getting adequate and regular sleep—if sleeping can be fairly called "an activity"—and meditation. Finding enough hours in a day for exercise, adequate sleep, and meditation can be a challenge for lawyers. We will stress later the importance of a balanced life, but let this be an early warning of the costs associated with a seventy-hour-per-week job. Relax with your favorite guru or yoga instructor and enjoy that voyage of self-discovery.

BECOMING A THRIVING PERSON

The Six Keys to Life Satisfaction

Across all cultures, six experiences have been found central to making a person thrive—and a thriving person is generally one who will be satisfied with his or her life. Those experiences are security, autonomy, authenticity, relatedness, competence, and self-esteem.[50] It is within your power to either develop or erode these core elements of a thriving person. If you play your cards right, you'll be happier.

Security is the odd duck on the list, in that it is more dependent on external conditions than the other five experiences, and is a prerequisite to a sense of well-being. A fearful, anxious existence is not consistent with thriving. Choices dictated by fear are not choices at all. People do not thrive in war zones when daily fears of bombs landing on their house crowd their minds. Most of us don't live in a war zone, but some of us do live in neighborhoods where security is an everyday concern. Others among us might worry about threats from someone living under our own roof. Still others may feel physically secure but be anxious about health or finances. When sources of deep anxiety are present, life satisfaction becomes impossible. Needless to say, then, anything that can be done to alleviate the anxiety should be done. Can you afford to move to a safer neighborhood? Can a psychologist or medical doctor or financial planner help you confront and control whatever it is that is the source of your insecurity? These feelings can be heavy and are really beyond the scope of this book—but know that without facing these issues first, everything else we can offer will be of little help.

Autonomy is the ability to make your *preferred* choices and not have them dictated either by fear or imagined or real constraints. Put simply, an autonomous person can do the things he or she wants to do. It should surprise no one that autonomy is central to thriving. When it comes to autonomy, Americans start with an advantage over Belarusians or North Koreans—at least we don't have a government severely constraining our choices. Nonetheless, we all sometimes have our choices limited. We might not have the money to take that dream vacation we want. Or we might have the money, but the demands of work make travel impossible. Or we have the money and the time, but we have an elderly parent whose needs we must care for. We can't always do what we want—so what else is new? Accepting that not every door is open to us is not only part of growing up but is part of becoming a happier person.

In fact, what is perhaps most worth noting on the issue of autonomy is that our freedom is enhanced, not constricted, when our universe of choices shrinks to a manageable number. More people today suffer from having too many choices than from having too few. Having too many choices can lead to a paralysis that prevents us from making any choice at all or, if we finally do make a choice, can cause us to suffer regret ("buyer's remorse") over all of those other possible choices not made. In his wonderfully insightful book, *The Paradox of Choice: Why Less Is More*, Barry Schwartz shows that people who overanalyze the vast array of choices modern life throws at us are less happy, less optimistic, and more depressed than people who are quicker to say "good enough" and make their choices. The overanalyzers, people Schwartz calls "maximizers," pay "a significant price in terms of personal well-being."[51] Choice overload becomes a nightmare for maximizers but not for "satisficers" who understand that no choice is likely to be perfect and that the time spent trying to select from a set of reasonably good alternatives can better be spent in more satisfying ways.

Authenticity is being who you really are. An authentic person makes choices based on his or her true values. Being "in the closet," whether on the issue of sexual orientation or political affiliation or spiritual preference, can be hazardous to your emotional health.[52] When your goals are consistent with your deepest values and not the values someone else chooses for you, your life has a clarity and sense of purpose that makes achieving happiness much more likely. What this means for you and your law career will be a topic for a later chapter, but it probably is obvious to you already that if you're a social conservative, your prospects for career satisfaction aren't enhanced by joining a pornography defense firm. Authenticity, however, isn't just about the big choices, it is about the little ones too. Do you prefer a Budweiser to that Sonoma County pinot noir, but go with the wine because you think your friends will think less of you if you ask for a beer? Does your choice of furniture reflect your taste or that of an interior designer your mother recommended? Almost everyone hides some part of their true self, but the less you do it, the happier you'll become. You can take a step in the direction of authenticity, and in the direction of greater happiness, by identifying the activities that truly make *you* (and not necessarily anyone else) happier—and then spending more time doing those activities. If your friends leave you because you suddenly start playing volleyball at nudist camps or going to pyramid conventions—well, they probably weren't the best of friends anyway.

The fourth key to thriving is relatedness, or feeling well-connected to others. People need people. People need to share, need to laugh, need support. Of course, creating deep connections takes time, and it usually involves a process of promise-making and promise-keeping that eventually leads to trust. The good news is that the very steps that can eventually create a close friendship often bring increased satisfaction along the way. Expressing gratitude frequently, for example, is one of the surest ways to increase your own life satisfaction. Forgiving others and moving on also increases satisfaction, while wallowing in and ruminating over past wrongs blocks happiness at the doorway. Acting happy tends to strengthen friendships and, interestingly, makes you happier than you were when you started acting. (Even a simple thing like forming a smile seems to bring a small amount of pleasure to the smiler.) Performing acts of kindness also increases satisfaction, as does joining with friends or relatives to reminisce over past events. We could come up with a much longer list here, but you get the idea.

A fifth experience of the thriving person is a sense of competence. The person who masters challenges or accomplishes a difficult task feels capable, feels valued, and is likely to feel happier. As a lawyer, you have already mastered (more or less) a difficult skill. If you have practiced in a specialized area of law, and your skill is in demand, you probably already feel valued by clients or by colleagues. (If you have that mastery, and no one in your firm seems to give a damn, maybe it's time to get out?) Apart from your legal career, however, competence in other areas such as woodworking or tennis might also give you a happiness boost. In particular, by developing competencies, a person increases their opportunities for activities that thread that happy needle between boredom and anxiety and which are highly correlated with feelings of enhanced well-being.

Finally, a thriving person has self-esteem. This experience, in fact, is so closely tied to satisfaction that the two terms are sometimes thought to be nearly synonymous. A person with self-esteem is satisfied with one's self. Self-esteem has been a large topic for many years, and we won't attempt to plow this field. Suffice it to say, adopting tools that increase self-esteem will also tend to make you happier. These tools include forgiving yourself, trying to imagine an ideal future for yourself, avoiding excessive rumination, and doing the things (such as practicing acts of kindness or meeting a difficult challenge) that could make you feel better about yourself.

How do you measure up on these six experiences of the thriving person? On a one-to-ten scale, which is your strongest suit and which your weakest? Focusing on these intrinsic (or self-development) goals produces more happiness than focusing on extrinsic goals, such as becoming rich or famous.

DO THINGS GO BETTER WITH HAPPINESS?

We don't seek happiness because it will make us a better spouse or friend or lawyer; we seek happiness because we like being happy. "People are strongly, perhaps even primarily, perhaps even single-mindedly, motivated to be happy."[53] As it turns out, however, happiness is more than its own reward. One of the side benefits of happiness, as we've noted, is that the happy person spreads happiness to others. Happiness also allows us to be more receptive to information, either coming from others or from our environment. It makes us mindful: we see things that we miss when in a sour mood. We become aware of the loveliness of a garden, the sound of the oriole, or the smell from the freshly fallen rain. Just as significantly, we become better at reading the signals that those near us are sending: we become better listeners and become more capable of satisfying the desires of our lovers and our friends. Finally, happiness makes us healthier. It produces better immune systems and makes us more resilient when we suffer setbacks. Happy people live longer than unhappy people.[54]

In this chapter, we've explored the components of happiness. We've learned that happiness has a significant genetic component, but it also can be strongly influenced by the choices we make and the strategies we adopt. In the next chapter, we will consider what aspects of a life in the law move us toward greater happiness and what aspects tend to pull us away from our goal. It's off to work we go.

CHAPTER 3

What Makes Lawyers Happy and Unhappy

W HEN A RESEARCHER AT THE UNIVERSITY OF Chicago's National Opinion Research Center (NORC) analyzed surveys of workers in 198 occupations, he discovered that the clergy ranked at the very top of the list in job satisfaction and roofers ranked at the very bottom.[1] The study did not attempt to determine why the clergy were so happy or roofers so miserable, but what we've learned about the sources of happiness in general gives us some pretty good clues. We'll see where lawyers stand on the happiness scale shortly, but let's start by looking at which occupations are the most and least happy to give us a measuring stick.

The first thing to note about the clergy is not only are they very satisfied with their work, but they are also unusually happy people. In addition to reporting the highest level of job satisfaction (with 87.2 percent calling themselves "very satisfied"), the clergy also reported the highest level of overall personal happiness (with 67.2 percent pronouncing themselves "very happy"). These results, of course, raise a "chicken-or-the-egg" question: Are the clergy so happy doing what they do because of the nature of the job, or do people who enter seminaries tend to be happier people and then let their personal happiness translate into higher levels of job satisfaction? The answer, it seems, is both: those who join the clergy are happy people and they love their jobs. Happy people tend to look at glasses as being half full and report above average levels of satisfaction across multiple domains, ranging from marital satisfaction to satisfaction with where they live.[2] It is quite likely that the typical seminarian is more purpose-driven, more extroverted, and more focused on relationships (all traits associated with increased levels of happiness) than the average person.

The evidence is compelling, however, that something in the nature of the work also makes the clergy so spectacularly satisfied compared to other workers. The number of clergy reporting themselves "very satisfied" with their work is a full 20 percent higher than the number of clergy calling themselves "very happy" in their personal lives. What explains this?

One factor is undoubtedly that the work of the clergy closely aligns with their own values. They identify paths to eternal life or personal fulfillment, and they then try to guide their flocks along that path. They comfort the afflicted and rail, when they wish, against the evils of the world. Happiness research makes it indisputably clear that people feel better about work when they think they are making a contribution to the public good than when they think their work either has no social value or actually undermines the public good.[3] The clergy have a benefit that lawyers, for the most part, don't enjoy. They can choose to attend a divinity school or seminary that closely reflects their own personal values, whereas law schools, with a few exceptions, generally are not associated with teaching distinctive sets of values.

Other factors help make the clergy so satisfied. Their work involves them in deep and meaningful ways in the lives of others, and deep relationships correlate with higher levels of happiness. Their job affords high measures of control. The clergy are usually free to shape church programs ("What should be the theme of my sermon this week?" "What field trip should we send the youth group on this year?"). They also have a fair amount of scheduling flexibility and the reasonable prospect of a good work-life balance. The clergy face creative challenges within their realm of competence and frequently interact with people less fortunate than themselves, both job characteristics associated with satisfying careers.

Compare the clergy to our oh-so-miserable roofers: up there, laying asphalt shingles in 100-degree temperatures or 20-degree wind chills and not feeling entirely secure all the while. Probably worse, laying shingles affords almost zero opportunities for creativity—the shingles are laid down in a preset order, and there's no opportunity for the roofer to let loose an inner Van Gogh. Control and personal interaction is limited at best; it's one long hour of tedium after another, often just you and your roof.

Jobs that align with values and involve helping others are those that rated at the very top of the NORC study. Following right behind the clergy in job satisfaction were physical therapists, firefighters, and education administrators (deans, principals, and school superintendents). Teachers came in sixth on the list, in-between two jobs offering bushel baskets of opportunities for creativity and personal control, artists and authors.

On the other hand, at the bottom of the list, just above roofers in reporting low levels of job satisfaction, were waiters, bartenders, packagers, and stock handlers. None of these jobs, with the possible exception of bartending, provides creative challenges or offers workers an opportunity to express their personal values through their work.

Given what the survey suggests about the most and least satisfying jobs, it should come as no surprise that lawyers rank slightly above the middle of the pack in terms of job satisfaction. Lawyers, with 52.4 percent reporting themselves "very satisfied," are below doctors (57.9 percent satisfied) and in-between occupations such as editors (52.9 percent satisfied) and accountants (49.7 percent satisfied). The jobs that fall between the extremes of satisfaction and dissatisfaction, including the practice of law, are those that score well on some characteristics of satisfying jobs (say, providing challenge), not so well on others (say, allowing control), and in-between on still others (say, opportunities for interaction or alignment of work with values).

Lawyers report so-so satisfaction with their careers despite the fact that law is a high paying and prestigious job. Those qualities don't matter very much in terms of job satisfaction. It is also a helping profession, and that is generally a positive indicator of happiness, except that, unlike clergy, lawyers don't see clients at their happiest moments.

An American Bar Association (ABA) study of how the practice of law matched the expectations that lawyers had when they entered the field is revealing. The study showed that the "intellectual challenge" of law practice was by far the aspect of practice that most closely matched expectations. Law is a great field for people who love mental puzzles, and almost everyone in the field seems to know that. Fully 70 percent of lawyers report that the intellectual challenge of law practice "very well" matched their expectations. Compare that to what seems to be the great disappointment of lawyers, the failure of their job to contribute as much to the public good as they expected. Only 16 percent of lawyers, according to the survey, found that their jobs afforded the "ability to contribute to social good" as much as they had expected. A full quarter of lawyers reported, on this measure, that their expectations were "not at all" met in their jobs. Falling in-between these extremes of expectation and reality was "financial remuneration," with 34 percent reporting their compensation "very well" matched what they thought it would be, while another 52 percent found that the financial rewards of law practice at least "somewhat" matched expectations.[4]

Depending on an attorney's specific job—small firm practitioner in a cultivated niche, in-house counsel with a template of corporate rules, or large firm associate—the attorney will have more or less control. But there are many things lawyers can't control, chief among them other lawyers, deadlines, and billing. According to a 2007 ABA study, 69 percent of lawyer respondents saw "declining civility" in their profession, and 90 percent of lawyers in the largest firms found "competition between firms" increasing, possibly forcing firms to abandon more traditional professional models in favor of more efficient models (i.e., more emphasis on billable hours and client development and less emphasis on building collegial relationships and doing quality work regardless of cost).[5] Especially telling is the fact that one-half of all lawyers now say that pressure to increase billable hours is a "very" or "somewhat" important reason that would make them consider leaving a firm.[6] A desire to have more time to spend with friends and family ranks well above the concern to earn more money or to advance within the firm's hierarchy.

These results clearly flag the trouble spots in a lawyer's search for happiness. Many lawyers, especially those in the private sector, are disappointed that their work doesn't more closely align with their values. Many are also dissatisfied with what they see as the overly competitive, zero-sum nature of much practice today. Finally, many lawyers are struggling, sometimes with limited success, to achieve a happy balance between their professional and personal lives. We look more closely at some of these issues in the next section.

WHAT ACCOUNTS FOR ATTORNEY UNHAPPINESS?

WORK STRESSES, HIGH BILLABLE HOURS AND LOW QUALITY OF LIFE

> Lying was a way of life—a necessity and therefore a virtue.... Our corporate culture required the show of enthusiasm in all circumstances. A partner would come into your office and ask if you had any plans for the weekend. The correct answer was "no." And you would then be given an assignment to fill your empty Saturday and

Sunday. The first time I was asked the question, I mumbled some-thing about having hoped to go to Vermont. The young partner, who was nicknamed "Dave the Barracuda," looked at me with a combination of incredulity and sympathy, as if I had just confessed to a subnormal IQ. "It's a rhetorical question," he explained with an exasperated sigh.[7]

Many lawyers are unhappy with the rigid billable hour require-ments of firm life and the long hours that the profession demands. The nature of the work is stressful: clients may have hopelessly unrealistic expectations; deals fall through; running a business while bringing in business is a constant pressure; cases have numer-ous unalterable deadlines that require late-night work; expenses of taking a case to trial can mount; clients can be convicted—and face life imprisonment or execution. Lawyers represent people who have been traumatized, people who are going through the worst crises of their lives, in sum, people who are unhappy.[8]

Overwork is a piece of the picture. In recent years, billable hour requirements have escalated. In the 1970s, associates at large law firms billed on average about 1,700 hours year (or thirty-four hours each week). In 2009, the national average billable hour requirement for firms of all sizes was 1,888 hours, but expecta-tions for associates on large firm partnership tracks can amount to 1,900–1,950 hours each year (an average of roughly forty hours each week).[9] A forty-hour week sounds manageable until you realize that forty billable hours means many more (some estimates range to 50 percent more) actual hours at the office. The bill-able hour meter typically does not run during firm administration work, pro bono cases, marketing and business generation activi-ties, attorney and staff recruiting activities, training and mentoring sessions for newer associates, or continuing education classes let alone during office face time, coffee breaks, or socializing oppor-tunities with colleagues. Compared to a median work week of forty hours for all full-time employees in America, lawyers work a median of fifty hours per week, and one-fifth of new lawyers work sixty hours or more each week.[10]

A 2009 study by NALP, the Association for Legal Career Professionals, offered billable hour estimates by firm size (see table 1).[11]

The difference in billable hour requirements between small and large firms seems modest, although attorneys in larger firms put in substantially more nonbillable hour time, when, for example, they perform administrative duties or have face time. Associates work these strenuous hours, but through attrition—both voluntary and involuntary—only about 15 percent of them become partners.[12]

It is not just that billable hour expectations are on the rise but that partnership and bonus systems are often specifically linked to billable hours. Slightly less than one-half of firms with more than one hundred attorneys used "meeting fixed goals" as a measure to determine bonuses.[13] The responses received from various studies and surveys revealed frustration among lawyers that their worth was quantified, and their career advancement determined, by the number of hours they worked. One associate commented, "devotion equals promotion. The more you work the higher you rise."[14] Similarly, The Rodent (an anonymous associate at a large firm writing an underground newsletter) reported that he was often criticized for not billing enough hours until one month, when

TABLE 1. Yearly Billable Hours by Firm Size

Firm Size	Billable Hours Required
50 or fewer attorneys	1,814
51–100 attorneys	1,847
101–250 attorneys	1,864
251–500 attorneys	1,904
501–700 attorneys	1,908
701 or more attorneys	1,938

partners lavished him with praise for high billable hours even though he was busy with "mostly clerical work—proofreading, sorting documents and making copies."[15]

Even some of the perks of large law firm life—on top of starting salaries beginning at $160,000 for first year associates—such as BlackBerrys, catered meals delivered to the associates' desks, and a chauffeur service to drive them home if the trains have stopped running—are props for billable hour production. One law professor commented, "Many associates feel they are working in nicely decorated sweatshops."[16]

Technology can also contribute to lawyer unhappiness regarding mounting billable hours and less personal time. While today's lawyers may be more productive and efficient due to various technological advances, they are also always "on call"—reachable by e-mail, cell-phone, or fax. One *American Lawyer* survey respondent complained, "Technology makes it possible for [partners] to encroach on all of your time, whether you're awake, asleep or on vacation."[17] Making work more portable has many advantages, but it increasingly blurs the line between being at work and away from work, and this contributes to attorneys' dissatisfaction.

Thus, we see that some of the primary reasons for lawyers' discontent with their working lives center on quality of life issues: the overwhelming hours coupled with the idea that the value of an attorney is measured by the number of hours billed; the stressful nature of the work; and the gap between the ideals they had when they entered the profession and the repetitive nature of their daily tasks.

LAW IS BECOMING MORE OF A BUSINESS, LESS OF A PROFESSION

Money is at the root of virtually everything that lawyers don't like about their profession: the long hours, the commercialization, the tremendous pressure to attract and retain clients, the fiercely competitive marketplace, the lack of collegiality and loyalty among partners, the poor public image of the profession, and even the lack of civility.[18]

The practice of law has become more of a business and less of a profession. Law firms focus on maximizing profits. Money is equated with firm prestige and individual career success. These economic forces are not unique to law. The uptick in greed and competition can be found in most occupations, industries, and social life. Economists Robert Frank and Philip Cook call it the "winner take all" society.

Law firms afford lawyers much less job security than in previous generations. Firms are willing to abandon practice areas that are less lucrative. They also have few qualms about jettisoning lawyers. The early 1990s saw layoffs of both lawyers and bankers in response to the bank credit crunch and junk bond market collapse. In recent years, the cascade of economic problems resulting from the subprime mortgage crisis has prompted slower hiring, attorney and staff layoffs, summer hiring freezes, rescinding of job offers, and "redeployments" of real estate and finance lawyers into other practice areas.

High rates of attorney turnover lead to reduced loyalty to firms. Within five years of graduating from law school, 80 percent of associates will have changed jobs at least once.[19] This is up from two-thirds in the 1988–96 period, and compares even less favorably to the historical view of Traditionalists and Baby Boomers of a lifetime career at a single firm.[20] Even when associates make partner, the relationship is no longer a permanent union. There are numerous different types of arrangements: typically equity (part-owners of the business) and nonequity partners, of counsel or senior counsel positions. These heavily stratified partnership structures create alienating hierarchies. In tiered partnerships, subordinate partners are often treated more like permanent employees than co-owners.

Law firm consolidations, dissolutions, and lateral hiring have always existed but increasingly have become routine. With the accelerating pace of consolidations has come a change in the nature of mergers. Law professor David Achtenberg says, "It would have been virtually inconceivable twenty years ago for a firm to merge into another one knowing that doing so would create a conflict of interest that would force a significant number of partners in the firm to have to leave or would strip many of its partners of any meaningful control in the newly created entity. Today it is common." Mergers and acquisitions add to feelings of instability and undermine trust.

Lawyers pay attention to the financial bottom line and try to maximize profits; success is measured solely in quantifiable terms—numbers of billable hours, hourly rates, fees, or favorable verdicts. Some lawyers may respond to economic pressures by doing what their clients want even if their behavior dances on the borderline of unethical conduct. Fee structures encourage continued combat. Examples abound of defense lawyers continuing litigation for years to protect their income stream of exorbitant hourly wage work.

Some lawyers cross the line and participate in unethical conduct. Others engage in offensive and unprofessional behavior that ranges from rudeness to obstructionist tactics. We turn next to dissatisfactions related to lawyer incivility.

Incivility

She wants to play dirty, I can play dirty . . . I went to law school, people.
—Bride Wars

One of the largest dissatisfactions with lawyers' professional lives is other lawyers. Incivility is rampant. In any gathering of lawyers, you will hear complaints about lawyer incivilities. Competitive tactics have long been part of the profession, but incivility is escalating, particularly in larger cities.[21] In smaller towns, everybody still knows everybody else; in more sprawling metropolitan areas, lawyers practice against opposing counsel they may see once and then never again. What is lost is not just a sense of a professional community but civility.

The adversarial system and the ethical obligation of zealous representation have spawned some mutant offspring. Some lawyers perceive that playing hardball brings a strategic advantage; others think litigation is a form of warfare. They may launch personal attacks and engage in insults, name-calling, threats of bar complaints, rudeness, and hostility. The unprofessional behavior extends from lawyer-to-lawyer contacts to depositions and into the courtroom. Examples of rudeness in reported cases include sarcastic and inappropriate language, diminutive names for female lawyers (e.g., "little lady"), references to defendants as, in one case, "snake[s] in the grass," and in another, "cowardly, dirty, low down dogs," and purely offensive and uncooperative behavior. In one survey of lawyers, 56 percent of those responding "cited obnoxiousness as the most common, unpleasant quality they encounter among other lawyers."[22] In a random sample of more than 4,600 respondents to an Eighth Circuit survey, nearly three-quarters of all female lawyers and one-half of all male lawyers reported that they had experienced general or gender-related incivility in the past five years.[23] According to two other polls, 69 percent of lawyers thought that civility in the profession had declined over time, and 80 percent of judges had observed uncivil attorney conduct in their courtrooms.[24]

Declining civility is due to an abundance of lawyers and an increase in competition for business, a decrease in mentoring of new lawyers, the absence of repeat interactions with the same small coterie of lawyers, and the rise of social incivility generally. Of course, part of the explanation may be a "good old days" problem. Older lawyers may remember practice thirty or forty years ago as more idyllic than it was. In 1932 Clarence Darrow wrote that "trials were not being conducted in a dignified effort to find the truth but more like a prize-ring combat."[25] (An interesting observation, coming as it does from one of the greatest courtroom prize-fighters of all time.)

The more contemporary scorched earth litigation tactics at times go beyond manipulation of facts, assertion of frivolous claims, hardball negotiation, disrespect for witnesses, ruthless cross-examination, discovery abuses, and unmeritorious appeals. State disciplinary boards have sanctioned lawyers for calling opposing counsel names like "punk," "boy," "fool," and "idiot"; shoving other attorneys; and in one case threatening an attorney-defendant who refused to settle with " 'the legal equivalent of a proctology exam.' " The Supreme Court of South Carolina issued a public reprimand to a lawyer who told a "deponent that he would like 'to be locked in a room with [her] naked with a sharp knife,' and that he needed 'a big bag' to put her in 'without the mouth cut out.' "[26] A popular YouTube video shows several prominent Texas lawyers devolving into colorful name-calling during a deposition.[27]

With the constant friction, lawyers feel isolated and learn to mistrust each other. It is stressful to go to war (er, work) each day having to anticipate Rambo litigation tactics and personal attacks—and not just from opposing counsel.

The competition and discontent also percolate into law firms. One of the first tensions is among peer associates in what Marc Galanter and Thomas Palay call the "promotion-to-partner tournament":

> Over a fixed period of time, the firm holds a contest in which all the associates in a particular "entering class" compete, with the prize of partnership being awarded to some fixed percentage of the "top" contestants. An associate's final standing in the tournament depends upon the size and quality of his production of two goods: (1) high-quality legal work; and (2) his own human capital, measured subjectively, not mechanically. After a specified period of time, the players in a particular class are ranked and those in the

top stratum are declared "winners." (This may vary from ten to ninety percent.) The losers are told that they can remain employees but will never become partners; or they may be given consolation prizes, such as severance pay or help finding another job; or they may be unceremoniously dumped.[28]

Partners can play too, although the games are somewhat different. Some partners engage in client-hoarding. The lateral mobility of lawyers, particularly those who control business, has created substantial incentives for those who currently have close relationships with a client to be certain that no one else does. By not sharing work with other partners, but instead delegating work to subordinate associates, a lawyer retains bargaining power within the firm and has a book of business to take down the road to a potential acquiring firm. Lawyers, as mercenaries who are always ready to pack their briefcases and head down the road—like a yuppie version of the *Grapes of Wrath*—also have little incentive to engage in meaningful social relationships with other people in their present firm.

A side result of this declining civility is the elevation of marketing over craft. The internal economic forces in a firm that prompt attorneys to hoard clients also create disincentives for lawyers to share work with the most competent lawyer for a particular issue to avoid risks of client-poaching. Attention to revenue undermines professionalism.

The adversarial system can also take its toll on your personal relationships. Professor David Guenther tells this story of winning an argument, while a good thing in the courtroom, can be a bad thing for a relationship:

> Several years ago a male student thanked me for what he had learned in my course. "For the first time," he said, "I'm winning arguments with my girlfriend." Coincidentally, a few months later, a female student asked me for advice on how to get her boyfriend to stop arguing like a lawyer. I told her about the time I thought

I was having a conversation with my wife when she suddenly retorted: "Stop cross-examining me!"[29]

KEEPING UP WITH THE JONES DAYS

Another dynamic that recently has entered the legal profession is the spread of information about co-workers' incomes, as well as the business-like calculation of partners' shares and associates' salaries and bonuses. The knowledge of relative wealth has exploded in the past twenty years. Accompanying this knowledge has been the conflation of wealth with worth.

Before 1975, when the Supreme Court held that the practice constituted price-fixing, local bar associations used to publish minimum fee schedules. Back then, few lawyers made astronomical amounts of money. Now there are more who do, whether it is through lucrative plaintiffs' practices or large draws by partners at firms. Not only has there been a surge in what the richest lawyers are making, but also there has been a vast change in the extent to which everyone knows all of the information.

In 1987 journalist and lawyer Steven Brill started *American Lawyer*. Before its publication, lawyers had a general understanding that it wasn't polite to talk openly about how much money they and their co-workers earned. Lawyers had a general sense of who was doing well, but it was not directly discussed. Brill's innovation, which made the magazine a huge success, was to blow away that inhibition on talking about what lawyers were being paid. The magazine published lists of starting salaries for new lawyers and of exactly what partners were making at all the big firms. That changed things, because lawyers became much more acutely aware of where they stood in the financial pecking order. Although *American Lawyer* concentrated on the biggest firms, it trickled down because the focus on what those top-paid lawyers were making generated envy and insecurity.

BIGGER IS NOT BETTER

Law firms are expanding in size and that has adverse consequences for lawyer happiness. In the United States, at least six hundred firms employ one hundred or more lawyers each. The 250 largest firms collectively employ more than 120,000 lawyers.[30] Firm size can make an enormous difference in the types of relationships lawyers have with both their work and other lawyers. In a thirty- or forty-lawyer firm, every lawyer knows every other lawyer. In a firm with two hundred lawyers, that doesn't happen. Bigger may not be better when it comes to happiness in law firms. People feel uncomfortable when substantial control over their future and success depends on people they do not know.

As firms grow bigger, the slices of work done on cases by individual lawyers get smaller. Attorneys work on minor pieces of huge cases and engage in endless review of documents with little human contact. When they do communicate with each other, they do so by e-mail and conference calls and through Fed Ex drops. Lawyers become alienated from the nature of their work, and they do not see how their work matters.

Yet people are different, and for some lawyers the big firm is the perfect choice. Most highly specialized, sophisticated litigation is conducted by large firms, and many lawyers report enjoying the intellectual challenges presented in those cases. Other happy large-firm lawyers point to the high-quality training and mentoring they received, or to their delight in having so many smart, interesting colleagues from whom to draw their circle of friends. For introverted lawyers, large firms typically offer a variety of research or transactional work that may reduce the discomfort they would feel in more socially demanding small firm settings. Finally, of course, there is the money. Money can't buy happiness, but sometimes it can be a shield against unhappiness. Big firms generally offer compensation at the top of the salary charts, and for today's many debt-ridden law graduates, a generous starting salary means one less big stressor.

FEELING UNLOVED

> Q: What's the difference between a lawyer and a bucket of pond scum?
>
> A: The bucket.
>
> Q: Why does California have the most lawyers and New Jersey the most toxic waste dumps?
>
> A: New Jersey got first pick.
>
> Q: What do you call six hundred lawyers at the bottom of the ocean?
>
> A: A good start.
>
> Q: What is the difference between a dead rattlesnake and a dead lawyer in the middle of the road?
>
> A: There are skid marks in front of the rattlesnake.
>
> Q: What's black and brown and looks good on a lawyer?
>
> A: A Doberman Pincher.

Of course, the ultimate anti-lawyer joke is that lawyers don't think anti-lawyer jokes are funny and that everyone else doesn't think they're jokes.

The public has a dismal opinion of lawyers. In a 2006 Gallup poll survey of Americans' opinions about the levels of honesty and ethical standards in twenty-three professions, only 18 percent of respondents gave lawyers a "very high" or "high" ethics rating. Lawyers ranked well below nurses (84 percent), doctors (69 percent), clergy (58 percent), and police officers (54 percent) but ranked above members of Congress (14 percent), insurance salesmen (13 percent), and car salesmen (7 percent).[31] An ABA survey revealed that nearly three-quarters of those responding believe that lawyers try to win no matter the costs and will "manipulate both the system and the truth."[32] Lawyers are perceived as crooked, unethical, greedy, aggressive, and untrustworthy: a combination of mistrust and dislike.

Why do people love to hate lawyers? A number of factors are at work. Lawyers inevitably suffer in reputation because they tend, just by the nature of their jobs, to be heavily involved in negative things. In other words, people don't need lawyers when things are going great, or at least they don't need them to be as visible. If a corporation is profitable, nobody is going to notice its lawyers, or think, "gee, they must have an excellent legal team." Lawyers take a more prominent role when things are bad—bankruptcies, accusations of crime, or divorces. People seek the services of lawyers when they are in trouble, so the "public will always associate lawyers with some of life's worst moments."[33] (Although clergy often step in during difficult situations too, they also celebrate the best of times with worshippers, and clergy don't absorb the blame when things go wrong.) It may be hard to avoid being tarnished by the negative associations, even if lawyers perform admirably and try to make the best of bad situations.

Lawyers are merchants of misery. They see people in times of stress or crisis and, unlike other professionals, can't always, perhaps not even often, make clients happy. As Professor Andrew McClurg observes, "Litigated disputes, by their nature, have winners and losers. Each one leaves someone hurting financially and often emotionally."[34] Aside from mediation, lawyers lose their cases about half the time, and even when they "win," their clients may not obtain all the relief they want.

While lawyers get dragged into the mud every time something bad happens, they rarely accumulate occupational brownie points for a job well done. Except for some fictional portrayals (such as Atticus Finch in *To Kill a Mockingbird*), civil rights cases, and actual innocence project cases, where lawyers championed the exoneration of incarcerated prisoners through DNA evidence, it is difficult to think of cases that prompted the public to react: "Wow, good lawyering!"

Lawyers must deal with clients' complaints about fees. The fee charged is often a large amount for the client and a small amount for an attorney. Very few clients feel the amount charged bears any relationship to the value received even when the lawyer is being responsible about fees.

Lawyers, particularly those who represent corporate giants or despicable criminal defendants, are perceived as hired guns whose values mirror those of their clients. A lawyer's function is not to be disinterested, impartial, or revealing; so, it is no wonder that the derogatory name "mouthpiece" has developed as a slang term for lawyer. The adversarial process encourages actions that may be perceived as lies, delays, and mindless posturing to create room for negotiation. "Those initial positions...may make lawyers seem hostile, aggressive and bloodthirsty, more interested in vicious battle than peaceful and prompt resolution."[35]

The public's attitude toward the profession is also formed by the media. Most Americans get the vast majority of their information about the legal system from the popular media, principally television. Hard news reports include spins about the "increases in the volume, cost and duration of litigation, as well as the number of lawyers, and the size of their incomes."[36] Much of the information about increases in the volume of litigation—and especially the size of awards in personal injury cases—is not true; but truth isn't the issue here. Sometimes the news and entertainment media blur together, resulting in the "entertain-ification" of the law. News reports about cases often come in sound bites from talking head legal analysts. Television personalities, such as Nancy Grace, urge the public to rush to judgment and portray lawyers (particularly criminal defense lawyers) as out to thwart justice at every turn. As a result, highly publicized circus trials occur, accompanied by "media misinformation about what was actually going on in some of those trials."[37] Every lawyer standing next to an unpopular client is tarnished by the association.

Part of the negative public impression comes from the pop culture spin. TV and movie depictions are often of bad lawyers in a profession characterized by greed, incompetence, and cynicism. While the prosecutors on *Law & Order* (especially Sam Waterston as Jack McCoy) are heroic, the defense lawyers are smug and insufferable. In the movie *Jurassic Park*, audiences cheered when the first human the dinosaur devours is the lawyer. In *The Devil's Advocate*, Al Pacino plays the managing partner of a law firm who actually *is* Satan. Being a member of a profession that faces a continual barrage of negative stereotyping from Hollywood and jokes from Jay Leno can be exhausting and saddening and can leave the human who holds the job "feeling empty and disillusioned."[38]

The cumulative effect of many of these dissatisfactions in the profession—the hours, fierce competition, incivility, and public aversion—may help explain why numerous people have had the same one-word reaction to the concept of happy lawyers: "oxymoron." We like to think of the idea as not an oxymoron but as a possibility.

We sometimes forget there are many upsides of being a lawyer—features of the job that are connected to attorney satisfaction. Let's remind ourselves of some of them.

LAW IS A NOBLE PROFESSION

> [I]t is we lawyers who create the mechanism for people involved
> in serious conflicts to peacefully resolve their conflicts in a sys-
> tem that places a search for the truth as a centerpiece of dispute
> resolution.[39]

Perhaps you are one of the many attorneys who not only like your job but feel that you are pursuing a passion as a well as a career. Being a lawyer can involve doing rewarding work. Law is a career in which you can make significant contributions, whether by handling adoptions, defending the Constitution, fighting race and gender discrimination, drafting legislation, protecting a battered partner, advising business entrepreneurs, tackling corporate Goliaths, or simply by being a trusted advisor. It also opens possibilities to contribute to the architecture of society: "Unfortunately, when one looks at a construction site or a building, one sees only the bricks and mortar, the workers, the cranes, the splendid architecture, and the engineering miracles. The myriad legal structures and devices are invisible. . . . Lawyers help build the world."[40] Social activists—those engaged in cause-lawyering—really can change the world because they can change the rules. Lawyers' words can become laws.

Lawyers are public citizens; they are vital in a democracy. Almost every lawyer-disparager, it seems, likes to trot out the line from Shakespeare's *Henry VI*: "First thing we do, let's kill all the lawyers." Few people realize, however, that the character offering the anti-lawyer remark, Dick the Butcher, is an outlaw and that his suggestion is made in the hopes of making life easier for lawbreakers everywhere. A world without lawyers would be a world in chaos. Economists have found remarkably strong positive correlations between the availability of lawyers in a society and the existence of civil rights and civil liberties.[41] Lawyers can engage in work that is socially significant and produces a relatively good income. But law is more about analytical challenges, intellectual stimulation, and the human dimensions of being a helping profession.

LAWYERS MAKE A DIFFERENCE

The *Legal Underground* blog tried to find out what lawyers enjoy about the profession, posing the question: "What do you like best about being a lawyer?" Some of the answers include:

> I like working with intelligent, thoughtful people.
>
> What I like best about being a lawyer has to do with the all-encompassing nature of the enterprise. Every day I am able to help people with disputes and issues that are beyond their own ability to handle.
>
> I enjoy counseling clients—they trust me. They listen to me. I tell them what to do and they do it. I solve problems for them.
>
> I like being a lawyer because I have the ability, access and opportunity to change, make or clarify law.
>
> I like knowing the rules. More than anything else, I like that fact. I don't have to wonder where I stand legally with regard to

much of anything. If I don't know something, I know where to find out about it.

What I love about being a lawyer is that I give a voice to people that otherwise have no one to stand up for them.

I like fixing problems. I am happiest when I am fixing a problem, regardless what kind of problem.

I went to law school in large part because I saw the impact that some lawyers had in their communities. That's really what I want to do with my life, try to make the community in which I live a better place.[42]

A repeated theme was making a difference in people's lives. One child advocacy lawyer said, "I love the work I do. It is an amazing feeling to be able to actually help people through such incredibly dark times."[43] In a later chapter, we will return to the stories of lawyers who find the practice of law satisfying, who are passionate about their work, and who have attained personal fulfillment in their jobs.

Professor David Guenther argues that "it is almost impossible to become a lawyer and not acquire a passion for justice." Exposure to people who have suffered injustice will cause you to "feel what they feel" and "understand it is not a game." If you are a lawyer worth your salt, "their cause will become your cause and you will become a passionate representative of their rights." Guenther maintains that this passion, if "channeled properly," will "bring out the best in you and inspire others."[44]

Law, as a helping profession, can claim many heroes. John Adams, late in an accomplishment-filled life that included playing a key role in gaining our independence and serving as our second president, wrote that it was his work as a young lawyer defending British soldiers who had opened fire on a mob of Americans during the Boston Massacre in 1770 that he was proudest of: "It was...one of the most gallant, generous, manly and disinterested Actions of my whole Life, and one of the best Pieces of Service

I ever rendered my Country." From abolitionist lawyers in the eighteenth century who dedicated their careers to fighting slavery to lawyers of today's innocence projects who work tirelessly to free the wrongly convicted, each generation has produced lawyer heroes. Lawyers have helped bend "the moral arc of the universe...toward justice."[45] You, as a lawyer, have it within your power to help people, to make a corner of the world better, to vindicate rights, to do justice, to become a peacemaker. In the words of Pope Paul VI, "If you want peace, work for justice."

Many lawyers are passionate about their work—they experience the nobility of law and truly enjoy making a difference in people's lives. Sometimes, though, when we are slogging through briefs and drafting documents late at night, we wonder if the rewarding parts of our jobs will outweigh the tedious ones in five years, or in ten.

THE ARC OF CAREERS

There is good news. Satisfaction with a career tends to increase over time. As the years go by, many workers manage to find ways to spend more time performing the tasks they enjoy most, while passing off to other—usually younger—workers some of the more annoying tasks. More experienced workers generally have achieved a higher level of competence and that makes for less job-related anxiety. They have a clearer understanding of what is expected from them. Finally, in the absence of excessive turnover, bad hires, or a repellant personality, they likely have accumulated a set of relationships that provide support and a source of fun.

Surveys of lawyer satisfaction show a clear upward trend in job satisfaction over time. According to an ABA study, lawyers with more than a decade worth of experience reported career satisfaction that was 40 to 50 percent higher than those with less than ten years work as a lawyer. Atlanta career consultant

Monica R. Parker offered this explanation for the happiness of more experienced lawyers: "Probably they've become partners or senior counsel, and by that time they've decided that the law is for them; they're going to stay and they like it."[46]

In addition to more satisfying work and more work product control, there is another reason for higher career satisfaction as the years go by. As we age, we learn to use more "mature adaptations" to deal with the inevitable setbacks and disappointments that come our way. Mature adaptations probably account for the higher rates of happiness reported by people in their sixties than in their twenties. When we are young and confronted by frustrations, we are more inclined to turn to repression, disassociation, projection, or passive aggression (consult your old Psych 101 text to jog your memory about these classic defense mechanisms). As we get older, we increasingly use healthier techniques, including altruism, humor, anticipation, suppression, and sublimation. For example, an older person is somewhat less likely to obsess about an office slight and more likely to shrug it off or laugh about it.

The central finding of George Valliant, in *Adaptation to Life*, an account of a classic longitudinal study of '42, '43, and '44 male Harvard University graduates as they progressed from their early twenties through middle age and into old age, is that developing mature adaptations to setbacks is the single best predictor of a successful life.[47] Of course, being mature in years is no guarantee of having developed mature adaptations, and many people—including many in the Harvard study—never mastered that singularly helpful ability. We all can think of a senior relative or colleague who still throws fits or turns sour and silent when things don't go his or her way.

As lawyers progress through their careers, they typically have a variety of work environments in which to practice their adaptations. By the time they hit midcareer, most lawyers have changed jobs more than once, and only 15 percent, according to a study of University of Virginia law grads, still hold the job they took when they graduated.[48] Some clear trends emerge from longitudinal studies of lawyers. While income continues to increase as a career goes on, fewer and fewer lawyers remain in private practice. Many migrate into smaller firms or accept in-house counsel positions. Substantial numbers of law grads in their forties, perhaps a quarter or so according to the Virginia study, have left the regular practice of law altogether and have instead moved on to jobs in academia and banking or became CEOs and small business owners.

While the story in many regards is the same for female lawyers as for male lawyers, there is one critical gender difference that emerges. Vastly more women than men interrupt their employment, usually to care at home for small children. The dramatic difference in this situation, although probably in decline, could hardly be overstated. For lawyers now in their forties, the percent of women who have at least temporarily left employment is about 40 percent while for men the figure is only about 1 percent. Despite the higher rate of interruptions and its effect on partnership tracks, the Virginia study found "no significant gender differences on any dimension of job satisfaction."[49] Women might complain more about "work-life balance" issues in law firms, but overall they still report levels of job satisfaction equal to that of males.

That lawyers change jobs, and that job-changing is occurring ever more often in our rapidly evolving economy, comes as no surprise. More often than not, the changes—when they are voluntary—seem to work out for the better. But it is important to remember that constantly being on the look out for a better job comes at a cost. Restless lawyers never seem to be able to enjoy what they've achieved or, more importantly, develop the sense commitment and deep collegial bonds that can lead to higher levels of career satisfaction. Psychologist Barry Schwartz observes, "there comes a point at which opportunities become so numerous that we feel overwhelmed.... Time spent dealing with choice is time taken away from being a good friend, a good spouse, a good parent, and a good congregant."[50]

What about career's end? What about that time when all the job-changing is done and lawyers either put away their briefcase for good or began finding time amidst the cases for rounds of midweek golf? Going from full-time work to a dead stop poses some risks, both to mental acuity and to relationships, making part-time work an attractive option for many older lawyers. This plan works well for some; others find, however, that going part-time is not a real option and that the nature of the work keeps them plugging away as hard as ever, despite their intentions. Retirement, interestingly, seems to have almost no effect on levels of personal happiness. Almost exactly the same percentage of retirees (36 percent) and full-time workers (35 percent) report themselves as being "very happy." The data are clear that busy people are happier than those with little to do: the most satisfied ex-lawyers are those who find hobbies, sports, and friendships to fill their free hours. Both working lawyers and retired lawyers, unsurprisingly, are considerably happier than the unemployed.[51] Only 16 percent of unemployed men said they were "very happy," less than half the percentage of employed men agreeing to the same statement. Daniel Nettle attributes the unhappiness of the out-of-work to a common feeling among this group that they have little control over their lives, not that they have lower incomes on average. Statistically speaking, Nettle notes, a sense of personal control is a twenty-times better predictor of happiness than income.[52]

Lawyers often sprinkle the introductory phrase, "But even if..." into their briefs. You may be thinking, "But even if...the arc of a career for most lawyers holds the promise of future satisfaction, will that apply to me?" Maybe you feel you are too competitive, too analytical or too much of a worrier—all qualities associated with lawyers (although not, of course, all lawyers)—to ever be happy. You might wonder if lawyers have distinct personality traits that undermine their happiness.

IS THERE A "LAWYER PERSONALITY" THAT AFFECTS CAREER SATISFACTION?

I fear that happiness isn't in my line, . . . blaming the disposition that was given to me at birth.

—U.S. Supreme Court Justice Benjamin Cardozo[53]

Do lawyers become unhappy people or do unhappy people become lawyers? Many of the existing works on unhappy lawyers posit that the practice of law makes people unhappy. When assessing whether a profession breeds unhappiness, it is important to keep in mind the difference between correlation and causation. Do people inclined toward unhappiness select law as a profession or does the practice of law induce, or perhaps exacerbate, those feelings?

The NORC career study suggests that happier people gravitate to some careers more often than others. It is also true that different personality types are disproportionately represented in different careers. It is likely that shy, helpful people are overrepresented in our nation's libraries; jobs in sales are disproportionately filled by extroverts; and that rodeo performers, by and large, are less risk-averse than the general population.

Is the practice of law disproportionately filled by people with certain personality traits? The answer is clearly "yes." When compared to the general population on a standard measure of personality types, a distinctive picture of lawyers emerges. Lawyers, as a group, are more introverted, more doubt-ridden, and more cool and logical than most people. They are less open about their feelings and less inclined to live in the present than most people. Lawyers are competitive, confident (sometimes a kiss away from arrogant), aggressive, and achievement-oriented; they can be argumentative.

We're not talking about you, of course, but many lawyers—including some very successful lawyers—express "high dominance" personalities.[54] High dominance personalities are associated with a strong competitive drive and are marked by frequently interrupting, controlling conversations, changing topics, offering unsolicited advice or instructions, and stating strong opinions.[55] In the courtroom, a strong competitive drive can be the difference between winning and losing for your client, so this personality type can be a career positive at the same time that it might sour the personal relationships so essential to both personal and career happiness.

Many lawyers are analytical problem-solvers who value thoughts and ideas, as opposed to feelings, in their interactions with other people.[56] Lawyers may also be exacting and tenacious, which are useful qualities for their work, but those are behaviors that can be noxious in interactions with opposing counsel. In short, the personality traits most common among lawyers are not those usually associated with happy people.[57] Of course, lawyers are a diverse group and some lawyers are as extroverted, confident, and inclined to live in the here-and-now as anyone, but the evidence is that many lawyers already have a strike against them in the quest for a happy career.

Martin Seligman, the father of positive psychology, and colleagues published a law review article exploring the question "Why Lawyers Are Unhappy," arguing that a major source of lawyer discontent stems from the fact that "lawyers are selected for their pessimism, or "prudence," and this generalizes to the rest of their lives."[58] A study at the University of Virginia School of Law showed that pessimists outperformed their optimistic peers in terms of law school success, such as grade point average and participation on law review.[59] People who choose law school are more often than not inclined to see glasses as half-empty rather than half-full, say the authors, and also more inclined to believe they are responsible for bad results, when they occur, and that those bad results will have lasting effects. These attitudes are not associated with good military leaders, insurance agents, or professional athletes, but they often do help people become better lawyers—at least better lawyers of a certain type. Transactional lawyers, in particular, owe it to their clients to anticipate and worry over worst-case scenarios. Caution and skepticism can help clients if and when things do later go to hell in a hand basket.

But the "downside" of pessimism, if you will, is fairly obvious. As the authors note, "the qualities that make for a good lawyer...may not make for a happy human being."[60] When they are not worrying about the future of their clients, pessimistic lawyers are likely worrying about whether they will make partner, whether they are really contributing to the public good in any way, or whether an airplane will fly into their skyscraper. Of course, these traits are compounded by psychological stressors of the job: high pressure and for many lawyers, particularly newer associates, limited latitude to make decisions or control their working conditions. The interplay of attorneys' personality traits and the professional demands of the job can prove toxic.

Law professor Larry Krieger and psychology professor Ken Sheldon take issue with the hypothesis that law is the career of self-selection by unhappy people. Instead, they hold law schools responsible for turning happy students into unhappy graduates. Krieger and Sheldon studied classes from two different law schools from orientation through graduation and compared these students to a population of undergraduates. They concluded that the "incoming [law] students were happier, more well-adjusted, and more idealistic/intrinsically oriented than a comparison undergraduate sample," but that the educational cues in law school culture create graduates that "are significantly different people from those who arrived to begin law school: They are more depressed, less service-oriented, and more inclined toward undesirable, superficial goals and values."[61] In chapter 5, we examine the extent to which the teaching methods, implicit messages, and career steerage in law schools help mold lawyer personalities.

To achieve happiness for some lawyers means struggling against their natures and against the very traits that contribute to their success. Poet Edgar Lee Masters had a day job as partner in the firm of famous defense lawyer Clarence Darrow. He wrote sympathetically about Darrow's "artist sense that drives him to shape his life to something harmonious, even against the schemes of God."[62] It may well be, for many of us in the legal profession, the schemes of God do not include our happiness, and we must work to steal from life what satisfaction we can.

If you have been doing a psychological self-assessment while you read the last few paragraphs, mentally checking off the boxes for ambition, tenacity, and perhaps functional pessimism, remember that personality has some plasticity. These personality characteristics are not fixed. Abundant research shows that behaviors change over time and are influenced by social arrangements, and that optimism is an outlook that can be learned.[63] If the psychological demographics of lawyer satisfaction do not work in your favor, there are things you can do within law to become happier.

This chapter has focused mostly on what makes lawyers unhappy. The next chapter offers a toolbox for achieving greater happiness. We turn next to the tools and tricks you can use to steal more happiness from your career as a lawyer.

CHAPTER 4

The Happiness Toolbox

ODDS ARE, IF YOU ARE READING THIS BOOK, YOU'RE not as happy with your job as you'd like to be. (If you've got the perfect job, congratulations—pass this book on to a friend who can better use it.) You'd probably like to know what you can do to become a happier lawyer. You've come to the right chapter.

This chapter will give you the tools you can use to build a happier practice or repair an unhappy one. As is usually the case with a toolbox, some of the items in it might be well-suited to a particular job while others might not. Look through the collection of tools we offer, and see which of them seem promising for your own situation.

The source of career unhappiness can be the nature of your job, or it can be the nature of you, but it is almost always a combination of both. What might be a very good job for someone with a particular personality just might make you miserable. But also, as we'll see, there are characteristics of certain jobs that are virtually guaranteed to undo the smile of any human being with a pulse.

People are more similar in their basic likes and dislikes than many people suppose. What makes you happy in a job most likely would also make your neighbor across the street happy.

Your neighbor might play classical music while you prance around your living room to '80s disco music, but still, at your cores, similar things probably make you happy at the most basic level. You and your neighbor probably, according to consistent social science research, seek a measure of control in your life, enjoy being connected to other people, feel a bit better about your situations when you see people worse off than yourselves, like to "get in the flow" of an engaging activity, and want—at some deep level—to do work that aligns with your values. These core desires are not satisfied equally in all jobs, and many of these desires are not satisfied at all in some jobs, but the degree to which a job fulfills them goes a long way to predicting how happy you are in your career.

Of course, if it were a simple matter of taking a checklist of near universal desires and applying it to a specific job opportunity in the field of law, we'd probably all have our checklists by now and be clamoring for the same jobs. Finding as much happiness as can be found in a legal career is not nearly so simple. It requires not only a deep understanding of a set of basic desires but also an understanding of how the various desires are weighted in your own hierarchy of values, plus an appreciation of what you can do to make a specific job do a *better* job of meeting your basic desires. Jobs are not objects set in concrete; they are goal-directed, behavioral systems that can be restructured to make those in them happier creatures.

So let's open up our happiness toolbox to see what can be found that might make you a happier lawyer.

MATTERING MATTERS: THE JOY OF FEELING IN CONTROL

If you want happiness as a lawyer, get control of your life. "Yeah, right," you say as you work frantically to meet the filing deadline for Acme's summary judgment motion while you speed dial your nanny to see if she can pick up your second-grader and get him to the baseball game that you're going to have to miss. Getting control of your life won't be easy, and there might be financial pain, but it has to be done for the sake of your emotional well-being. When we sense our lives are spinning out of control, we are very unhappy creatures.

THE RAT RACE

Eduardo Punset argues that loss of control is "the ultimate origin of unhappiness and depression."[1] As he sees it, the brain hidden away in its "dark room," removed from the actions it interprets, needs to feel that it is in charge. What is true for humans seems to be true as well for our animal brethren. Punset points to an experiment conducted in the late 1970s. Researchers put five rats in separate cages. The rats were subjected to strong electric shocks at random intervals. One rat, however, had a lever which, when pushed, ended the shocks for all five rats. By the end of six weeks, the immune systems and emotional systems of four rats had broken down and they died—essentially of depression. The rat with the lever survived many months after the deaths of his fellow rats, even though all rats had received exactly the same doses of electric shocks.

Numerous studies confirm that humans feel the same way about control as rats do. Studies with subjects ranging from college students to British civil servants to elderly nursing home residents consistently show that control is closely related to happiness. When, for example, nursing home residents were put in control of watering and tending a plants, they reported higher levels of happiness (and, remarkably, *half* the death rate) compared to residents in a low-control group who were told that a staff person would take care of the plants. In another study, happiness levels among British civil servants turned out not to depend on their salary levels but on the degree to which the various jobs allowed them to exercise control.

A sense of being in control is critical to happiness in virtually any domain, from relationships to bodily functions to motoring down highways. But we're interested here in jobs. Thinking about those unhappy experimental rats, Punset sees control as the most important key to job happiness. He writes, "When my students...ask me for my opinion on possible job positions, I always suggest that they only accept posts with a control lever, however small, and that they never accept, even if offered a lot of money, a post where no one and nothing depends upon what they do."[2]

It is a fact of life that most lawyers do not have the same degree of control in their jobs as do people in many other occupations. A shop owner controls when the shop opens, what products are sold and for how much, how the products will be displayed, and who will do the selling. A football coach has control over what plays will be run, how long practice will be, and who will start at quarterback. An artist wakes up each morning free to create anything within his imagination. But a lawyer? As a lawyer, you pretty much do the work a client needs done, whether it's your idea of an interesting project or not. True, you might have control over what arguments are made on a client's behalf or the exact form a contract will take—but compared to some other occupations, that control might not seem like much. This lack of control might well account for the fact that lawyers had the highest rates of major depressive orders among surveyed occupations. Researchers suggest that lack of control is linked to depression and noted that lawyers and secretaries (two of the three highest risk groups) had relatively little autonomy.[3]

To understand what might be done to better our lives, given that control is not one of our occupation's selling points, it is helpful to recognize what brings on a feeling of control. The feeling comes only when a number of things combine in a job. Control, it turns out, has several aspects.

THE FACETS OF CONTROL

What are these several facets of control? One comes when you feel that you've achieved an appropriate balance between the demands of your job and the demands that come from being a parent, spouse, relative, or friend. A sense of balance also requires that you take care of your own emotional needs, whether by simply making time for beers after work with colleagues, catching that new episode of your favorite television show, or fitting in an after-work golf game on an inviting May evening. How often on a late Friday afternoon have you seen your plans to catch your kid's school play or have dinner with friends all go up in smoke? That motion for a summary judgment has to be filed before the courthouse closes and you still have three voice messages and seven e-mails that need some sort of response before you're out the door. "Work-life balance?—you've got to be kidding!" It's what everyone you know talks about, but no one in your office seems to have. We feel the demands of life are pulling us along and that our own internal compass is helpless to determine our direction.

A sense of being out of control is commonplace today, especially in the large firms, where career dissatisfaction is the greatest. Seventy percent of lawyers in an American Bar Association (ABA) study said that "wanting more time with family" is a reason that might justify leaving one job for another.[4] Nearly 20 percent of lawyers are "not at all" happy with the work-life balance in their present employment.[5] Women, unsurprisingly, are far more likely than men to complain about the stress work is placing on their family life.

A second key aspect of control in the workplace is job security. Peter Warr, a British professor who has extensively studied job happiness, identifies a sense of job security as one of the twelve most important keys to worker happiness.[6] Worrying about whether the next slip to cross your desk will be pink, it seems, is incompatible with happiness. Nothing is really secure in this world except the prospect of death and taxes (and perhaps, therefore, the jobs of probate and tax attorneys), so all levels of job security are relative. Relatively speaking, however, lawyers in large firms may feel their jobs are less secure than those in smaller firms. Your job in a two-hundred-person firm might well depend upon the whim of a single supervising attorney, the decision whether your firm merges with another mega-firm, or whether an important account picks up and leaves. Although smaller firms also have job security issues, notably attracting enough business to stay afloat, colleagues who know you well are less likely to show you the door.

A third aspect of workplace control depends on believing that your contribution matters. As Daniel Gilbert succinctly notes, "Mattering makes us happy."[7] Unfortunately, this sense of mattering through one's work is relatively rare today. Punset observes, "What now prevails is a growing feeling of powerlessness to influence the product, the company, society, or what is going on in the rest of the world."[8]

A sense of mattering, in turn, has varied sources. It can come from supervisors or colleagues praising your work, or at least letting you know that what you did was important. It can come from your clients—their sense of relief (and, one hopes, gratitude) from winning a favorable verdict, having a deal close successfully, or getting that speeding violation off of their motor vehicle record. Study after study shows job feedback to be critical to happiness on the job. Not all feedback is equally likely to produce happiness, of course. The most unambiguous feedback is generally the most appreciated. When we're doing something wrong, we prefer to know exactly what that is, so we have the best chance of making the necessary adjustments.

Not all law jobs are equally likely to produce a sense of mattering. The ABA's 2007 survey of lawyer satisfaction found that public sector lawyers, the group most satisfied with their professional lives, were also the lawyers most likely to feel appreciated in the workplace. Seventy percent of all public sector lawyers felt that way.[9]

A sense of mattering can also have an internal source. You might know—and no one needs to tell you, but it wouldn't hurt—that what you do has real consequences for real people you care about. It's when we don't give a damn what happens to the people affected by our work, or don't see our work as affecting anyone in particular, that we grow dissatisfied. We want to feel our work has some purpose beyond simply bringing home the bacon. Some of us are more capable of realizing these internally generated rewards than others, who seem unhappy without recognition from other people.

Finally, a sense of control can come from, not surprisingly, the number of opportunities in the workplace to control things. These things can relate to the content and timetable for a work product. Lawyers tend to feel happier when they can decide which file to pick up and which to put on the back burner, which paragraph should be deleted to reduce the brief to the maximum length allowed by the court, or who should be deposed this Tuesday and who the following week. People in first-chairs in the courtroom are generally happier than those in the third-chair.

Unfortunately for lawyer happiness, our adversarial system of justice places the parties, and not you, in ultimate control of cases. You might want to settle and get the stinking file off your desk, but that's not acceptable to your client bent on a measure of justice. You might think a paragraph you wrote in a contract was a stroke of brilliance, but your client might think otherwise and want it out. You might want to spend a day leisurely exploring an interesting angle of your client's civil case, but your client might not have the deepest of pockets and wants to reign in your billable hours. The system is what it is, and you are never going to have the freedom of a novelist. Accept what you cannot change, as the serenity prayer urges.

Finally, personal control also means the ability to alter one's work environment. Is it okay to put a valued family photograph on your wall? Will anyone complain if you bring in a comfortable chair, move your desk, or change the lighting in your office? The more power you are given to affect your own working environment, the happier you will be. One commentator notes, "Small freedoms... are very good for satisfaction."[10]

GETTING CONTROL

If control in its many senses is so central to happiness, then giving lawyers more control over their work lives should be one of the highest priorities—maybe *the* highest priority—for a firm. Work-life balance issues, according to ABA surveys, are a leading cause of stress among lawyers. More generally, the tilt toward long workplace hours in the United States may explain why happiness levels in this country have stagnated since 1975 while rising in increasingly laid-back Europe. While the average American puts in about 2,000 hours a year at work, the average Dane, Italian, or German works less than 1,700 hours a year.[11] Working 15 percent fewer hours, and spending the additional time socializing or beachcombing, could give a much-needed happiness boost.

For some workaholics, however, dialing back the hours at the office might actually increase distress. As psychologist Jerome Kagan notes, once people establish an association between hard work and rewards, it is hard to break. For the person whose diligence paid off first with a good college experience and then with the landing of a high-paying job, the link between work and reward might have become hard-wired.[12]

One good thing about law firms is that they are filled with smart people. People who are certainly bright enough to identify ways, beyond the first step of reducing the required number of billable hours, to give lawyers in the firm a better sense of control. Depending on the firm's goals and economic situation, a wide variety of changes might be considered. A partial list might include offering flexibility in hours and work location, allowing lawyers to bring children to the office, providing lawyers flexibility in choosing clients and work assignments, letting lawyers choose how they approach and complete work products, and encouraging lawyers to alter their personal work environments—lighting, hangings, furniture—to suit their own taste and work style.

If you are a lawyer whose firm seems unable or unwilling to give you the control you need, a change of jobs might be the best option. The firm down the street might accept your proposal to shift to part-time work or a more flexible schedule. A smaller firm might promise you greater control of your work product and work environment. Of course, a solo practice offers the maximum degree of control—perhaps even too much control, if promotion and marketing is not your strong suit. In short, consider what aspects of control are most important to you, and then determine where you are most likely to gain it. Control of your life is just too important to give up without a fight.

IT COULD BE WORSE: THE JOY OF DOWNWARD COMPARISON

Max, who knows barely half of what you do about corporate law, commands a gorgeous view of the Quatzawatamie River from his corner office. You look out over the backside of the Acme Building. Jane, who didn't even make law review at Middlebrow, earns $10,000 more per year than you—you, the former articles editor at a law school that *U.S. News & World Report* proclaims to be one of the five finest in the land. These things gnaw at you. The injustice of it all! How can the firm's managing committee be so clueless? You'd prefer to focus on the tasks at hand (that memo on *Snerk v. Google* needs to get out soon), but your mind returns to that corner office or that extra ten grand that should be yours.

You are suffering the pains that come from upward comparisons.

Sometimes, it turns out, finishing worse is actually better. Researchers evaluating the happiness of Olympic medal winners discovered that bronze medalists generally were happier with their finishes than were silver medalists.[13] Why? The silver medalists tended to compare themselves with gold medalists, the athletes who achieved the goal they long sought; bronze medalists, on the other hand, were just happy to be on the medal stand, thinking about how close they came to joining all those other hard-working athletes who failed to medal at all.

The acerbic social commentator H. L. Mencken observed, "A wealthy man is one who makes $100 more than his wife's sister's husband." We seem to understand that happiness depends less on income than how we're doing compared to the Joneses. Asked whether they would prefer to have an income of $50,000 when the average is $25,000 or an income of $100,000 when the average is $250,000, most persons polled chose the first condition. Everyone knows that $100,000 will buy a better standard of living than half that much, but being *relatively* well-off is seen as clearly superior to being *relatively* poor. We are okay without that sixty-inch plasma screen so long as most of our neighbors don't have one either.

As we indicated in chapter 2, earnings have little to do with happiness once they rise above middle-income levels. When per capita incomes in the United States shot up 300 percent from 1970 to 1990, there was no increase in the happiness of Americans.[14] Money really can't buy much happiness.

Relative income, however, matters much more to people than absolute income. Being in a higher social class *does* correlate with increased levels of reported happiness. The nonincome benefits of being in a higher social class, such as increased status in workplaces and leisure places, seem to make people happier.[15] People who perceive themselves as being in lower social classes are people who most often make upward comparisons—and get grumpy when they do. It grates to see their neighbors and colleagues doing much better financially than they are. In the terminology of British economist

Richard Layard, the wealthy spew a "social pollution" that incites toxic envy among those around them.[16] A *New Yorker* cartoon, showing a mid-level executive in a supervisor's office, makes the point. Standing at his boss's desk, the employee is saying: "O.K., if you can't see your way to giving me a pay raise, how about giving Parkinson a pay cut?"[17] It should be no surprise that the egalitarian nations of Scandinavia, where social class is largely a nonissue, consistently rank among the happiest countries on the planet—with Scandinavian residents reporting significantly higher happiness levels than U.S. residents. (Proving Shakespeare wrong, Denmark is about the least melancholy place on earth—it appears either at or next to the top of list in the most recent polls of happiness levels.)

Whether the question is the amount of compensation, the size of offices, or plum case assignments, it is human nature to compare our situation with those around us. When we compare ourselves to persons better off than us, we are unhappy because, as Sonja Lyubomirsky observes, "You can't be envious and happy at the same time."[18] On the other hand, if we find our fate better than our comparison group we tend to be happier. So happiness turns in part on the group we choose for comparison. Bigger fish in smaller ponds really do turn out to be happier—consider that the next time you are deciding where to go for a swim.

Of course, it is no simple matter. You cannot just choose a group to downward compare against and then get happier. To some extent, our genetics and our upbringing will force comparisons—either upward or downward—on us. Nonetheless, we are not powerless to affect our choice of comparison groups. We tend to compare ourselves most against persons with whom we spend a lot of time, so by hanging around those less fortunate than ourselves, we set up more opportunities for downward comparisons.

We spend a lot of time working, especially Americans who work longer hours than people in just about any other country. Who we choose to work with, and who we choose to work for, are choices. We could have been undertakers or roofers or nurses or architects.

We chose to be lawyers. Moreover, we decide to be small-town lawyers or big-city lawyers, immigration lawyers or securities lawyers, solo practitioners or associates in three-hundred-member firms.

Survey data suggest, as previously noted, we might well have been happier had we chosen one of the nurturing occupations: social work, nursing, physical or mental therapy, or Peace Corps work. The higher-than-average happiness levels reported by people with those jobs most likely has a lot to do with the opportunities those occupations afford for downward comparisons: "I might have problems and my pay is low, but I'm not a single mom on drugs, quadriplegic, crazy, or stuck in a malaria-infested third-world nation for the rest of my life." People with those jobs are more inclined than the rest of us to see their own lives as half-full bottles, not half-empty ones.

All this suggests one way in which lawyers might increase job satisfaction: begin spending more time working for clients who have at least a few more problems than you do. Along with the positive feeling that comes with helping acts, you're likely to come home feeling better about where life has taken you. Yes, there is some status that comes with churning out the billable hours for zillionaires who want a few more zillions than the next zillionaire—but odds are you'll be a little happier helping Farmer McDonald save the family back forty from the I.R.S., helping that well-intentioned Latin family obtain citizenship, or making sure that the little boy crushed by the falling anvil will get his medical expenses paid for by ABC Anvil Company (or whatever negligent bastard let loose the anvil). On the whole, careers in elder law, social security law, personal injury law, and immigration law—where you can make a direct contribution to other people's lives—produce more job satisfaction than careers spent defending companies whose sole goal is to maximize profits. Somebody has to defend pyramid schemers and monopolists, but it doesn't have to be you.

There's another way to increase the likelihood of downward instead of upward comparisons. You could become the proverbial bigger fish in the smaller pool. Because size is relative, you'll feel bigger in the small pool and feel just a little happier when you think of yourself swimming along with all those smaller-finned creatures. Instead of taking that higher paying job at the prestigious firm of Thurston, Howell & Gilligan, how about accepting that slightly less lucrative offer from the seven-person firm in your hometown? If you really want to build a life of it in Metropolis, you still have an array of choices—and you don't have to opt for the one that would most impress your fellow alums at the next law school reunion. You might be less smug once every five years, but happier day-to-day as the go-to lawyer in the somewhat less power-lunching firm. Sure, you might also have moments of daydreaming misery when you imagine the good life (which isn't really that good) of classmates in those high-paying prestigious jobs, but you're not getting corner-office envy every time you trot to the water cooler.

There's one last way of increasing the likelihood of downward comparisons, at least for those lucky enough to be in a firm that provides such opportunities. You can volunteer for pro bono work that will increase your contact with persons whose problems seem vastly larger than your own. Survey data show that increased pro bono work correlates with increased levels of happiness. Besides, the volunteer work you do is likely to be a departure from your typical tasks, and the data is clear that when we look at back at life from our rocking chairs a few decades hence, the odds are much greater that we will regret more the things we didn't do than the things we did. Do good, and be happy.

REAPING THE REWARDS OF RELATIONSHIPS: IT'S THE PEOPLE, STUPID

Without social connections it's next to impossible to be happy. In fact, according to one happiness expert, about 70 percent of our controllable happiness stems from relationships.[19] We could debate whether control or connections is *the most important* determinant of happiness levels, but there is little disagreement that they are the two biggies. We not only define ourselves in terms of our social ties, we also derive much of the meaning in our lives from those ties.

It should come as no surprise that your fellow human beings can be a source of happiness. People need people. Ever since writers have been putting words on papyrus, the praises of close relationships have been sung. "Of all the things that wisdom provides to help one live one's entire life in happiness," wrote the Greek philosopher Epicurus, "the greatest by far is friendship."

Next to sex, socializing is the activity that makes us happiest. Interaction with friends gives us the biggest happiness boost, followed by time spent with spouses and children. We do not, as a general rule, enjoy interaction with co-workers and clients quite as much as our time with close friends and family, but it still beats—by a wide margin, according to a survey of workers—interaction with supervisors and, especially, time alone on the job.[20] Most people like to be in contact with others much of the time, and for the 75 percent of Americans who are extroverts, this is especially true. Contact with others, both in quantity and quality, has been identified as one of the twelve factors most important to job happiness.[21] This explains why one of the reasons that losing a job is so devastating: it severs the relationships with co-workers.

Although socializing is our most common pleasure-inducing activity, working ranks near the bottom on the same scale. Working falls below exercising, eating, shopping, worshipping, watching television, and even (believe it or not) housework. Among daily activities involving significant amounts of time, only commuting makes us less happy than working.[22] If socializing makes us very happy and working does not, one might wonder whether the workplaces that provide the most opportunities for interaction—even if the interaction is less satisfying than raising toasts with your buddies on a Friday night—tend to be the happiest? It turns out that they are.

CAN LAWYERS CONNECT?

The workplaces that produce the highest levels of happiness tend to be those where workers deal directly with other people. The deeper the connections between co-workers or people served on the job, the happier a worker generally is. When it comes to recruiting new associates, law firms understand the critical role that positive interaction with co-workers plays. As a summer intern, you are feasted, trotted out to luxury suites in ballparks, toasted in pubs, loaded into kayaks, and provided with a host of other bonding opportunities. Too often, unfortunately, when you join the associate ranks, the tool that worked so well to make you happy as an intern is forgotten.

The depth of job-related relationships may explain why, when 27,500 randomly selected people were asked to rate their jobs, the happiest of occupations turned out to be the clergy.[23] Two of every three clergy reported being "very happy" as opposed to an average of just one out of three for all workers. One key reason for high levels of happiness among clergy is the opportunities the job provides for close personal connections. Jackson W. Carroll, a professor at the Duke Divinity School, had this explanation for the poll results: "A pastor does get called on to enter into some of the deepest moments of a person's life, celebrating a birth and sitting with people at times of illness or death. There's a lot of fulfillment."[24]

Lawyers rarely find it within their job description to celebrate a client's newborn or hold hands with a client on her death-bed. Clients often do, however, call on lawyers during periods of difficulty and crisis—as any divorce, personal injury, probate, or criminal lawyer could attest. These encounters can sometimes be intense. They probably do not produce the same happiness benefits as the clergy experiences during important passages because the lawyer and the minister have different goals. The minister focuses on establishing a bond that can enhance the church member's sense of peace and well-being. The lawyer, in contrast, usually aims at meeting a more immediate, and often monetary, goal of the client. Those lawyers who develop personal bonds with clients, even while serving clients' pressing legal needs, tend to be happier lawyers than those who do not. Lawyers in public service positions report higher career satisfaction levels than other lawyers, and part of the reason might well be the greater client contact those jobs usually afford.

Everybody Needs Somebody Sometime

For many who practice law, the deeper connections established in the workplace are likely to be with fellow lawyers rather than with clients. The quality of those connections is closely linked to our happiness. Everyone longs to belong. We want to be welcomed into a tribe and learn the secret handshake; we want to be accepted. It is not surprising, therefore, that we seek to spend time "with people who like us and are like us."[25] If your law firm colleagues share your interests and values, and they enjoy your company, you are more likely to be among the lawyers reporting themselves to be happy. The odds increase further if your firm is one that doesn't think building human connections is just for summer recruiting but instead provides numerous opportunities for interaction with colleagues, whether through collaborative work projects, brown bag conversations in the lunch room, or office parties and firm softball games. Robert Putnam observed in his important book, *Bowling Alone*, that social connections are fraying in our cocooning modern world.[26] The more a firm can do to rebuild some of these connections, the better it and its workers are likely to be for it.

You can do your part for the bonding process. Expressing gratitude has been shown to be especially rewarding, both for you and the person on the receiving end.[27] Whenever a colleague offers helpful advice, performs a favor, or just makes a contribution to the firm's greater good, let that person know their gesture was appreciated. Handwritten notes are better than e-mails.

An ABA survey of lawyers suggests than smaller firms are happier places than large firms.[28] This finding is consistent with other survey data involving nonlawyers and the size of workplaces. Smaller is usually better. But why?

The answer likely has a lot to do with trust. Survey after survey show trust is critical to happiness. Loss of trust in a personal relationship, such as might come with awareness that a spouse is having an affair, is devastating. Workers who trust their co-workers tend to be happiest.

Among all nations, the ones where citizens have the most trust in their government and their fellow citizens—including Denmark and Switzerland, the world's two happiest countries—are also the happiest.[29] The quality of a society seems to have a much greater effect on personal happiness than an individual's specific role in that society. What goes for countries probably goes for workplaces as well. Where a sense of trust exists, workers are most likely to be happy.

Smaller workplaces are more conducive to trust building than large workplaces. Trust is something that develops over time. It comes from positive engagement, especially when co-workers share stories and keep their promises. In a large firm setting, where you might not work on two projects in a year with the same colleague, trust can't develop as it can in a smaller workplace with more regular interaction between colleagues.

Obviously, however, small firms are not for everyone. If, for financial reasons or reasons relating to specialized expertise, only larger firms are viable options, then investigate the quality and quantity of interaction the firm will afford. Find out whether the firm has a high turnover rate—high turnover makes it next to impossible to build trust. Try to determine whether you are likely to spend the majority of time in "a firm within a firm"—working as a member of practice group with a specific mission and a nonrotating set of colleagues. Learn about firm culture: Do lawyers know each other's names? Do lawyers and staff hit it off? How common are water cooler conversations, retreats, collaborative work, group lunches, and social events? Does the firm provide a sense of play? How much emphasis is there on billable hours? Clearly, some big firm experiences provide better interaction than others.

COMMIT

A firm with satisfying levels of interaction that promote trust will, over time, produce another great good. It will allow you to feel a sense of commitment to the larger enterprise. Without commitment, you're mostly just spending time. You cannot, it has been noted, love either a person or a place or a job with a foot out the door.[30] Just as with marriage or other long-term love, career satisfaction over the long haul requires adjustments and compromises.

Lawyer career coach Hindi Greenberg deals often with mid-career boredom: "The first couple of years, it's exciting to say, 'I'm a lawyer.' You carry a big briefcase and even the minutiae are new and exciting. But then the routine sets in."[31] In addition to trying to do more of what they do like at work, Greenberg advises lawyers to make "a change in attitude": look at "the glass as half-full" and "get over it."[32]

No job is perfect. Lawyers spend a lot of time reviewing documents, filing motions, and pushing paper or electronic files. Newly appointed Supreme Court Justice Sonia Sotomayor reminds us, "The vast majority of lawyering is drudgery work—it's sitting in a library, it's banging out a brief, it's talking to clients for endless hours."[33] Irritations sometimes crowd out satisfaction. When this happens, remind yourself what it is you really like about your job. Make a list, and see if that helps elevate your mood. Still, if you are like most people, there will be days when you think you'd rather be working somewhere else. But wondering whether the grass is greener on the other side of the hill (or office tower) comes at a cost. Besides diminishing the possibility of love, if that's a word you can wrap your head around in the job context, there are other costs associated with being in a perpetual job hunt. You can't really relax, for one thing. A multitude of job opportunities can leave you feeling overwhelmed—"So many to investigate, so little time." And all that time checking out other career options is time taken away from your family, friends, and favorite leisure activities.

There comes a time in life when you really should enjoy what you've achieved. Commitment is a big and serious word that we spend the first two or three decades of life running from—but deep satisfaction comes to those who are able to embrace it.

FINDING THE FLOW

When does time fly for you?

The sense of time flying comes when we are so absorbed in an activity that it crowds out the worries and self-consciousness that dog so much of our existence. The activities that absorb vary with our individual skills and interests. For some, time flies when they are rock climbing. For others, time whizzes by during a round of golf. For others still, minutes race during a foot-stomping guitar set with their neighborhood band. What all these activities provide, for someone with the right skills and interest, are stretching experiences—or creative challenges.

When everything is going just right, and the challenge is enough to test our skills and demand our attention but not so daunting as to produce anxiety, we are in what has been called in positive psychology circles "a flow experience." The term "flow" is most associated with Mihalyi Csikszentmihalyi who defined flow as "a dynamic state that characterizes consciousness when experience is attended to for its own sake." It is a state where "action and awareness are merged."[34] Athletes recall fondly their flow experiences, typically speaking of times they were "in the zone."[35] During a flow experience we are in the *now*, not the past or the present—and utterly mindful. Of course, over time, thoughts of the past (that critical comment a partner made about my last memo) and future (will I finish the brief in time to join the gang for lunch?) assert themselves and the flow ebbs. It is probably more accurate to say that we can experience various degrees of flow experiences, with true flow being their short-lived essence.

It is not entirely accurate to say we are *happy* during flow experiences. We're so focused on the task at hand that where the dial is on our personal happiness meter seems irrelevant. Moreover, if we interrupt our flow experience to consider the question of how happy we are at the present moment, we almost certainly become markedly less happy and lose our sense of flow. When we are feeling the flow we are living actively in the present and living intensely. Is that being happy? Perhaps. Asked afterward to reflect on our flow experience, most of us would probably describe the activity as fulfilling, engaging, even fun—but we'd pause before characterizing our feelings at the time because the one thing we know is that we were not thinking about our feelings. When you're intensely focused on making contact with that high-velocity serve of your opponent, you have no time to think about how happy or sad you are—and that's the beauty of it.

When asked about flow experiences, we are likely to draw examples from nonwork related activities such as athletics, outdoor recreation, hobbies, playing music, or writing poetry. Yet the characteristics of flow experiences can be found in workplace tasks as well.

What are the features of an activity that might cause it to induce a flow experience? First, it has to be an activity that requires you to apply a skill that you have, or at least one you think you have. Self-delusion seems to be sufficient here. Second, the demands on the skill must not be so great as to produce anxiety yet must be sufficient to avoid the boredom that accompanies less-demanding tasks. As a colleague of ours notes, "It's no fun to play tennis with someone who can't return your serve, but it's also no fun to play tennis with someone whose serve you can't return."[36] Third, there must be clear goals so that the direction of your activity is not in doubt. Fourth, the activity should be one that frees you from the flights of mind and distractions that accompany the more humdrum experiences of life.[37] It helps if there is a mystery or unresolved question that will be unraveled or answered by your efforts. The mind far prefers puzzles to certainties. Finally, the activity should be one that is not interrupted by phone calls, police sirens, bathroom breaks, daydreams, or sports score searches on espn. com. A flow activity has our full attention.

Flow is not the first thing to come to mind when we consider our work as lawyers. Most hours in law firms are occupied with nonflow experiences such as answering e-mails, filling out billing forms, or digging around in files for an elusive document that suddenly has become important. It's worth asking, however, when work time does, more or less—it's not a magic carpet ride—fly. If you are a fire-in-your-belly trial lawyer, it might come when you cross-examine that key witness or reach the final flourish in your closing argument or ponder how to use your last precious preemptory challenge in jury selection. If you are a transactional attorney, it might be the eureka moment when you see a path to contract language that might spare your client costly litigation and months of potential worry. If you are a law professor, flow might come when classroom discussion gets buzzing and light bulbs go on amidst that sea of student desks. If you are a lawyer who takes pride in writing skills, flow can come in the simple task of putting one clear and significant sentence after another on a page. Flow is where we find it, given our own skills, interests, and goals.

We all want more flow. It might not be synonymous with happiness, but we recognize that it's pretty darn good. To get more flow, it helps to seek out more of those work experiences that have provided it the past. Take stock of those activities during your workday that give you a sense of flow and find a way to do them more often. If planning the firm retreat last year provided flow experiences, volunteer to do it again. Work more, if possible, with colleagues who you find engage your interest and challenge your intellectual skills. If trials do it for you, do more trials. Lose hours when writing appellate briefs? Then find a way to write more briefs. Needless to say, not all our hours will flow by like the Columbia (some chores are boring, but still have to get done), but improving the ratio of flow hours to nonflow hours should be every lawyer's goal.

Research tells us that some work conditions are more likely to produce flow experiences than others. Jobs with variety in tasks are better than jobs without. Offices and work spaces with views of outdoor life (especially with natural beauty) are more conducive to flow experiences than spaces without windows or with views of brick walls or vacant lots. Jobs with novelty are better than jobs without. Jobs without frequent interruptions, and work environments that are free from excessive noise, are better than work places with noise and other distractions.

Puzzles are especially good at increasing the odds of a flow experience. Puzzles can come in many forms and still perform the trick. If we have a problem that offers no obvious solution, yet is a problem that we believe we have the skills to solve, there's a good chance that "the flow" will soon be with us. Puzzle-solving demands our attention. There's another bonus with puzzles, too: when we solve a puzzle, we garner a little happiness reward at the end—that same sort of positive reinforcement that basketball players experience when their shots swish through the nylon net.

The practice of law, thankfully, affords numerous puzzles. How do we avoid enough estate tax to allow our client to keep the family farm in the family? How do we get a particularly helpful fact before the jury without exposing our witness to damaging impeachment? What case holds the key to convincing an appellate court to finding in my client's favor? The list goes on and on—if you can't think of any puzzle in your work that gives you any pleasure to solve, you're undoubtedly in the wrong line of work.

We can become happy for good reasons, bad reasons, or neutral reasons. Helping others brings happiness for a good reason. Becoming happy because a romantic rival has just contracted a life-threatening disease is a bad reason. Becoming happy because you're passively consuming an enjoyable piece of fluff entertainment is a neutral reason. Flow, if it can be said to bring happiness (and we'd argue that it *does*), is almost always happiness for a good reason.

LEARNING FROM THE HAPPINESS (OR UNHAPPINESS) OF OTHERS

You think you know what will make you happy? You're most likely wrong. That is one of the principal lessons Gilbert offered in his bestseller, *Stumbling on Happiness*. Piling study on study until it can scarcely be doubted, Gilbert demonstrates how remarkably inept human beings are at predicting their own future levels of happiness.[38] Our imaginations fail us when we try to picture what life would be like for us in new situations.

We think we will be as happy as a lark five years after we win the lottery. We won't be. We think life will be all downhill after we lose a limb in an automobile accident. It won't be. Far better than we imagine, we learn to adapt after setbacks. And far sooner than we think, the initial jolt of happiness brought on by a surprising success dissipates as we run on the hedonic treadmill.[39]

We make numerous assumptions about happiness that aren't accurate. We think we'll be much happier if we move to California than Iowa, but it turns out that we aren't. We imagine how much we'll enjoy the mountains and beaches of the Golden State, but we forget about the horrendous traffic congestion and the higher cost of living. We think Iowa will be duller than cornflakes, but it turns out we'll find good friends and realize that there's some culture on the prairie after all. We fail to think about the vast majority of our time that won't be spent sunning in the sand or swooshing down slopes, including all that time stuck in traffic or groaning at the tab in an overpriced restaurant.

One cannot review Gilbert's mountain of research without gaining a little humility. We really don't have much of a clue as to what will make us happy. Asked what one thing could make them happier, Americans say "money," according to a recent University of Michigan study.[40] A worse answer could scarcely be imagined, from what a consistent body of happiness research shows. But there it is: Americans think more money is the key to future happiness.

If our imaginations are grossly deficient in predicting our future happiness, what can we do? Gilbert says he has the answer: "Surrogation is the best way to predict if we'll be happy."[41] We should "observe how happy people are in different situations," he suggests. The best source of information about the future is other people who are presently experiencing events that we are contemplating experiencing. Chances are that our own happiness in those different situations will approximate those of the people we observe. Human beings are much more alike than they are different; we all tend to be made happy by the same sorts of things—connections with other people, a sense of control, a sense of mattering. If a situation we observe has enough of those happiness contributors, it's likely to produce happy campers—someone else today, perhaps us tomorrow.

A recent experiment involving speed dating provides surprising evidence as to just how powerful a tool surrogation can be. Researchers set out to discover whether examination of a prospective date's personal profile and photograph was a better predictor of how much a subject would enjoy a five-minute speed date than the single report of another woman who previously participated in a speed date with the same prospect. Even though most of the women believed that they individually would be a better judge of how well they would enjoy the five-minute speed date based on the profile and photograph, they actually "made more accurate predictions about how much they would enjoy a date with a man when they knew how much another woman in their social network enjoyed dating the man than when they read the man's personal profile and saw his photograph."[42] The researchers concluded that although information from surrogates may produce a better affective forecast, people will tend to underutilize surrogation because they mistakenly think their own mental simulation will be more accurate.

What works for dating also works for career shopping. "Snooping in on other people's lives"[43] gives us our best shot at an accurate prediction of the workplaces and types of work that will make us happiest as lawyers. Our learning from the experience of others should come from observation. Asking another person if they like their job won't do. Most everyone says that they like their jobs, and their answers have virtually no bearing on how good their job actually is.

Observation requires getting off your posterior. For practicing lawyers, this means taking mental notes on lawyers you interact with. If you're looking for a job, you might be better able to put yourself in a variety of workplaces. Visit courtrooms, law offices, judge's chambers, law schools, press conferences, administrative hearing rooms—visit any place you can see lawyers acting as lawyers. Talk to any lawyers you can about their professional lives. How happy do they seem to be? Remember, of course, that happiness only rarely will be shown by laughs and big smiles. Happiness might be revealed by the focused attention of a lawyer engaged in a flow experience. The negative signs, the signs of unhappiness, will probably be at least as revealing as the positive signs. Boredom is hard to hide. Stress shows. So do anger and distraction.

Having said all this about there really being no substitute for observation, is there still something helpful that survey data can tell us about what workplaces produce the happiest lawyers? Yes, but the survey data are ambiguous. They come loaded with qualifiers. Make the best you can of it, and then go boldly out into the real world of lawyering with open eyes and an attentive mind.

KNOWING YOURSELF CAN MAKE YOU HAPPIER: IDENTIFYING YOUR PLEASURES AND YOUR STRENGTHS

IDENTIFYING PLEASURES

The idea is so simple that you would think everyone would do it: Reflect on what things you like to do, then resolve to do them more often. Yet this most direct of all paths to a happier life is rarely taken. Instead, our daily activities are determined more by our *wants*—and wants turn out to have relatively little to do with happiness.

At first blush, it might seem that what we want is what is likely to make us happy. But evolution has designed us to be competitive creatures and to seek out the prizes that come from competition rather than activities that give us pleasure. We strive to get the promotion, to earn more money to get the biggest house on the block, or to acquire the firm's most high profile clients. We believe, more than ever before, that being financially well-off is an important key to happiness, despite study after study showing only a modest correlation between the two.

Make a list of the activities that give you pleasure, large or small. Your list might include reading the morning paper in your bathrobe, playing doubles tennis or games of Scrabble by the fire with a couple of old friends, traveling to new places, or having beers with office mates after work on Fridays. Take special care to identify the small pleasures that occur each day. They may be something as seemingly insignificant as a moment of rest by a sunny window in the late afternoon or a cup of that really good coffee from the café. Now, if at all possible (it's hard to make more Fridays, but maybe you could also have lunch with co-workers on Tuesdays?), do the things on your list more often. What could be simpler?—and you'll be happier. Recent research from the University of North Carolina backs this conclusion up. When people appreciate the daily "micro-moments" of happiness, those "positive emotions blossom"—and help people develop resilience against adverse events.[44] As Lyubomirsky counsels, "Enjoy little things, for one day you may look back and realize that they were the big things."[45]

In the context of your law job, unfortunately, things might *not* be quite so simple. You might love making closing arguments to juries, but you cannot just decide to give more closing speeches and go do it. Giving more closing arguments requires taking more cases to juries—and taking every case to a jury hardly serves your clients' interests. It might also mean doing more of something you do not like, such as pulling all-nighters preparing for examination of key witnesses. Still, there are likely to be certain pleasurable tasks on the job that can get more of your time without any obvious downside. Whatever it is you love to do—whether it is "rainmaking," searching Lex-isNexis, planning firm parties, deposing witnesses—if you are any good at it, perhaps you can do more of it. Of course, you still must meet whatever other expectations your colleagues have for you, but the evidence is compelling that by doing more of what you most enjoy doing, you will become at least a little happier.

IDENTIFYING STRENGTHS

Three questions deserve your attention: What activities give you meaning? What activities give you pleasure? What activities allow you to exercise your personal strengths? The jobs with the greatest long-term satisfaction are those that provide a source for each of these three activities.[46]

Identifying your strengths is no harder than identifying what gives you pleasure. If, ever since kindergarten, teachers have told you that you work well with others, you probably do. On the other hand, if every written project you've ever submitted came back filled with scribbled critical margin notes ("What's this mean?," "Poor word choice!," "Bad organization!"), writing is probably not your strength. The list of possible strengths is long and varied. It runs the gamut from being a great proof-reader to having the empathy necessary to really connect with jurors in personal injury cases. List your strengths. Think hard about what jobs allow you to exercise those strengths. Happiness correlates with being good at what you do and having the feeling of control that comes with professional competence. Seligman argues that people who find jobs that allow them to use their strengths stand a greater chance of deriving the "authentic happiness" that is the most erosion-resistant of all forms of happiness.[47]

Whether law provides opportunities that lie at the intersection of your values, pleasures, and strengths is a question only you can answer. But it is a very important question. You should try to answer it and find the job (if one exists) that offers all three in the best proportions. You're almost guaranteed to be happier if you do.

FINDING A JOB THAT ALIGNS WITH YOUR VALUES: FOLLOWING YOUR HEART

If you could pick your clients' legal causes, what would they be? The ones you fight for now, or some entirely different set? If you're like most lawyers, many of the legal battles you wage on behalf of clients concern matters that are of little significance beyond the parties. Sure, an indifferent or bad cause pays as well (often better) than a good cause, but we'd be happier if we earned our bread in some other way. Poet, lawyer, and Librarian of Congress Archibald MacLeish wrote that he knew it was time for a different line of work when he lost the ability to care very much "whether $900,000 belongs this way or that."[48]

The happiest lawyers tend to be those who do work that they think make the world at least a marginally better place. Law professor Deborah Rhode, one of the nation's leading experts on the legal profession, states that attorneys experience "the *greatest* source of disappointment in practice" when they feel that they are not contributing to the public good.[49]

Unlike some other sources of lawyer unhappiness, feelings about not serving a larger social purpose come from a choice you made. No one forced you to take the job with the fancy downtown firm with its list of well-heeled clients. You could have taken a job with the county prosecutor or the public defender (which one would have given you a sense of contributing to society's betterment depends upon your own views on law, order, and justice). Maybe that dream job with the Justice Department or the Sierra Club wasn't going to happen, but there probably was *something* out there that would have aligned better with your own values than the job you took. If you have sympathies that run to the little guy, perhaps a job in a personal injury plaintiff's firm would have been a good fit. On the other hand, if you believe, as did President Coolidge, "the business of America is business," corporate law or a job as corporate counsel might have been a surer route to a happier practice. What are *your* values?

If you cannot readily answer the question that ended the last paragraph, make a list of people, causes, and things you pay attention to. (And, if you don't pay attention to *anything*, get some professional help, because only attentive people have a clear shot at long-lasting happiness.) You might pay attention to some things that you'd rather not tell your mother about—craps tables, pornography, bongs carved by hand. Cross them off the list. You might pay attention to other things that provide personal pleasure but hardly seem substantial in the big scheme of things—your favorite football team or rock band. Cross them off too. Look at what's left on the list. It could be the environment, your family, gay rights, free trade, or the homeless. Now, think hard: What can lawyers do to aid your cause, and where do you find the lawyers who provide that aid? Go look for them. Beg to work for them. Honest passion sometimes pays off.

If you work at something you care about, you are much more likely to be happy. One reason for the higher satisfaction among public sector attorneys[50] relates to their greater success in achieving a desired work-life balance, but another key factor is that they care about the causes they work for. A job that aligns with your values allows you to emotionally connect with your work. "Without emotion," as Punset reminds us, "no project is worth its salt."[51]

We can't all work to save endangered species or defend civil liberties; most lawyers work in the private sector. In some private firms, pro bono opportunities provide a source of serving the public good that might not come from the firm's usual run of clients.[52] Pro bono work has been clearly linked to increased self-esteem among lawyers. As one attorney sold on its benefits put it, pro bono work is an "enormous morale booster for the entire firm.... No office parties or picnics could give you that."[53] A side-benefit of pro bono work is that it improves the profession's decidedly poor reputation among the public. A survey suggested that two-thirds of persons surveyed would think more highly of lawyers if they engaged in more pro bono work.[54]

What is true for lawyers is true for persons in other lines of work. Professions that involve helping others rank high in general happiness. To be more precise, occupations that allow workers to *think* they are helping others do well in happiness rankings. The fact that the help provided might seem rather modest in the eyes of those outside the profession is of little matter. Gilbert notes that often when a job doesn't provide an obvious sense of meaning, people will figure out how to add it. As an example, he points to hairdressers who derive satisfaction from seeing themselves as key confidants of their clients.[55] There's a lesson here for lawyers: If you don't presently see your job as making the world a better place, perhaps you could give the matter a bit more thought.

The perfect job is the one that lies at the intersection of our deeply held values, our personal strengths, and our pleasures. Rarely do people stumble into such jobs; to find these jobs requires a great deal of reflection about what truly matters to us, as well as what sorts of tasks test our strengths and give us the most pleasure.

Not All Happiness Is Created Equal

We suggested at the outset that happiness has many meanings. There is the happiness of the moment, what Seligman called "the giggles and pleasures and joys of life,"[56] but there is also the happiness that comes from commitment. Aristotle used the word "eudaemonia" ("good spirit") to describe the feeling that accompanies a life well spent: one of engagement and immersion in activities that contribute to a better society. True happiness to Aristotle comes not simply from feeling good, but from feeling good for good reasons—a feeling that generally comes from *doing* good.

The type of happiness that results from doing work that you find meaningful, after giving serious reflection to that question, is an especially resilient form of happiness. Fulfillment through important work is less prone to "set-point reversion" than other forms of happiness, such as the shorter-term happiness boosts that come from pay raises or promotions or captures of coveted corner offices. Being engaged in the good work of building a better world brings the sort of happiness that tends to sticks with you for a good, long while.

Enhance your happiness by either finding a legal career that aligns with your values or, at a minimum, finding one that allows you to believe that you are somehow improving the world. If your job involves strictly fights over money, money that you really do not care goes to whom, then you're not likely—in the long run—to enjoy much job satisfaction. Commit to a cause you believe in and be happy.

It's a Toolbox, Not a Recipe

It's the rare construction project that requires every tool in a toolbox, and it's the rare lawyer who could successfully adopt every one of the suggestions we've made in this chapter. Consider each tool and its possible application to your career. Use the ones that make sense for your situation and your skills and personality. Now, get to work building the framework for a more satisfying life in the law.

Ways to Become a Happier Lawyer

1. Make sure your job is one that matters to you.
   - choose meaningful projects over busy work
   - try to become a key player in your firm and legal community
2. Think about the way your job positively affects other people.
   - identify how your work has bettered lives

3. Strive for a comfortable work–life balance.
   - be willing to sacrifice income if necessary (it won't matter)
   - consider telecommuting or "5 days work in 4" options
   - discuss work flexibility with sympathetic partners

4. Work to make your job more secure.
   - know and become friends with those who control your fate
   - meet or exceed firm expectations
   - develop expertise in noncyclical or countercyclical areas

5. Take control of your work product and work space.
   - set, when possible, a timetable for finishing work
   - develop your own strategy for meeting goals
   - personalize your work space with photos, art, etc.

6. Connect with people.
   - work on collaborative projects when possible
   - eat lunch with colleagues or clients
   - participate in firm social events
   - seek help and offer feedback
   - praise colleagues who do good work
   - remember birthdays and write personal notes
   - choose face-to-face work when possible

7. If happiness seems possible in your job, commit to that job.
   - don't always look for greener grass (water your own)
   - remind yourself what you really like about your job
   - trust those who earn it and remember that building trust takes lots of interaction

8. Increase the frequency of your "flow experiences."
   - think about projects that have "made time fly"
   - identify common characteristics of those projects

- look for tasks that challenge you but are within your abilities
- avoid, when possible, tasks that are so easy as to bore you
- find a work setting where distractions are minimized
- try to include a variety of tasks within your work day
- work in places with natural light and views of nature

9. Avoid making upward comparisons.
   - focus on internal goals, not keeping up with colleagues
   - remind yourself that money has little to do with happiness
   - choose, when possible, projects that benefit the less fortunate

10. Find out what experiences have made other lawyers happy.
    - remember that people are more alike than different
    - talk with other lawyers and ask about their experiences
    - observe what seems to make other lawyers happy
    - choose jobs and projects that have made other lawyers happy

11. Know your strengths and what gives you pleasure.
    - identify tasks and events that give you pleasure, and do them more often
    - recognize your strengths and find ways to use them

12. Align your work with your values.
    - identify your values and look for work consistent with those values
    - consider volunteering for pro bono work or work that you care about

CHAPTER 5

Preparing for a Satisfying Career: The Law School Years

 THE DAYS WHEN SOMEONE COULD BECOME A LAWYER by "reading the law" and apprenticing with an experienced attorney are largely in the past. Today, for most people hoping to practice law, the only road runs through law schools. It's a three-year-long stretch that can spell the difference between a happy career and an unhappy one.

Our focus in this chapter is not on surviving law school. There are numerous good books available on that subject.[1] This chapter is addressed to law students and would-be law students, but the focus is on how to approach law school with an eye toward developing a career in law that will be satisfying to you. Implicit in this chapter is the vision of an ideal law school—one that is committed to its students' future career satisfaction.

IS LAW SCHOOL FOR YOU?

Not everyone is cut out to be a lawyer. Every year, thousands of students decide that law school is not for them—and thousands more have that decision made for them by law schools. Between 2002 and 2008, first year law school enrollment across the country remained consistently between 48,000 and 49,000 per year.[2]

If you're thinking of going to law school, ask yourself why. If the answer is "I want to make a lot of money" or "It will make my parents happy," we strongly urge you to reassess your options. There are a lot of good reasons to go to law school, but those aren't two of them.

Think twice if you are going to law school expecting the glamorous life of lawyers in movies or television series, such as *Law and Order*, *The Practice*, or *Boston Legal*. "Law in prime time media offers some combination of wealth, power, drama or heroic opportunities. Law in real time is something else."[3] Through the cinematic lens, the profession looks dramatic and exciting: compelling stories, novel legal issues, exculpatory forensic evidence, riveting courtroom scenes, and flamboyant oratory. But the daily lives of most working lawyers do not offer the courtroom adrenaline rush and only sometimes, maybe even rarely, is there the opportunity to champion a victory for an underdog. Most lawyers spend their working days researching statutes, cases, or administrative regulations; reading the fine print in contracts; writing memoranda, motions, or briefs; preparing for or conducting depositions; and meeting with clients. "Truly realistic portrayals of lawyers' work would hardly make for entertaining or interesting movies. Few, for instance, would line up to see a film titled *Adventures in Document Production* or *The Man Who Did Due Diligence*."[4]

Come to law school because you think you will enjoy learning about law and legal institutions. Come because you love problem-solving, critical thinking, and helping people.[5]

You are most likely to fit well into law school if you are open to new ideas and approaches—a trait that is one of the better predictors of both academic and career success. The single *best* predictor of both academic and career success, by the way, is conscientiousness, defined as "the degree to which a person is organized, persistent, and goal-directed."[6] If you are open to new ideas, conscientious, and you like the activities that law school demands—including tons of reading—you not only are on course for a satisfying law school career, but a fulfilling professional career as well. Those qualities are "a pretty good predictor of the ability to make a satisfying career out of the degree."[7]

There's nothing necessarily wrong, if you have the time and money to spare, with giving law school a shot even when you have some uncertainty about your passion for practice or doubts about your ability to succeed. Many people attend law school as a generic grad school while they figure out what they want to do with their lives. Law school is often the default graduate program for smart college students. You'll have three years to make a decision—and even after that there is time for a career correction. But go in with your eyes open. And yes, there are worse things that can happen than learning a thing or three about the law while falling short of a degree.

When deciding whether you really want to be a lawyer, you should consider that the classic model of a lawyer working for a law firm, large or small, is on the wane. Only about two-thirds of lawyers are in private practice. The remaining third may work in corporate legal departments or state or federal government positions, but many of them use their law degree in fields outside of law.[8] This is a significant demographic shift since 1950 when there were fewer than 250,000 lawyers (a quarter as many as there are now) in this country, and 80 percent of them were in private practice.[9] These changing demographics mean that during the span of your career, you will likely be doing something other than serving clients in a law firm setting.

Keep an open mind about the possibilities of using your law degree to pursue some path other than practicing law.

Law degrees offer tremendous flexibility. If you go to dental school—well, plan to spend years looking at teeth. A law degree, on the other hand, can open doors in politics, business, health care, journalism, law enforcement, and other fields where clear thinking and a knowledge of our nation's laws is valued. Don't limit your career vision to traditional law jobs. You can consult in an area of your expertise (such as business valuations); be a headhunter; go into arbitration or mediation; look at human resources jobs (such as affirmative action officer); develop real estate; write thrillers (think Scott Turow or John Grisham); become counsel for a school district; use the law degree to teach at the college, junior college, or paralegal level; become an agent in the entertainment or sports industries; manage a baseball team (Tony La Russa); coach football (Vince Lombardi); write poetry (Edgar Lee Masters); create crossword puzzles (Will Shortz); become a sportscaster (Howard Cosell) or broadcast journalist (Geraldo Rivera); become an actor (John Cleese); become a Presidential speechwriter and a game show host (Ben Stein); or even become a community organizer and then President of the United States (Barack Obama). In short, don't start law school thinking that the sole career outcome is to practice law with a law firm.

CHOOSING A LAW SCHOOL

Choosing a law school is a big decision. Not only will the choice influence the next three years of your life, but it may also very well determine what type of law you practice, how you practice it, and how much you enjoy being a lawyer.

Nearly two hundred American Bar Association (ABA)-accredited law schools exist in the United States. In many ways they are remarkably similar. Because of accreditation requirements, all law schools require at least two-and-a-half years of study. All teach many of the same courses, and almost all teach many of the basic courses in similar ways—in large lecture halls using a case analysis method. All offer many of the same extracurricular opportunities, from law review to student bar associations to mock trial teams.

When most people set about choosing a law school, they start by comparing law school rankings; weigh considerations such as the credentials of the faculty or the impressiveness of the building; and factor in geography, course offerings, and perhaps whether the school has a good football team. This is the wrong way to go about picking a law school.

CONSIDER THE IMPORTANCE OF YOUR PEERS

By far the best indicator of a good law school match for you is how well you like, respect, and trust the students who will become your peers and whether you are stimulated by them. We think, when we decide to go to law school, that we are buying a legal education. In fact, it may be more relevant to say we are buying a peer group, choosing the people who will shape our values and approach to practicing law and who, in many cases, will be the people we deal with on both a professional and social basis in the decades to come.

We've already discussed how critical relationships are to happiness and how important it is to trust those people with whom you spend your days. But it is also increasingly evident that our peers determine our values and influence our behavior to a degree most people find surprising. In *Connected: The Surprising Power of Our Social Networks and How They Shape Our Lives*, Nicholas Christakis and James Fowler show how our peer groups influence everything from our weight to our sexual practices, not to mention our happiness.[10] In fact, Christakis and Fowler come to the startling conclusion that not only is getting a $10,000 raise less likely to make you happy than having a happy friend—it's also less likely to make you happy than having *a friend who has a friend* who is happy! "Network contagion," the phenomenon explored by Christakis and Fowler, is incredibly powerful and is rooted deeply in our evolutionary history.

So with that in mind, consider carefully the peer group you select. Do the students at a school you are considering have the ethical values you would like to have? Do they see the world as you see it, or would *like* to see it? Are they, in general (there's a grouch or two everywhere) the type of people you would be proud to call your friends? When you go on your campus visit, remember to pay at least as much attention to the students as to the architecture. Interact as much as possible with students and ask yourself if they are the type of people you would like to be— because they, in fact, will pull you in their direction for the next three years (at least). Their joys and sorrows will, to a larger extent than you ever imagine, be your joys and sorrows.

CONSIDER VARIOUS TYPES OF RANKINGS AND SOURCES OF INFORMATION

You might be tempted, given the surface similarity of most law schools, to choose your school based on external ratings that emphasize the entering academic credentials of students, the financial resources and outside reputation of the school. You might decide to pick your law school based on the *U.S. News and World Report* rankings of American law schools. For some of you, especially those of you interested in fast-tracking to judicial clerkships or high-salaried jobs at the nation's most prestigious law firms, that might well be a sound basis for your decision. No one can doubt that the ranking of a job applicant's school does influence hiring decisions for certain positions.

You may want to consider other factors as well in choosing your law school. It is worth noting, for example, that graduates of "fourth-tier" law schools (the lowest in the *U.S. News* ranking system) actually report the highest level of job satisfaction.[11] There are many possible reasons for this, including the satisfaction that comes from downward comparisons. Fourth-tier grads, like the bronze medalists at the Olympics, might be happy they made it through law school at all and thus appreciate their profession more than other law graduates. It might also be the case that the extremely competitive and intellectualized atmosphere of top-tier law schools, leading generally to highly paid and stressful jobs, is not conducive to a happy career path. The school that is most impressive on your resume may not be the one that will make you happiest in the long run. When you are thinking about attending law school, evaluate which law school will best launch you into a satisfying career.

Instead of simply accepting admission to the highest ranked law school you can get into, consider carefully which law school seems to care about your future and can best guide you to a lifetime of happy lawyering. Contact law students and graduates and faculty at a prospective law school. What do they think about the place? Look at surveys such as the Law School Survey of Student Engagement, which evaluates law student happiness on many measures ignored in the typical national rankings of schools.[12] Each year the *Princeton Review* publishes its *Best Law Schools* guide, which rates law schools based on more than 18,000 student responses in categories such as quality of classroom experiences, quality of life (including aesthetics of the law school and community ties), and professor accessibility and discusses the degree to which the school welcomes older students.[13]

Take a look at the school's catalog and see whether the school offers courses in areas of practice you especially care about. In short, kick the tires. Get a real sense of whether the school you're considering is truly a happy place likely to produce happy lawyers.

Visit the Schools

When you are comparing different law schools, visit them, ask upper-level students about their experiences, and go for a test drive—sit in on several classes at each school you might want to attend. Is the law school one that makes efforts to equip its students to handle the stresses of practicing law? Is it one that encourages you to identify your own morals, beliefs, and standards? Are students encouraged to solve real-world problems? Is it a school where professors offer feedback and care about civility? Do the professors address the plights of people whose stories are the textbook cases? Do they seem to be trying to prepare students to have positive relationships with future clients?[14] Supportive educational cultures promote student academic achievement, lead to success on the bar exam, and foster career motivation.[15]

The best elixir is not money, but people. Search for a law school where professors understand and teach the importance of social bonds. Is your prospective law school one where students and faculty play together? Does it hold poker tournaments, faculty-student softball games, or annual skit shows? Do members of the law school community participate in Habitat for Humanity or other charitable projects? Ask current students if they have ever had a beer or a cup of coffee with a faculty member.

Is the school one that prizes professional and personal mentoring? Historically, apprenticeships were the way that new lawyers were trained and socialized into the profession. Today, however, the interaction of professors and students at many schools begins and ends in the classroom.[16] Check to see if your school offers a formal advising system by assigning each law student an individual faculty advisor. Formal advisement programs set the expectation that faculty are supposed to be more accessible to students. Several law schools have integrated members of the local bar into mentoring or inns-of-court programs to offer students both faculty advisement and attorney counseling.[17]

Does the law school you are considering train for collaborative law practice? Does it encourage, or even permit, collaborative work among students? While students sometimes collaborate informally with peers on assignments, the "vast majority" of law students typically are not assigned to "work together with other students on projects."[18] Although numerous studies demonstrate the benefits of cooperative learning—that it fosters engagement, depth, and critical thinking[19]—students at numerous schools still risk honor code prosecutions for cooperative behavior.[20] Outside of some work in clinics and journals and a few team events such as moot court, most law schools "make competition something of an art form to be practiced in relative isolation."[21]

A few schools are developing interdisciplinary and problem-solving courses, primarily in the clinical context, to encourage student teamwork in developing real-world solutions to problems of child and family services or healthcare.[22] A very few schools are expanding these collaborations into the business curriculum—for example, forming teams of business students and law students to teach entrepreneurial lawyering.[23] Ask about the sorts of training your future school offers in collaborative law skills that will prepare you for the legal world you will enter. The practice of law is increasingly interdisciplinary, multidisciplinary, and collaborative. Trials are vanishing. In 2006, fewer than 1.5 percent of federal civil cases ended in a trial.[24] The past quarter century has witnessed an exponential rise in the use of alternative dispute resolution mechanisms such as arbitration and voluntary mediation. Collaborative law practitioners report high rates of both client and lawyer satisfaction with the process and outcome.[25] Not only is choosing a school that promotes collaboration likely to lead to a more satisfying career, it should also help prepare you for the changing nature of legal practice.

Choose a Law School Where People Matter

I'd rather learn from one bird how to sing than to teach 10,000 stars how not to dance.

—e. e. cummings

Law is a people profession. As some of the stories you will read in Chapter 7 illustrate, the vast majority of the best and worst experiences reported by lawyers we interviewed centered on the highs and lows of their interactions with other people. When you visit law schools, observe how faculty members treat their students. Try to find a school where professors respect students, their time, and their needs. An obvious form of respect, for example, is the learning and using of students' names. Students prefer to be called by their names rather than be identified as "You in Back with the Green Shirt" or have a professor's finger pointed in their direction. Other forms of demonstrating respect for students may be equally simple. See, for example, if classes start and end on time. Ask current students what's best and what's worst about their law school experiences.

More broadly, determine whether professors are adept at giving the subtle cues that people matter. It is easy to ask a student to give the opposing view to arguments made by another student; it is more difficult for a professor to communicate that she expects that student to look for and acknowledge the best in the argument made by the first student and then develop the other side. Were different points of view valued? Was explicit praise given when the students helped each other in class? Try to find out if the professors care about the students. As a student once told us, "Good teachers care how students are doing in the classroom; great teachers care how students are doing in life."

Teachers that care about people help counter declining civility in the legal profession and convey the idea that people and their feelings matter. They understand that in using the case method to push students to separate the "relevant" from the "irrelevant" this idea can be lost. Typically, if a fact or feature of a case is one that might affect the outcome of the case, it is "relevant." If a fact or feature of the case, however much it might matter to the parties or even society as a whole, is unlikely to determine a legal outcome, the fact or feature is deemed "irrelevant." Intense personal suffering, gross indignities, and abstract notions of justice all get thrown under the irrelevancy bus as the class discussion moves to its oh-so-logical conclusion. While this analysis might sharpen students' minds, professors risk signaling to students that all matters deemed legally irrelevant are, in the larger world of human experience, also irrelevant there—when, in fact, they are anything but. There should come a time, in a discussion of a case, when we pause to measure the situation without our lawyer lenses. The practice of law is about more than winning or losing cases: it is about doing right for our clients while, consistent with that goal, doing as little damage as possible to everyone else.

In a school where people matter, professors will not over-emphasize the combative or adversarial nature of the profession. Too often, the lesson drawn from professors' war stories is not the concept of intellectual engagement with ideas—students begin to see a world filled with enemies:

> Law students quickly learn to see other people as adversaries. Success means finding fault with the other side's, or the lower court's, position. If we focus on the positive, our words are deemed vacuous. This facet of our professional lives exacts a heavy toll on our ability to connect with other people in our lives, whether in professional or personal relationships.[26]

The practice of dispassionately flipping legal arguments can cause lawyers-to-be to become insensitive to the people involved and their suffering. People behind the cases in textbooks can become dehumanized "plaintiffs" and "defendants."[27] Each case you will read was a series of real events—perhaps life-altering—for the people involved. The people in those cases lived with various social, economic, job, and familial pressures. None of them had, as we do now, the luxury of distance from the events in their lives. Christine Hurt, a torts professor at Marquette University Law School, reminds her students "that every person in our textbook's cases, whether plaintiff or defendant, was a real person who had either been injured, or caused injury to others, and would therefore never be the same."[28] How you think about the people behind the sterile appellate cases in the casebook lays a foundation for the ways you will think about clients in the future—as demanding interlopers in an otherwise great relationship between the exchange of money and ideas or as complex people with frailties, needs, and hopes. If you learn to care about the people you represent, you will become a better professional and a more satisfied practicing lawyer.[29]

Choose a School That Cares If You Become a Happy Lawyer

The traditional law school curriculum too often ignores career satisfaction. While more than one hundred colleges and universities offer classes in happiness research, we reviewed the available curriculum and course descriptions posted on the websites of almost two hundred ABA-approved law schools[30] and found only six schools that offer specific classes in happy lawyering.[31] Nine other schools address issues of career satisfaction as a small portion of much broader courses on law practice management, trial advocacy, or professional responsibility. Harvard Law School boasts more than four hundred seminars and courses but no courses on happiness or career satisfaction, although its undergraduate college offers one of the best-attended happiness courses in the country. The University of Michigan Law School lists the intriguingly named course "Bloodfeuds," but again, no course on happiness. Perhaps law schools consider the topic the exclusive province of the career services office or one not worth academic inquiry—or maybe the topic has simply not been considered at all.

Ideas about job happiness, of course, may surface from time to time in other classes, such as legal ethics or professional responsibility. Discussion of these issues may help set expectations for careers and thus reduce dissonance between students' ideals and the later realities of legal practice. But the fact remains that more than 90 percent of all law schools in the country do not offer a single course that explicitly proclaims it will address issues of career satisfaction or lawyer happiness. How can law schools help students make good career choices if they offer no courses on career satisfaction?

What If Your Law School Doesn't?

Maybe you are already in law school and as you read the above wish list, you realized that your law school was missing a few key features. Being the optimist that you are—surely, there's a pony in here somewhere—you might be wondering what you can do to make your law school more successful at promoting happy careers. You can always push for changes at your current school. Many, if not most, law schools make students participants in the schools' decision-making processes by giving them positions on law school committees affecting student life, including curriculum and appointment committees. Find the student organizations that host forums and invite speakers to your law school. Voice your desire to bring to your school speakers who can address lawyer happiness issues. You can request specific panels or presenters from your career services offices as well.

Why not approach a professor or a curriculum committee with the idea of creating a new course on satisfying legal careers? The course could introduce students to the general literature about the science of happiness and the different definitions of happiness. It could also provide comparative data on the satisfaction levels in various professions, identify characteristics of jobs with high and low levels of satisfaction, and consider dimensions of career satisfaction among lawyers in different types of practice. The class could include information from decision theory about how people respond to an overabundance of choices and what types of heuristic errors people make when predicting their reactions to events and situations.[32] Course exercises could include projects that help students identify their own values or could require students to interview practicing lawyers.[33] Finally, the course could weave in stories of lawyer heroes and heroines to remind students that they are embarking on a noble journey[34] and to teach them, as philosopher Sidney Hook said in his 1943 book, the *Hero in History*, the importance of not only doing their job well, but also of "mak[ing] a unique contribution to the public good."[35]

DEFINING SUCCESS IN LAW SCHOOL

All students applying to law schools write a personal statement telling why they want to be lawyers and what distinguishes them from the other 80,000 plus applicants. In encouraging students to present a sense of themselves, law schools echo Cyrano de Bergerac's Roxanne: "Speak to me...be eloquent, be brilliant for me. Improvise, Rhapsodize...Please gather your dreams together into words."[36] You probably wrote that you approached law school with the desire to make a difference. Perhaps you described your aspiration to fight for justice and make the world a better place. (We're generously assuming here, in these cynical times, you didn't just say whatever you thought would get you admitted.)

So what happens to your dreams?

When you enter law school, it is easy to get on "the institutional glide path."[37] Law schools often define success for their students in terms of grades, class standing, and journal participation that lead to well-paying jobs at prestigious law firms. Law students report hearing about these prizes during law school orientation even before their first day of class.[38] Consequently, students tend to internalize these prescribed measures of success and feel pressure to perform. As Harry Lewis, former dean of Harvard College, wrote in *Excellence Without a Soul*, students try to obtain high grades as a form of credentialing rather than seeking understanding or mastery of the material.[39] You can easily get sucked into believing that success and meaning can only be found in attaining a top ten percent grade point average, making Law Review, and having a full dance card for on-campus interviews. If you let these extrinsic markers of achievement define you, you are setting yourself up for unhappiness.

One of the first questions to ask yourself is whether other people are setting school and career expectations for you? Many students aspire to work in large law firms: some because of the exciting big impact cases those firms take, others in part because of the money or the prestige. Still others think they *should* aim for big firm practice because law schools send the message that this is the pinnacle of success; at some law schools it is simply easier to find one of these jobs. Working at a big law firm and earning a high salary are not bad things. But three-fourths of law students in any given geographic area will not practice law with a large law firm.[40] Ninety percent of law students will not graduate in the top ten percent of their class. (Go ahead, do the math.) And virtually all law students who embrace these traditional markers of success will be afflicted with the problem that these numeric measures are not good predictors for future career happiness. Buying into these metrics of success also has the unpleasant side effect of feeding a competitive law school culture and aggravating individual vulnerability, self-doubt, and isolation—in other words, making your law school experience pressure-cooker miserable.

Two of the most important things the happiness literature reveals are that people who have a passion or purpose in their careers are happier and that those who define the meaning of their work for themselves will be happier doing it. Law schools tend to define success for people in narrow terms that begin and end with big numbers, judicial clerkships, and jobs at elite firms. That is a very limited vision of what is possible—and it may have little or no relevance to what will make you happy.

Remember your dreams. If you don't have dreams going in or just don't know what you want to do yet, explore widely, consider the kind of law *you* want to practice, pay attention to the common errors you might stumble on as you try to make your future self happy, and consider whether you even want to practice law at all.

THE LAW SCHOOL EXPERIENCE

> *The Universal Fallacy: that the road to happiness runs through the top of the class.*[41]

The first year of law school is transformative. It is a time when you recognize that most legal problems do not have single, correct solutions—that law is indeterminate. Recognizing that incoherence is embedded in law is unsettling, particularly for those of you who were drawn to law because you like rules. The reading assignments consist of a voluminous number of pages per night, much of it in what seems at first like a foreign language. Terms like *res ipsa loquitur* and *mens rea* may stump you even after you translate them from the Latin. In Contracts, "consideration" is not kindness. And "horizontal privity" in Property? Well, it doesn't mean what you think it means.

You must be prepared each day, if called on, to demonstrate your understanding of the material and perform in front of your classmates. The Socratic method, which is intended to probe students' understanding of the law and to show that factual differences can lead to different outcomes, can be wielded (highly improperly, we think) in ways that intimidate students and undermine self-esteem:

> Mr. Jones, can you please tell us the facts in the case of...? Mr. Jones, what was the issue confronting the court in the case of...? Now, Mr. Jones, do you think the court was correct in finding that...? I see. Well, Mr. Jones, what would you have the court do instead? But Mr. Jones, now I am confused. You are telling us that.... Whereas, a few moments ago, you told us that.... Which is it, Mr. Jones...? What do you mean you're not

sure, Mr. Jones? Not sure about what? Well then, let me change
the facts a bit for you, Mr. Jones....[42]

Sometimes the Socratic method seems like a cruel game of "hide
the ball." This can lead to a loss of trust. And, as we've seen,
research in disciplines from social psychology to neuroeconomics
shows that trust in relationships is crucial to happiness.[43]

Competition and alienation from fellow classmates surface
outside the classroom as well. Embedded in law school culture
are other very public contests—for positions as research or teaching assistants or on the moot court team or for clerkships, internships, and jobs. The architecture of law school is reminiscent of
high school, with assigned classes, lockers, and relentless gossip.
At some law schools, but certainly not all, students engage in
more aggressive forms of bullying or hazing. They instant message each other during class to ridicule other students or play
"Gunner Bingo."[44] Acts of aggression among law students may
be the training ground for later incivilities among lawyers. This
emphasizes the importance of selecting a school where you will
like your peers.

Most of you enter law school with high expectations. You
were an academically successful undergrad or you wouldn't be
here. Maybe you are also the sort of type-A personality that makes
other type As look like B minuses. Grading systems are competitive; law school curves pit students against each other in class
ranking battles. The nature of the rankings is that they create
a small number of winners and a large number of losers. You
may feel like a failure if your law school grades don't resemble
your undergraduate grades, even though the curve is different,
and your self-esteem may take a hit if you don't perform as well as
your peers. First-year grades often determine who joins the law
review and who wins prized summer clerkships, both of which
pave the way for later jobs. What's worse, and makes you all the
more anxious, is that all of those grades still typically ride on a

single comprehensive test at the end of the semester.[45] You will usually receive minimal individualized performance feedback before that single exam.

In response to these cumulative pressures, you may be seduced into changing both your life style and your attitudes: you will probably worry much more than you have before, give up regular exercise, and socialize much less with your family and friends. "You'll have some significant changes in your personal habits: you'll lose your appetite or you'll want to pig out all the time; you'll want to sleep all the time or you won't be able to sleep; you'll want sex all the time or you'll never want sex again."[46] You may suffer some manifestations of stress-induced illness: depression, headaches, viruses, allergies, or a host of other ailments—and you may experience despair, difficulties concentrating, and anger at friends, family members and professors.[47] You may try to anesthetize yourself with alcohol and drugs.[48]

You might wonder whether law schools are admitting people destined to be unhappy.[49] Law schools don't use a GPA-LSAT-MMPI admissions index, but studies show that law students start out with psychological profiles that are normal. Law students look very much like other students except for a couple of personality variables. They may be more competitive than the general undergraduate population, have a higher need for dominance or leadership, and have a tendency to be oriented to external measures of validation; but pre-law students have "no greater incidence of psychological distress than the general population."[50] Psychologist Kennon Sheldon and law professor Larry Krieger evaluated law students at two different schools during the course of their three years of legal education. They found that students entering law school were equally well- or better-adjusted than a comparable population of undergraduates. Then the students became increasingly unhappy in law school.

Accompanying the intense competitive pressures to succeed is an insidious attitude transformation. Students are drawn away from intrinsic (inherently enjoyable) and idealistic motives such as helping others or curiosity and toward extrinsic motivations (activities that are "a means to an end"), such as "impressing others, or gaining status and affluence."[51] Success in law school is defined by these external measures and law students—smart creatures—internalize the goals of grades, law journal positions, clerkships, and high starting salaries.

In short, students buy into a system of superficial goals over which they may have little control, and they then suffer a loss of self-esteem from the competition. Krieger says simply that it is "likely that your *attitudes* (and anxieties) about the possible results, coupled with life style distortions, are wearing you out physically and emotionally."[52] Even worse, many of these dysfunctional patterns established during law school—the anxiety, depression, and drug and alcohol dependence—carry over into practice. The competitive atmosphere of law school and the transition to practice can cement good or bad habits, especially for those for whom law school represents their first real experience with the full-time work world. Changing bad stress management habits once you have begun working is neither easy nor likely.

In the sections that follow, we consider the things you can do to avoid laying a poor foundation for career happiness. Before we do, though, let's examine an alternative outlook on law school. You often hear about the dark sides of the law school experience. What about the upsides?

A DIFFERENT VIEW OF THE LAW SCHOOL EXPERIENCE

Is law school really *that* bad? Does it inevitably set most law students up for disappointing careers? Just as many lawyers find the profession satisfying, many law students enjoy the ride. There is no one generic law school experience. Law schools are different. Law professors are different. Students will find professors at each end of the continuum measuring their concern for the well-being of their students.

Law schools across the country boast numerous graduates who have had a very different sort of experience than the stress laden competitive expedition described above. A 2007 survey of more than 27,000 law students showed that the vast majority of students were "satisfied with their law school experience. Eighty-two percent of all students rated their law school experience 'good' or 'excellent.' Only 3% said their experience was 'poor.'"[53] Some students thrive in law school and emerge feeling excited about their upcoming careers. Some talk enthusiastically about the atmosphere of mutual support and sense of tight-knit esprit de corps they found in law school. An extension of that camaraderie is the network of fellow former students who will become your professional colleagues: "Many of us look back to our law school days and see that as the time when we made some of the most enduring friendships of our entire life."[54]

The wide array of clinics and externships offered at law schools gives students a window on career options that may be personally satisfying.[55] Contrary to the bleak view of some commentators— that law schools are creating disillusioned students who anticipate "brutal hours, inadequate training and unfulfilling work" at a large firm so "they can hope to pay back their enormous debts"—a survey of third year students showed that 79 percent were either somewhat or very optimistic that they "will have a satisfying career after law school."[56]

Perhaps one of the greatest services law schools can offer students in preparation for a satisfying career is to enable students' expectations to match the realities of practice. Law schools outfit students for fulfilling careers by preparing them for what is to come. The hard work that law school demands is appropriate training for a profession that has fairly grueling hours.

You may look back and realize that law school did equip you to handle many of the slings and arrows of practice: that you learned teamwork in sharing notes, that the Socratic dialogue prepared you to sharpen your thinking and articulate positions for your clients and to understand that there is no single right answer to "most of the hard questions that real world practice poses," and that as a litigator—and unlike Yogi Berra—you need to be ready to "tak[e] both forks in the road."[57]

Students may have better or worse experiences in law school because of their own personality characteristics or the schools they choose to attend. The next section explores the types of attitudes that are associated with greater measures of satisfaction in law school and suggests some approaches you can take during law school to build a sound base for later satisfaction in practice.

DEFINING SUCCESS FOR YOURSELF IN LAW SCHOOL

KEEPING YOUR OWN COMPASS

> It is practically a "given" that great success—top grades, high salary, or a prestigious job represent the fast track to happiness. This pervasive belief is false.[58]

So much of learning how to actually practice law is on-the-job training. Yet there are a few keys to future career happiness that you can learn in law school. Surprisingly, they have little to do with pure academic successes. A recent study of more than 6,000 law students at fifty law schools showed that high LSAT scores are "slightly negatively related to life satisfaction."[59] The researchers concluded that "one's ability level, as assessed by standardized admissions tests, does not predict life satisfaction; rather, rewards gained through hard work and engagement with the material predicts life satisfaction."[60] In short, highly engaged law students are more likely to become happier lawyers.

Those keys to life satisfaction have everything to do with learning to let internal motivations guide you. Students who define success in terms of their own values are better at avoiding the distress-depression-substance abuse triad.[61] The individual values can include personal qualities that are important to you, such as integrity, responsibility, or openness to collaboration. Or they can shape intrinsically satisfying goals, such as representing clients effectively, telling a client's story, championing civil rights, or serving the public.[62]

Having intrinsic focus does more than enhance self-esteem, build competence, and help avoid the competitive nature of a law school's system of extrinsic rewards. Research in learning theory shows that when students study toward the goal of mastering a topic and concentrate "on acquiring the skills or knowledge that are the subject of study," they actually perform better academically than those students who set performance goals that focus "on grades or other performances relative to . . . fellow students."[63] In other words, if you are studying Property "hard" and agonizing over whether you are studying "hard enough to get a B," you are likely to perform less well than if you study with the goal of being able to explain various rules about covenants that run with the land to a future client. If you learn to focus on your own objectives and consider what fulfills you personally, you will be more likely to pursue individually satisfying—rather than socially-prescribed—career directions.

Another key to success in law school that lays the foundation for future career satisfaction is to make friends. Your fellow students will be your professional peers for the rest of your career. Reach out, even if it makes you uncomfortable at first. Remoteness and a lack of sociability are not characteristics of either happy law students or happy lawyers. Studies show that those lawyers who have more close friends and a greater amount of social interaction are more likely to be successful (according to ratings of external evaluators) than lawyers who report they are isolated.[64] Building connections to other people, and remaining close to your support network, takes work; but you will happily discover that much of what you will learn during law school and the best part of the overall experience takes place outside the classroom.

Developing positive relationships with your professors is also important. Law students may perceive faculty as distant, particularly in first-year, large-section classes. Females and racial minorities in particular may be less comfortable than males and whites in seeking out professors for conversations about the course material or career advice.[65] Developing social connections with faculty outside the classroom not only enhances learning, it "makes the educational process more meaningful" because professors can often help students reflect on their own values better in one-on-one meetings.[66] To boot, professors may also have early notice of career opportunities.

Just as you will ultimately want advisors outside of your own firm as well as inside once you start practicing, you should search for mentors outside the walls of the law school. Seek out mentoring. Learning to find mentors is part of your professional training. Networking and mentoring will be crucial to your career. Fortunately, you will probably discover that lawyers in the community are more than willing to be mentors. When asked to describe a peak experience he has had in the practice of law, Greg Castanias, a partner in the Washington, D.C., office of Jones Day, said that it was not any one event, "Ultimately, it seems to come down to the mentoring I have received, and the mentoring I have been able to provide to others."

Avoiding Debt-Driven Career Choices and Subtle Steerage

The literature on job satisfaction in particular law careers shows that on average those in government and public interest work are more satisfied with their work than those in private practice. However, many law students wonder whether they can afford to pursue their public interest passion and still repay their school loans. Studies show that when students enter law school, between

40 and 70 percent of them say they want to work in the public interest area. Yet, when exiting law school, only a fraction of those who expressed such a preference actually start work in public interest law.[67] Looming law school debt provides an incomplete and perhaps partly misleading explanation for the crowds detouring away from public interest work. The other explanation is that the curriculum of most law schools is not geared toward training students in the administrative, practical, and human skills they will need to enter public interest work.[68]

Median tuition at public law schools for in-state students was approximately $15,600 in 2008, $26,400 for out-of-state students at public schools, and $34,000 at private law schools.[69] In 2009, the typical law school graduate entered practice with debts of approximately $100,000.[70] Let's look at what that debt load means in relation to starting salaries.

For the class of 2008, the National Association for Law Placement (NALP) reports that the median starting salary among all law firms was $72,000, with a mean of $92,000.[71] These figures can be misleading. Salaries are significantly stratified into a bimodal distribution: the mapping of them looks like a double-humped camel, with clumps of salaries at both the high and low ends. New lawyers are, upon graduation, salary-sorted into the "haves" and the "have nots." Many law graduates received low starting salaries, a smaller number obtained large starting salaries, and there was not much middle ground.[72] See figure 1.

The far right hump (really, more of a spike) of the camel shows that larger firms enter this salary competition believing their reputations are tied to their ability to compete with other big firms in terms of starting salaries. The other hump reveals that most other firms don't feel compelled to, or can't, enter the salary race—and instead offer salaries that match their own markets.

The actual starting salaries vary significantly with the size and type of firm and the geographic area of the country. For instance, the national median starting salary in 2007 for firms with 2–25

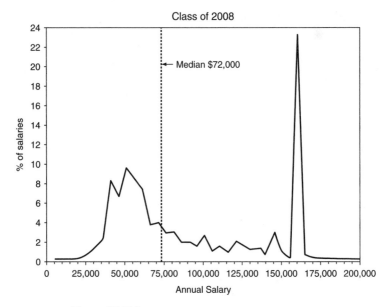

FIGURE 1: Class of 2008
Source: NALP

lawyers was $68,000, for firms with 26–50 lawyers, it was $81,000, and for firms of 101–250 lawyers, it was $105,000, with salaries starting at $130,000 for firms of more than 250 lawyers. First year prosecutors and judicial law clerks earned about two-thirds of the median salaries at the smallest firms ($46,000), while first year legal services lawyers earned only $38,000.[73]

Consider how many of your current decisions are motivated by economics—what you can afford to do, and whether you can repay your student loans. Fortunately, this debt may be more manageable than the looming large numbers first make it seem. Lawyers are not minimum wage earners and make a good salary over time. Tapping into recently enacted federal loan forgiveness programs—programs that completely or partially relieve debt for lawyers working a certain number of years in particular legal services jobs—is an option for some.

Loan Repayment Assistance Programs

Sixteen states and the District of Columbia offer loan repayment assistance programs for lawyers entering public service jobs.[74] These typically provide a yearly amount of from $2,500 to $12,000 of assistance to lawyers in specified public interest jobs whose annual income does not exceed $40,000–$65,000, depending on the state.[75] Equal Justice Works lists 109 law schools that either have their own loan assistance repayment program or participate in one in their state or both.[76]

In 2008, Congress passed the Higher Education Reauthorization and College Opportunity Act, which created four new loan forgiveness programs for public interest lawyers.[77] Finally, the Department of Education has created a plan for Income Based Repayment (IBR) of federal student loans. Starting in July 2009, IBR creates a sliding scale based on income and family size for federal loans made to students (not parents), allowing them to qualify for reduced payment options.[78] If you are interested in public interest work, examine these sources of assistance in debt repayment.

Income and Subjective Well-Being

As you explore various career options, keep in mind the literature on the limited ability of money to make and keep you happy. Maybe money is the one thing you think will make you happy, but people overestimate the effect that money will have on their levels of happiness. Remarkably, even having higher income aspirations leads to reduced life satisfaction.[79] People who look upward when they make comparisons and then evaluate their own situation in relation to their financial ambitions pay a price. Also, as our discussions of the "hedonic treadmill" revealed, the pleasure boost from a raise in income is transitory; then consumption levels increase, and you find yourself again in the position of wanting to have more than you do. What's more, particularly in certain types of law practice that emphasize billable hours, you will likely find that you do not have the time to enjoy the new toys your money provides.

IDENTIFYING A SATISFYING CAREER

> [F]or over twenty-five years, the National Association for Law Place-
> ment (NALP) has surveyed the nation's law schools and reported
> that over 90 percent of those seeking employment find it within
> approximately six months of graduation....The fact that you will
> ultimately find a job does little to assuage the nagging fear in the
> minds of many law students that *they* will be the ones left out in the
> cold, $100,000 in debt and panhandling outside the Grand Central
> Terminal just to stay alive....Actually, the real danger is not that you
> will fail to find a job, but that you will find the wrong one.[80]

Students attend law school for many different reasons and,
thus, contemplate myriad career paths after graduation. When
you start thinking about what job you want after law school, it's
good to keep in mind that old law adage that there is no one
right answer. Eduardo Punset cautions that because reality is too
complex, we create ideals—imaginary perfect models—of lovers,
of careers, and so on.[81] There is no ideal job, but lots of jobs could
be satisfying. There can also be jobs that are wrong for you.

Avoiding the Institutional Glide Path

When you consider possible jobs, evaluate the sources of information and institutional pressures toward certain types of jobs. Law
schools face a number of tensions that may undermine their steering students toward individually satisfying careers. Many of the
subtle messages students receive about worthwhile occupations
come from faculty members who, for the most part, worked for
large law firms and did not have a large amount or a wide range of
practice experiences.[82] For law professors across the country the
average time in practice prior to teaching is only 3.7 years.[83] This
is part of the glide path problem: professors may have a tendency
to steer students toward the model with which they are most
familiar—a federal clerkship that rolls into a stint at a big firm.

Schools also have a reputational interest in placing students in the biggest, best-paying jobs possible. This creates a prestige boost and produces more lucrative donors down the road.

Career services offices in a variety of ways cater to larger firms, which are their recurrent visitors during on-campus interviews (OCI) seasons and typically are the most frequent employers of graduates. The exposure of students "to a significant level to a large firm presence ... often leads to a perceived hierarchy of post-law school jobs, with employment at big firms being seen to be more prestigious than other non-large firm jobs."[84] Another factor plays into the tilt toward "Big Law." Career offices are judged in large part by their placement statistics. This may leave directors of career development in the position of spending buckets of time tracking students down for employment reporting purposes, a task low on anyone's list of favorite pastimes, and with much less time to do individual advising to assess career options that match interests and skills.[85] Although law school personnel know that a mismatch between a given job and a student's interests and skill set will not result in a happy outcome, the traditional steerage toward the most prestigious job offered remains a well-embedded default position at most schools. Keep in mind that the conventional path may not be the one that will bring you the most long-term satisfaction. Although high status jobs and high salaries are "seductive—they create a nice picture of life ... they are actually correlated with relative unhappiness."[86]

Career service offices receive little encouragement to widely disseminate information that might put law schools into conflict positions with large firms in their areas, many of which are probably the law schools' principal supporters: the lavish donor firm that put the Jackson Pollock in the faculty lounge and the fountain in the student center. Although this may not be a conscious sentiment of those people giving career advice to students, there may be the vague concern that if law schools focus more on finding happiness-producing jobs for their graduates than high income-producing jobs, there may be an impact on law school finances over the long term.

The absence of information about which law jobs are more satisfying or firm-specific information about billable hours and work-life balance policies is compounded by firms having a marketing interest in the disclosure of less information rather than more. Remember that the lawyers who come to law schools for on-campus interviews are there, at least in part, to sell their individual firms.

What all of these ingrained interests, default positions, veiled facts, and traditional ways of doing things imply is that you will need to be proactive in seeking out unfiltered information about measures of career satisfaction in various types of jobs. The Internet makes information about law firms (e.g., size, salaries, practice groups, services, and clients) instantly available. Rankings from various groups are splashed across its pages. Law Students Building a Better Legal Profession provides a website that provides an interactive "report card" on almost 350 firms in major markets across the country, based on factors such as the number of billable hours required. In 2008, *Working Mother* magazine and the national consulting group Flex-Time Lawyers compiled its second annual list of the fifty best law firms for women.[87] More information is available than ever before. Just as law professors have had to face the verdicts of their student reviewers on websites such as www.RateMyProfessors.com, law firms now are being reviewed on the Web by their associates and clients alike.[88]

Maybe your career services office is one that tries to ensure that the expectations of students match the realities of the firms or organizations they are joining. Perhaps it offers a chart of area firms' billable hour requirements, parenting leave policies, and approaches to work-life balance. Your career office might even keep data on alumni who go to different firms and whether they are happy there or whether they leave those firms to get a sense of personality matches between individuals and firms. If your career services office is one that doesn't do these things, consider asking why not?[89]

EXPLORING WIDELY VERSUS THE PARADOX OF CHOICE— WHY THINKING LIKE A LAWYER MAY NOT HELP

When you begin your search for jobs in law, the sheer number of possible paths can be daunting. You can have too many choices and be unhappy. You can also have too few choices and be unhappy. It's the law careers version of the Three Bears' dilemma.

If you take the path of least resistance, you wind up with only a narrow slice of possibilities. You participate in the on campus interviews, while moaning a little that the OCI favor the top 10 or 20 percent of students, and then pretty much limit your searches to the online lists of job postings on the career services website. This is a mistake.

There is often much more than OCI going on at a given school. Attend various career forums and panel discussions about career possibilities, meet-the-firms, and bar association networking events. Explore public interest job search guides, participate in mock interview programs, review binders with students' evaluations about their summer experiences, and attend educational programs about topics such as how to make yourself profitable to a firm or how to assess your values, personality, and career choices. Peruse the bar directory and write letters to firms in your interest areas. Seek out government internship or fellowship opportunities and inquire whether your career services office has a reciprocity arrangement with that of law schools in other cities where you might like to work. If you have a specific idea about your career path, pursue it by taking relevant courses, attending seminars or continuing legal education programs, and finding out how attorneys in the area landed their jobs. Explore widely, at least initially. But you can have too much of a good thing.

Remember *The Paradox of Choice*? An overabundance of choices produces anxiety, undermines happiness, and leads to disappointment.[90] Being able to select from among ninety different types of mutual funds and seventeen brands of toothpaste makes people feel overwhelmed. That same sprawling array of options—coupled with the search for the perfect fit—awaits you in the legal field. Too many options can paralyze you with indecision: "Perhaps there comes a point at which opportunities become so numerous that we feel overwhelmed. Instead of feeling in control, we feel unable to cope."[91] Even the possibility of too many choices can create inertia—which is why most people stay with their telephone providers rather than shop calling plans.[92]

People feel most in control of their lives when they have choices—but not too many choices. One way to deal with hyperchoice is to whittle down the multiplicity of options into a smaller number of clearly differentiated paths, a distinct variety of possibilities. The first step is distinguishing between "choices that matter" while "unburdening yourself from the choices that don't."[93] Don't spend all of your decisional time pondering the relative advantages of living in Pittsburgh versus Philadelphia—and which city has the better baseball team. Think instead about the type of practice that interests you and best aligns with your values.

Choosing an alternative that is good enough—"satisficing"—often leads to greater happiness than holding out for the perfect choice: "With 'good enough' rather than 'best' as a criterion, the satisficer will be less inclined to experience regret if it turns out that an option better than the one chosen was available."[94] Too often, we imagine that there is a perfect job and hold out for it. There are bad jobs and good jobs—even some great jobs—but there are no perfect jobs.

Michael Melcher, a career coach and author of *The Creative Lawyer*, says that many of the analytical strategies of "thinking like a lawyer" you learn in law school won't serve you well in thinking about your career path. Lawyers, he says, "analyze rather than explore, focus on flaws and potential problems, look for clear precedent, require solutions of general applicability ('what would work for lawyers') rather than specific applicability ('what would work for me'), defer action in situations of uncertainty, [are] skeptical about possibilities, [and] avoid taking risks."[95] It is not possible to imagine your whole career, see how it is going to play out, and know where you will be happiest. As Melcher concludes, "the path from here to there is a zigzag, not a straight line, and...you are better off exploring and experiencing than assessing things through detailed analysis."[96]

So, bearing in mind the paralysis that too many choices can cause, the worry that comes from too few choices, and your inability to reason your way out of this mess in a lawyerly fashion, what should you *do*? Is taking a job that passes the threshold of acceptability a good start, particularly given that your first job in law is highly unlikely to be your last? Or might that approach lead you down a path that locks you in to a particular type of work? We're going to give the typical law school answer: That depends. It depends on what your emotional and financial needs are, what jobs are available, and what ability you have to tolerate uncertainty. Too often, students seem desperate to Get A Job. Anxiety and fear tend to drive the job search. The best approach is to consider very specifically what would make you happy and what values, skills, and interests you have.

REMEMBER YOUR PASSIONS

There are ways to both pursue your passion and distinguish yourself from the other 43,500 new law graduates who will flood the market each year. There may not be "clear precedent" for the type of law you think you might like to practice.[97] If you have a combination of skills that permits you to offer a distinctive set of services to clients, you may be highly marketable and also very content. Consider the experiences of Kevin Travis, a lawyer who lives in the Midwest, but whose primary client is several states away in the South.

I worked my way through both college and law school as a mechanic, and once I got my law license, I thought I'd never use my mechanical knowledge again. But that one client for whom I ended up spending all my time as a litigation associate at my first firm was a vehicle service contract administrator, and when they got sued over claims they had denied, they not only needed someone who knew how to defend a lawsuit, but also someone who could understand what had gone wrong with the car, and why, and could explain the mechanical aspects of the claim to the finder of the facts. Because I had the combination of legal and mechanical skills, I could do both, and suddenly, I'd found a specialty where I could stand out...not only in my town or my state, but in the whole country. I'm now doing the same type of work for a different client, but in the same industry, that is a thousand miles away. I get that work, rather than one of the many hungry local lawyers in the large town where my client is located, because of the unique combination of skills I can offer.

Or take Julia Belian, now teaching in Michigan, who earned a master of divinity degree and then a law degree. With this set of degrees, she entered estate planning. She says she found a "special joy" in probate work because "it really *matters*, whether it is rich clients or not, because we're all mortal, and we all want to take care of our loved ones.... This isn't just *law* we're discussing, it's life and death, quite literally." She is also particularly trained to help clients discuss their fears and make estate plans—"because to plan, you must first accept that you will die." Having these discussions with client, she says, is "a ministry of the highest order."

Or perhaps you liked horses when you were growing up. When Denise Farris was little, her family "always had a horse in the back yard." Her "horse hobby" continued after law school. When she noticed the enactment of statutes creating liability shelters for equine professionals, she created a newsletter addressing those statutes and mailed the newsletter to stables in a tristate area as a public service. She was invited to speak on the topic by the Missouri and Kansas Horse Councils as well as the University of Kentucky Law School, and quickly became one of the nation's experts on equine law, which is now a substantial portion of her practice. She addresses numerous intriguing facets of equine law for clients: risk management contracts, stallion syndication agreements, "who's your daddy" testing following artificial insemination, zoning and environmental issues regarding manure and carcass disposal, and estate planning for owners wanting to ensure ongoing care for that special horse. Farris says it is richly rewarding to discover new practice areas can be created around life-long passions.

Based on your interests, hobbies outside law, and special expertise, you may be able to create your own niche practice. But, if you don't have a pre-existing specialty area, then what?

YOUR STRENGTHS, INTERESTS, AND VALUES

Ever since 1880, when John Venn introduced his famous diagrams, students have been taught to use overlapping circles to depict the intersection of information sets. Harvard University psychologist Tal Ben-Shahar proposes using Venn diagrams as a job finding tool. We believe this approach could benefit law students searching for that satisfying job.

Ben-Shahar urges job-seekers to use what he calls "the Three Question Process." He identifies three inward-looking questions most helpful to the search: (1) What gives me meaning? (2) What gives me pleasure? (3) What are my strengths?[98] Sources of meaning might include, for example, working with the elderly, solving problems, promoting religious values, or protecting nature. Sources of pleasure could include, for example, hiking, singing, solving crossword-puzzles, or reading books about history. Strengths might include problem solving, meticulousness, knowledge of history, and an ability to relate to a wide variety of people. Preparing lists of your own sources of meaning and pleasure and your strengths is an exercise that requires considerable reflection and time on your part. You might aim to identify, say, ten entries in each of the three categories. In identifying strengths, consider subject areas of expertise (for example, environmental law, intellectual property), your skill sets (for instance, writing, oral communication, analytical skills, organizational ability, ability to relate well to others), and your personality (are you compassionate, risk-tolerant, extroverted, patient?).

To complete the exercise, put your entries in circles and then, in Venn diagram fashion, examine the overlap between your circles to sharpen your thinking about what jobs might be the most satisfying. If you find meaning in working with the elderly (source of meaning), enjoy spending time with others or like discussing history (sources of pleasure), have expertise in the area of elder law or estate planning, and are patient and compassionate (strengths), then you might do well to consider positions with the Social Security Administration or an estate planning firm, to name a couple of obvious job possibilities. If you like helping underdogs, enjoy performing and strategizing, and relate well to people of all types—well, we suppose you have already thought about becoming a plaintiff's personal injury lawyer.

Ben-Shahar warns that your own list is likely to be messy. Jobs might not come jumping off of your page of Venn diagrams. The real benefit of the Three Question Process for most of you is likely to be to sharpen your thinking about meaning, pleasure, and strengths and to gain an appreciation for how those concerns are central to your job satisfaction.

Another way of viewing your strengths comes from noted University of Michigan psychologist, Christopher Peterson, and Martin Seligman, former President of the American Psychological Association, as well as fifty-five other social scientists. They developed a classification of character strengths by examining concepts of positive characteristics of humans to identify six core virtues that religious and moral philosophers have, over history and across cultures, tied to human flourishing and achievement of the good life. The six virtues, according to these social scientists, are courage, humanity, justice, temperance, transcendence, and wisdom. These larger categories break down into twenty-four virtues or character strengths that are valued universally.[99]

Peterson, Seligman, and their group posit that people have a handful of these characteristics as their signature strengths. Indications of a signature strength are that people feel that the strength is an authentic reflection of who they are, have a fast learning curve for activities tied to that strength, and are invigorated and excited when using that strength. The idea is that people are better off trying to build on their individual signature strengths rather than trying to correct deficiencies. On his website, Seligman offers a questionnaire to help you identify your signature strengths.[100] The key connection between these character strengths and happy lawyering is that "[i]dentifying your strengths can help you find new work that is personally fulfilling and meaningful or alter your current work to become more personally fulfilling and meaningful."[101] Peterson and Seligman suggest you consider a deep sort of happiness. Their focus is on ways to build on character strengths that may lead to longer term life fulfillment. Is what you are doing on a daily basis drawing on your strengths?

So you have answered Ben-Shahar's three questions and have taken Seligman's self-assessment to help identify your signature strengths. Where do you go from here? We suggest that you write not just a job description, but a sketch of the path you want your career to take.

YOUR CAREER PATH

Using the questions below as a guide, draft a two-paragraph vision statement for your career. Paragraph one: What kinds of jobs would best match your personality, values, and skills? Paragraph two: Where do you want to be in ten years? Twenty?

1. Do you have a general idea of what kind of career you want? Do you plan to practice law? What do you envision yourself doing in twenty years—at the height of your career?

2. What are your values? Do you value financial security? Time with your family and friends? Autonomy? Stability? Creativity? Do you want to have children? Do you like to take risks? Do you like variety? Do you like excitement and pressure or do you prefer life without stress? Do you desire leisure time to pursue various interests? Are your career plans consistent with your values?

3. How do you want to spend your day? Do you like dealing with people? Do numerous meetings make you crazy, or do you welcome the time to noodle issues with colleagues? In what size groups do you work best: all alone, with one or two other people, with a larger group? Do you like spending large blocks of time researching and writing? Do you like detail work? Do you enjoy or hate business development? How do you feel about the prospects of litigation? Do you like to travel? Do you prefer new challenges or handling matters over which you have some mastery? Do you know what kinds of law do *not* interest you?

4. What kinds of hours do you envision yourself working as a lawyer: a mammoth number of hours, a 9 to 5 day, part-time? Are you someone who is able to create work life balance for yourself, or do you take on too much work?

5. When you are considering a job, will the salary and benefits meet your basic minimum needs? Will some other factor be paramount in your job search (for instance, whether the work is meaningful to you or can keep your interest)?

6. Are you interested in entering a type of law that might dictate that you live in a particular region (such as

international law or water law)? Do you prefer cities? Large or small? Suburbs or rural areas? Domestic or international travel?

7. Do you feel that other people (perhaps family members such as parents or partners) have specific expectations for what you will do with your law degree? Do they match yours?

8. What are your signature strengths as they relate to a legal career? Weaknesses?

9. What are your interests or hobbies? Do they relate to your career plans? Can they?

10. If you could not be a lawyer, what would you do? Do any of these alternate careers suggest what you could do with your law degree other than practice law?

Once you have a sense of the possible path you think you want to take, then you need to assess whether it is the right path. This is where you could encounter some cognitive stumbling blocks.

THE FUTURE IS NOT EXACTLY CLEAR

Research in cognitive psychology shows that people systematically make inaccurate predictions about what will make them happy. In thinking about how to make your future self happy, you are likely to make two types of errors: prediction mistakes and, on the other hand, failures to follow those predictions that are accurate.[102]

Like other people, lawyers wrongly predict their emotional reactions to both positive and negative future events. They overestimate the joy that winning a multi-million dollar verdict will bring them, and they underestimate their ability to rebound from a denied promotion. In both circumstances, the context will moderate the effects of the event, and people will hedonically adapt and tend to return to their happiness set point. When you are considering that job offer from Parker, McBain & Chandler, LLC, you might assume that accepting an offer from one of the most prestigious firms in your city will bring you happiness. And it will—for a while. Soon, however, the drudgery of day-to-day work will dampen the joy of the associational prestige.

You might also suffer from projection bias. People tend to assume that their future likes and dislikes will be similar to their current preferences. (This explains the tendency to overfill the grocery cart if you shop for food while you are hungry.) Daniel Gilbert observes, "Because we naturally use our present feelings as a starting point when we attempt to predict our future feelings, we expect our future to feel a bit more like our present than it actually will."[103] Your own behavior and many external factors will influence how your future self will react. If you are in your first year of law school, you may gravitate toward fast-paced jobs that promise the endorphin rush of trial work, such as being a prosecutor or public defender. You may, at present, have no other responsibilities so you can devote countless hours to trials. Three years from now, however, you may want a job with somewhat less excitement and more regular hours, so you can spend time with your nine month-old who isn't even a gleam in your eye at the moment. Gilbert suggests: "if we want to predict how something will make us feel in the future, we *must* consider the kind of comparison we will be making in the future and *not* the kind of comparison we happen to be making in the present."[104]

Even when people make accurate predictions about the kinds of work that would make their future selves happy, they often fail to follow their predictions. Christopher Hsee and Reid Hastie, both professors of behavioral science at the University of Chicago, note that "[a] major cause of sub-optimal decisions is impulsivity—the choice of an immediately gratifying option at the cost of long-term happiness."[105] You may have been a victim of your own impulsivity in the past if you have ever overindulged in food or drink. In the world of legal employment, at times people make impulsive decisions, accepting a job that has some immediate appeal—it was the first one offered or a parent's good friend is a partner at the firm.

Another paradox of decision-making is that people are drawn to make rational or rule-based decisions, even if they predict that another type of experience would make them happier. For example, thinking they should follow a "rule" of seeking variety in experiences, people may choose a menu item other than their favorite when in fact they would be happier to repeatedly select the old standby item that they like the most. People also tend to assume that financial aspects of decisions should matter more than experiential aspects. Hsee and Hastie offer this example: "when asked to choose between a 50¢ small chocolate that looks like a heart and a $2 large chocolate that looks like a cockroach, most respondents opted for the larger cockroach-shaped choco-late, even though when asked to predict which they would enjoy more, most favored the smaller, hearted-shaped chocolate."[106] If you are just embarking on your career, you may assume that the primary goal of the job search is to obtain the highest paying or most prestigious position possible. Instead, the evidence suggests that you should look for jobs that would give you the most experiential satisfaction or that would use your signature strengths.

How do you avoid the cognitive pitfalls? What if you think you would like a particular kind of legal job, but you just aren't sure? Or you were sure, at least until you read the last few paragraphs. We turn next to one of the best methods to steer clear of the shortcomings of our imaginations.

INVESTIGATING POSSIBLE FUTURES

> *Before we set our hearts too much upon anything, let us first examine how happy those are who already possess it.*[107]

The best way to estimate your future happiness in a job is to ask people who currently hold that job whether they like their work—look at surrogates for your future self.[108] This is especially important for those of you just embarking on your law careers. Bill Davis, formerly a partner with a mid-sized law firm in North Carolina and then in-house counsel, suggests: "look for 'success' stories in the environment you are considering and picture yourself relative to them, their skill sets and their personalities."

You need to get a picture of what, physically, you will be doing every day when you go in to the office. The actual day to day tasks and interactions can be as important as practicing in a particular substantive area. When you get up in the morning, you want to look forward to going to work. Every job has multiple dimensions, but two are key to happiness: what you will be doing on a daily basis, and with whom you will be doing it. "Some days, one is more important than the other; but you need to have both," says Joan Heminway, a Tennessee law professor, who used to work in corporate mergers and acquisitions at Skadden Arps.

People who practice the type of law that you think might be of interest can help you envision a day at the office. If you want more accurate information about whether you would like to try a capital case or write a patent application or conduct discovery in a behemoth class action, find people who are presently doing those things and ask them what they spend their days and night doing and particularly about the peaks and valleys in their work. One way to do this is to ask a lawyer in a particular specialty area for an "informational interview." Don't just ask people whether they like their jobs—most people say that they do.[109] Ask them what the most satisfying parts of their jobs are, what aspects cause them the greatest stress or anxiety, what training they found most useful for their practice area, and whether they think their experiences are typical for that type of work.

The personal interview is not the only way to glean information about different careers from sources. Take advantage of public lectures. Approach professors who teach in the substantive areas that interest you. Most law schools also provide clinical opportunities and internships. According to a study done by Affiliates legal staffing service, "90 percent of lawyers surveyed said internship experience was a key factor in selecting candidates for full-time positions."[110] Internships or externships provide opportunities to assess your own reactions to certain types of practices. Summer associate experiences are also valuable, but courted and coddled "summers" would be well-advised to examine the lives of the junior associates they will become if they join the firm.

There is another source of potentially important information that could guide your job choice. After you get an offer and you are doing a final check on one or two firms, try to find out what has happened to associates from that firm from four or five years ago. Use Martindale-Hubbell (the books, the ones in the basement of the law library, not the up-to-date online version) to find the entering class of a firm from five years ago, compare that to the current associates list, see who left, and track several of them down to see why they moved to a new firm or position. By expanding your sample to include those who left and not just those who stayed, you can get a more accurate picture of the costs and benefits of your possible future job.

Interviewing for a More Satisfying Workplace

Most career services offices offer a standard battery of books and handouts containing suggested interview guidelines. Most of these lists of sample questions are targeted toward impressing interviewers. Very few address ways to assess what a law firm's values are or the quality of life in that firm. We offer below a different sort of list, one that is attentive to both favorably impressing interviewers and helping you to probe more deeply for the kinds of things that will lead you toward a satisfying career.

INTERVIEW STRATEGIES

Presumably, before you have your first interview, you will have done your homework. You will know whether the firm's representative client list is big tobacco and axe murderers, or if it consists mainly of innocent victims of toxic mold and Bernie Madoff. You will know whether a senior partner has just been indicted or has just won the Congressional Medal of Honor. As you interview for a legal job, collect information about whether this is a place that fits with your values and interests, will appreciate your strengths, and will offer a satisfying work environment.

Think about interviewing as roughly a two-stage process, corresponding in many instances to an initial round of on-campus interviews and a later in-house callback. An opening conversation with a firm or organization may not be the most opportune time to probe about the firm's work-life balance policy. During the initial interview you are trying to present yourself to law firms, rather than to assess all the benefits the firm can bestow upon you.

Initial Interviews

For openers, most legal employers will typically ask a fairly standard series of questions, such as: Why do you want to practice law? Have you enjoyed law school and did you have a favorite course? What qualities do you have that you think will make you a good lawyer? Tell us about an obstacle you have overcome in life? Where do you see yourself in ten years? In these early conversations you can ask questions that reflect your interest in the firm's structure and your eagerness to work hard. Use your questions to glean information about the control the firm gives to associates, the feedback and training offered, and the interpersonal relations. May associates specialize in particular practice areas? Does the firm have any formal training, mentoring or business development programs for associates (e.g., are junior lawyers included in client pitches)? How does the firm evaluate associates' work, and are there any formal feedback systems? You should also ask what is the firm's governing structure (e.g., a single managing committee or several committee's on different issues), and what is the firm's overall growth plan? What is the typical length of the partnership track, and are attorneys expected to have an independent book of business for partnership? For litigation (or transactional work), what kinds of cases (or deals) would an associate be able to work on or exclusively handle?

Depending on the available time and how the interview is going, you may also be able to ask additional questions about the kinds of people, qualities, and activities to which the firm attaches importance. Who are the heroes and heroines of the firm? Do you have a story about the way your firm has handled a case or some aspect of a case that is representative of your firm's values? You can learn a lot about whether a firm's values align with your own by hearing the victory stories (and war stories and horror stories) of a firm. The anecdotes people choose to tell you convey their own stories.

Later Interviews

During a second-round or in-house interview, you may be able to ask more probing questions designed to reveal how a firm or agency will match up with your happiness agenda.

Below are some questions that you might want to ask of prospective law firms.

These questions do come with a warning label (forgive us, disclaimers are an occupational hazard): these aren't questions to ask as you would in a deposition or you will probably self-destruct during the interview. They are certainly not the only, probably not even the primary, questions you should ask during that second round. And they should be sprinkled in gently, over time, in between other questions, or you might want to figure the answers to them out for yourself without asking the questions directly.

1. What are the firm's billable hour expectations? Do attorneys receive bonuses (or compensatory time off) if they exceed their targets or expectations?

2. What kinds of responsibilities and decision latitudes are given to associates on cases? How about on personal matters? (e.g., Will I be able to arrange my own office, hang my own paintings, or bring in my own lamp?)

3. Are attorneys able (or even encouraged) to set their own schedules? Are reduced hours, telecommuting, and flexible full-time schedules options for all lawyers (or only upon certain events, such as pregnancy or illness, or only after a certain number of years of service)? What percent of all associates and all partners opt for a reduced hours schedule? Are associates or partners who opt for reduced hours or flextime evaluated in the same manner as those working a traditional or set amount of hours? To what extent does the firm outfit home offices or provide technology reimbursement?

4. How much vacation leave do attorneys get, but perhaps more importantly, do people really take it, do they feel

pressured not to use it all, and are they tethered by e-mail and BlackBerrys during vacations?

5. Is this a firm that plays to individual lawyers' strengths and interests? If lawyers want to pursue a new practice area interest as an associate or in midcareer, are there examples of the firm supporting lawyers to move in new directions?

6. What amount of subsidized family (maternity, paternity, partner) leave does the firm provide? What percent of lawyers take the leave that is offered? Can lawyers negotiate unpaid sabbaticals apart from family leave?

7. What type of personality does best in this firm? Are you looking for people who are driven or more laid back? How are conflicts (regarding cases or salaries or personnel) resolved?

8. What efforts is the firm making to promote females and racial minorities into the top leadership positions at the firm? Does the firm have a director of diversity or a director of professional development? Do women/racial minorities/sexual minorities head practice groups? Sit on the firm's managing committee?

9. What are the firm's turnover rates—how many associates (and partners) leave each year?

10. Apart from events to woo summer associates, in what kinds of events do members of the firm participate to play together (e.g., poker nights, sports, or a new parents group)? Do the lawyers in the firm go out to lunch together or get together regularly outside of work? What sorts of community involvement does the firm encourage and support?

After the interviews are over, there is a question you need to ask yourself: do you think you will really like the people with whom you will be working?

FINAL THOUGHTS

Let's end our conversation about your future on a fun and cheery note. Let's imagine your funeral.

Professor Larry Krieger, who is at the forefront of the humanizing legal education movement, offers a thought-provoking exercise: write your own eulogy.

> I ask participants to imagine a future time when they are retired and away from their current environment, perhaps traveling in a pleasant place. I have them imagine visiting a small, quiet gathering which then turns out to be a preview of their funeral. I then ask them to briefly write down the eulogies about themselves that, if they could attend their own funeral, they would like to hear from important others—their life partner or best friend, a respected lawyer or judge that has known them in practice, a member of another community they valued during their life (church, neighborhood, service club, etc.), and if time allows, their child or another young person they had known. They may also be asked to write down the things that they would most like to be able to say about themselves—the things about which they feel best when looking back on their life.
>
> The results of this exercise are illuminating, because they show students and lawyers the kinds of things that matter most deeply to them. Participants are often surprised by the results. Almost invariably the qualities and values expressed in these eulogies are the most traditional human values and virtues: patience, decency, fairness, humility, courage, caring, integrity, willingness to work hard for worthwhile goals, helpfulness to others (family, friends, clients or community), and so forth. No one thus far in my experience has drafted a eulogy focused on a luxurious home, high grade point average, law review membership, or extraordinary income.[111]

While this exercise might seem to invite some of the predictive flaws of misimagining the future, it asks you to think now about how you want other people to think of you later. The point of it isn't to imagine an accurate future but to envision a future shaped by a life lived according to your personal values and intrinsic goals. It also brings home the point that these intrinsic virtuous qualities are unlimited and noncompetitive: "In law school parlance, everyone can be in the Top Five Percent in kindness, patience, etc."[112] If your focus in law school is on your own goals, and not those defined for you by the well-worn default paths, you are more likely to emerge from law school ready to embark on a career that will satisfy you.

CHAPTER 6

What Law Firms Can Do to Make Lawyers Happier

We're a law firm. Time is billable. The client doesn't pay for small talk. Every minute you spend away from your desk is a minute the firm isn't making any money off your presence, even though you're still using the office supplies, eating the muffins, drinking the coffee, consuming the oxygen, and adding to the wear and tear on the carpets. You're overhead. And if you're not earning your keep, you shouldn't be here.[1]

JEREMY BLACHMAN'S SATIRICAL EXPOSE ON ELITE LAW firm life, *Anonymous Lawyer*, a blog that became a book, is not the only bleak depiction of law firm life. William Keates kept a diary of his first year at a prestigious firm and published *Proceed With Caution*. Numerous other blogs, such as http://abovethelaw.com, catalog gossip, dubious achievements and horrors of law firm recruitment techniques, billable hour demands, associate abuse, office politics, and layoffs.

Is it really that bad? Maybe not, but there is evidence that life, especially in larger firms, has taken a turn for the worse. The 2009 recession prompted salary freezes or cuts, delayed start dates for new associates and led to layoffs of both associates and partners. Beyond recession-induced turbulence, focus on the bottom line increasingly has made the comforts and relative stability of big firm life a thing of the past. From experienced attorneys the refrain is heard so often as to seem a mantra: "Law is becoming just another business." Implicit in the complaint is the suggestion that law should be more than "a business"—it should be a profession that places a high value on quality and service to the community. Older attorneys bemoan the emphasis today on meeting ever-higher billable hour requirements, the foregoing of face-to-face contact in favor of more efficient electronic communication, and the compromises in work product quality that are made to placate client cost concerns. They remember with fondness the clubbish colleagiality of their firm in days gone by, and they lament the loss of civility in their profession.

The good news is that, in response to these disturbing trends, some firms, corporations, and government agencies are reconsidering their personnel practices. A number of firms are implementing policies that allow their lawyers to find work-life balance or to reconnect with colleagues. If you are a partner at a law firm, the supervisor of in-house counsel, or the manager of a government or public interest organization (for shorthand reference, we will talk in terms of "law firms" for the most part), this chapter is for you. It addresses what you can do to make your firm a happier place and why you should do it.

FOUR REASONS LAW FIRMS SHOULD CARE ABOUT MAKING THEIR LAWYERS HAPPY

REASON NUMBER 1: HAPPY FIRMS KEEP GOOD LAWYERS

The primary resources of your law firm are your lawyers. If your firm is perceived as performing work of exceptional quality, you get the cases, the clients, and the fees. Your top talent can be lost if the lawyers are unhappy. The National Association of Law

Placement conducted a survey of associate attrition at large firms in 2007 and found that within three years 37 percent of associates leave their firms, a figure that skyrockets to 77 percent within five years.[2] Of course, there are a thousand reasons why a lawyer might leave a firm, but one of the most common is that the grass seems greener elsewhere—in fact, the grass in the lawyer's former firm might have withered in the associate's eyes.

REASON NUMBER 2: KEEPING LAWYERS HAPPY SAVES MONEY

Estimates of the amount it costs to replace a departing associate range from $200,000 to $500,000—roughly one and one-half to two times the annual salary of that lawyer.[3] If your firm loses five lawyers in a year, that is a one to two-and-a-half million dollar loss. The explicit costs of attorney turnover may include: severance pay and accrued vacation benefits, job advertisement for the now vacant position, recruiter's time and salary, interviewing expenses (including travel, meals, and hotel), reference checks, expenses for relocation, orientation and training of the new employee, and, possibly, signing bonuses. The behind-the-scenes costs—such as lost productivity time, covering the work of the departing lawyer, client notification and perhaps mollification, as well as a morale drop among lawyers who remain—can dwarf the explicit expenses.[4]

REASON NUMBER 3: HAPPY LAWYERS ARE MORE PRODUCTIVE

Evidence is mounting that happier workers are more productive and that happiness enhances performance. Happier people (who are more likely to have jobs in the first place) get better work evaluations and earn higher pay. They have less absenteeism and lower medical costs; they set higher goals and persist longer at cognitive tasks. In occupations outside of law, studies have shown that happiness is tied to numerous measures of better performance: people in a good mood are better negotiators than those in bad moods; they will make better managerial decisions, be more creative, and compliment the performance of those around them.[5] It is reasonable to assume that positive expectations and happiness present the same correlations in law.[6]

This is not to say your goal should be to keep lawyers in a constant state of euphoria. While happiness promotes creativity, it undermines precise focus because happier people are open to a variety of different kinds of information and lack the attention filter that negative emotions supply.[7] Euphoria and detail work, the latter of which can be considerable in law firms, do not go hand in hand.

Reason Number 4: Happiness Is Its Own Reward

In addition to saving valuable human resources and increasing productivity, creating a happier law firm will make you and the other lawyers in your firm happier. That, of course, is a reward in itself. As happiness begins to develop in a firm, it will spread of its own accord. You can "catch" happiness. If the lawyer next door is happy, if your secretary is happy, there's a good chance that their happiness will improve your mood as well.

We are social creatures, and our affective state is influenced by the emotions of people around us. People tend to spontaneously mimic the expressions and behaviors of other group members and to absorb, match, and mirror emotions of others through largely unconscious feedback mechanisms. Studies in organizational behavior show that group emotions—such as morale, rapport, and cohesion—and mood contagion in a workplace can be affected by words, nonverbal cues, policies, goals, and priorities.[8] Negative moods also transfer between people and spread through a group. If you spend a significant amount of time around Debby

Downer at your office, you may catch her negative mood. Disgruntled lawyers can spread their unhappiness like cold germs. The ability to infect other people works with cheerful as well as negative emotions. In short, both happiness and unhappiness are contagious.[9]

OPTIMIZING, NOT MAXIMIZING, LAW FIRM HAPPINESS

Your goal is not to maximize happiness but to optimize it. Ringing the party bell at 4:00 PM every day might boost firm happiness, but there are obvious costs to that as well. Your firm, after all, has clients to serve and income to earn.

If you want to just have a happy law firm, we'd suggest you hire a bunch of people with high happiness set points, typically optimistic extroverts. Hiring happy people, and only happy people, is the easiest way to improve firm happiness. But the serious business of law firms is better served by a mix of talented people with different happiness set points. Lawyers who have a tendency to be unhappy can still be excellent lawyers, better perhaps at worrying about details and negative outcomes. Remember Martin Seligman's observation about the positive dimensions of pessimism for lawyers. Happiness is a good thing, but it is possible to have too much of a good thing. For law firms today, however, too much happiness doesn't seem to be the problem. Too little happiness is.

ADDRESSING FIRM HAPPINESS: IT'S A WHOLE NEW GAME

Forces are driving law firms to revolutionize their traditional structures and ways of doing business. Push for change is coming from a variety of quarters—not just from lawyers who would like time with their families but also from clients who prefer flat rate (per project) billing and who demand diversity in the law firms that do their work, from the American Bar Association (ABA) (which urged lawyers in 2002 to rethink the billable hour), and from students who will be the next generation of lawyers. Moving towards a happier law firm sometimes involves swimming with the current.

Understanding Generational Differences

> *Generation Y and women want a life balance.... The 50-year-olds don't understand that, but they're in a bind because there are not enough bodies to do the work. It's forcing law firms to think in different ways.*[10]

Just when you were beginning to understand some of the generational differences of your firm's newest partners, the Gen X'ers, you realize that the next generation of your firm will be staffed by the Gen Y associates you recently hired. Seventy million strong, Gen Y'ers (or "Millennials") are the next wave of the American workforce. Lawyers from Generation X (born between 1965–79) and Generation Y (born between 1980–2000) often work in law firms where the senior partners are either Baby Boomers (born between 1946–64) or members of a Traditionalist generation (born before 1946).

As arbitrary as these labels might be for people born just a year apart (and odd that the "generations" vary from fourteen to twenty years in length), generational research can still offer some useful information. Obviously, these are group characteristics as well as sweeping generalizations. Some Gen Y'ers might have old-time values and some Baby Boomers have work attitudes indistinguishable from their younger co-workers.

Work-life balance is more important to more contemporary generations than income. Ellen Freedman, a law practice management coordinator, says that Gen X'ers "value flexibility in the work environment and expect significant recognition and rewards but are willing to take significantly reduced compensation in return for a more balanced lifestyle."[11] Gen Y lawyers are sociable and want mentoring, teamwork, and feedback; they are also "'intolerant of drudgery.'"[12]

Gen X'ers and Gen Y'ers have much less firm loyalty or interest in a career commitment to a single firm. More than half (58 percent) of Traditionalists cited commitment to the company as most important, while less than a third (32 percent) of Gen Y'ers did so.[13] For Traditionalists job changing carries a stigma; if you are a Boomer, you may see shifting jobs as creating a competitive disadvantage; for younger lawyers, changing jobs is necessary, expected, or routine.[14] Remember that studies show that commitment is important to job satisfaction. If you are busy looking for your next job, it is hard to develop trust, commit to, and engage in your existing job. The reluctance of younger generations to commit to their present jobs might be an obstacle to happiness.

Different generations come to the firm with different expectations. Boomers and Traditionalists are accustomed to face to face communications, including face time at the office, while younger generations who grew up with cell phones and computers are used to electronic communication and working from remote locations. Newer generations, raised by supportive, engaged parents who included them in decision making, expect transparency and the ability to participate in making decisions: "They prefer egalitarian leadership, not hierarchies."[15] Members of Gen Y have been treated as important and special, and they desire immediate and frequent positive feedback. "'Older workers think no news is good news. [Gen Y'ers] want pats on the back. Older people tend to be thankful for a job and younger workers really want some praise and recognition.'"[16] Members of this multitasking generation (known in some circles as "the iGeneration"), who text message at the speed of wifi and TiVo television shows, expect instant access to information and are accustomed to an unprecedented amount of control over their lives. While Boomers prize recognition in tangible forms, such as money or a corner office, Gen X'ers see freedom as the ultimate reward, while Gen Y'ers seek work that is meaningful to them.[17]

What does the current generational mix mean for sound law firm policies that promote overall happiness? It underscores the importance of recognizing that different things may make different cohorts more or less satisfied and appreciating that each generation brings helpful ideas to the table. The commitment espoused by Traditionalists is good for happiness and so is the feedback and mentoring promoted by Gen Y'ers. Gen X'ers want to work smarter rather than harder, and they tend to like flexibility. Gen Y'ers each have their individual playlists: they want to be judged based on their productivity and the quality of their work, not their seniority. As we discuss later in this chapter, some firms are moving to differential incentive systems, more family-friendly work arrangements, greater social interaction opportunities, and more explicit feedback systems. While there is no perfect recipe for law firm happiness, each generation offers promising ingredients.

> X'ers are looking for a team where they can make a meaningful contribution. Boomers did, and still do, want the same. X'ers want sufficient access to information. Doesn't everyone? X'ers want entrepreneurship, defined as room in the work to define problems, develop solutions at their own pace, and produce their own results. This is the very essence of a lawyer's work for her clients. X'ers want personal attention, mentoring, and loyalty. All successful lawyers feel the same.[18]

ADDRESSING CLIENT DEMANDS

Across the country, clients are calling for changes in traditional hourly billing methods—the same thing that lawyers complain about from a different direction. Studies have demonstrated "the potential conflict of interest between resolving disputes efficiently and billing clients by the hour."[19] Financial incentives discourage efficiency and encourage padding of hours.[20]

In some circles use of hourly billing may diminish due to pressures from clients. A number of large companies that outsource their legal work have begun to negotiate a fixed fee (one price for handling a series of matters) or a flat rate (a set cost per task) rather than billable-hour arrangements. Alternative fee arrangements still remain an alternative lifestyle for now: 83 percent of the general counsel responding to a 2008 Altman Weil survey said that, excluding discounted hourly rates, "they used alternative fee arrangements less than 10 percent of the time."[21] However, three-quarters of managing heads of Am Law 200 firms (the nation's two hundred highest grossing law firms) think that in the next decade "'many if not most' big firms will change their billing practices," and two-thirds said that some form of fixed-rate deals were being negotiated.[22]

Some of the country's largest corporations are also beginning to demand that the law firms to which they outsource their work not only hire appropriate numbers of female and minority attorneys but have those attorneys billing their time on the companies' work. In 2004, Rick Palmore, general counsel of Sara Lee, issued an open letter entitled A Call to Action: Diversity in the Legal Profession, urging corporations to insist that law firms performing work for them make a commitment to diversity. Since then, the commitment statement has acquired 136 corporate signatories, from such corporations as General Mills, General Motors, Hewlett Packard, Johnson & Johnson, Microsoft, Shell Oil, Starbucks, Target, and Walmart.[23]

This corporate insistence on diversity has practical consequences for lawyers. To obtain the work of these corporate giants, law firms have responded by heeding the Call to Action and staffing their cases with lawyers who are women or racial minorities.[24] Law firms are learning that diversity makes business sense. But does diversity lead to happiness?

Contemplating Workplace Diversity

Firms used to be good ol' boy networks, with no pressures to become more diverse along any dimension. Partners and associates were white, male, and upper middle class and played golf. Law firm demographics have changed enormously in the past several decades: law firms today are diverse in numerous ways. Although golf is still a constant, now it is as likely to be played with a Wii on a "virtual golf course" as it is at a country club.

Whether a diverse law firm is, for that reason, a happy law firm, remains an open question. On the one hand, among the happiest nations in the world are those that are homogeneous, such as Scandinavian countries.[25] The same can be said of homogenous neighborhoods, according to Robert Putnam, author of *Bowling Alone*. Putnam's study of diversity in communities found that ethnically diverse communities had substantially lower levels of "neighborly trust," lower levels of voter participation, lower levels of confidence in government, a reduced rate of volunteerism, and "less happiness and lower perceived quality of life" than more homogeneous communities.[26] At the level of personal interaction, considerable evidence suggests that people empathize more readily with others to whom they are similar in key ways.[27] Much of this evidence (other country, community, and interpersonal relationship data) does not specifically apply to the workplace, and it is not clear what conclusions should be drawn for workplace happiness until more studies are conducted.

On the other hand, diversity unquestionably has educational and economic values, and differences enhance creativity.[28] Lawyers who are members of GenY get satisfaction from being around others from different backgrounds.[29] Social critic Malcolm Gladwell observes that "in embracing the diversity of human beings, we will find a surer way to true happiness."[30] Law firms are also seeing that attention to diversity—training about micro-inequities, creating accommodations for attorneys having child or elder care responsibilities through part-time status or the ability to work from home, and developing "parenting leave" handbooks and mentoring programs—improves satisfaction with working conditions and retention of women and racial minorities.[31] The same individualized attention and flexible work policies are good for members of majority groups as well; firms that are family-friendly and sensitive to the individual needs of their lawyers tend to be happier places to work. And Putnam, despite the evidence he accumulated questioning whether diversity promotes happiness, ultimately concluded that diversity was a value worth pursuing. He noted that while diversity initially makes people uncomfortable, "One great achievement of human civilization is our ability to draw more inclusive lines of social identity. The motto on the Great Seal of the United States (and on our dollar bill)—e pluribus unum—reflects precisely that objective—namely, to create a novel 'one' out of a diverse 'many.'"[32] While the jury is still out on whether a more diverse law firm is a happier firm, we conclude that a more diverse firm is—no small thing—a better firm.

TEN STEPS THAT COULD MAKE YOUR LAW FIRM A HAPPIER WORKPLACE

Happiness at a law firm has several aspects. The overall reputation of a firm—is it a happy place to work or not—is one dimension of employee satisfaction in the job domain. At the firm level, positive behavior, such as focusing on enhancing employees' attributes of loyalty, resilience or compassion (as opposed to criticism), correlates with employee commitment, retention, and productivity as well as various measures of corporate success.[33] There is also "facet-specific happiness,"[34] or attorney satisfaction with specific tasks while working at the firm, such as the degree of control over their own cases, clarity of directions, or feedback. Managers who are successful in raising attorney satisfaction will attend to generalized domain (or job) satisfaction as well as "facet-specific" happiness having to do with the attractiveness of different tasks. We will address some aspects of both of these dimensions throughout these steps.

1. PROMOTING LAWYER AUTONOMY

Studies of attorney satisfaction show that if your job gives you significant autonomy, you are more likely to be happy. Conversely, satisfaction is lower if you are subjected to constraints on your decisions and work setting and circumstances. In 2001, the nonprofit research group Catalyst surveyed a sample of 1,400 lawyers who graduated from one of five elite law schools: University of California-Berkeley, Columbia, Harvard, Michigan, and Yale. Catalyst asked the participants to rank the top five sources of satisfaction for them in their jobs. Control over work was the leading source of satisfaction for men (68 percent) and the third highest source of satisfaction for women (57 percent).[35] This result is consistent with other research on reported dimensions of job satisfaction.[36]

An absence of control (low decision latitude), combined with high workload demands and high stakes outcomes, describes the work life of many associates.[37] For firms that find ways to provide associates greater freedom to choose the cases they work on, or greater ability to control the cases they are assigned, the satisfaction, loyalty, and productivity payoffs could be immense. A step in the direction of greater lawyer autonomy, one that probably would not undermine other firm goals, would be to turn over smaller files to associates (combined with good mentoring of progress). If this were done at a significantly reduced hourly rate, more junior lawyers could gain valuable experience—and clients would be more satisfied with the fees.[38] Another approach might be to have younger lawyers, who are researching projects, explain their research results to the partner and then be the ones to brief the client. "You learn how to practice law by practicing law"[39]—and newer lawyers need meaningful responsibilities to acquire skills.

Associate happiness is also likely to be increased if you encourage development of each lawyer's specific strengths and skill sets. When you have a series of projects, rather than following the traditional route of individual partners tapping particular associates, send a memo to several associates with a brief squib about the projects and permit them to self-select work assignments. If you have a mentoring program, allow the junior lawyers who are being mentored to choose their mentors or express preferences for one of several possible mentors. This is essentially a no-cost proposition for firms, and it is a way of affording choices to newer attorneys. (If one partner is the perennial favorite and another is never selected as a mentor, perhaps that should indicate something about the appropriate compensation of those partners?)

Finally, your firm can make its lawyers happier by letting employees make choices about their own work environments. Is it really necessary that every office have standard-issue furniture and the same antique white walls, or could employees be allowed to exercise some personal choice? Could that edict addressing the removal of personal pictures from office walls be rescinded? Could employees be given a greater say concerning what neighborhood in your sprawling four-stories of offices they are housed?

2. Taking Off the Billable Hours Straitjacket

When asked what they dislike most about the practice of law, many lawyers will answer "billable hours" or some variation on the theme: "that my worth is tied to billing hours"; "unrealistic billable hour expectations"; "because of the hours I work, I have no outside life." In response to a 2005 National Association for Law Placement (NALP) Foundation survey asking attorneys the single most influential factor prompting them to change jobs, the factor checked by the largest percentage of respondents was "reduction of work hours."[40] Of the more than 2,300 respondents to an *ABA Journal* survey, 84 percent said they would be willing to receive less income in exchange for a lower billable hours requirement.[41] These are not just associates or younger attorneys. Almost half of the attorneys in management positions would gladly give up some portion of their salary in return for more family or free time.[42] But, if lawyers have to ask for release time, flexibility, or alternative salary arrangements, rather than have the firm offer those as clearly available options, the lawyers who seek them may be seen as subpar or undedicated players. It will take structural changes to get around the perceptions that alternative time and salary arrangements are perversely different.

3. PROVIDING WORK-LIFE BALANCE

> *Nearly two-thirds of all lawyers report difficulty managing the demands of work and personal/family life.*[43]

Lawyers want more work-life balance than they have now. The buzz-phrase is rampant; it's just that nobody seems to have much of the real thing. More than one-third of the male lawyers and almost one-half of female lawyers cited "work-life balance as one of their top three reasons for selecting their current employer."[44]

The Law Student Revolt

Pressure for change is coming from law students at some of the nation's most elite schools. In the spring of 2007, a group of students at Stanford Law School and other law schools calling itself Law Students Building a Better Legal Profession (BBLP) sent letters to one hundred prestigious law firms urging them to reduce billable hours and implement work-life balance policies. The organization also produced rankings of firms based on how compatible firms' policies were with a balanced life for associates. BBLP urged firms to lower the number of billable hours expected per year, move toward flat rate or transactional billing, increase diversity, offer more time for pro bono work, and make work expectations transparent by publicizing the median hours that associates and partners work. Specifically, the group called for firms to implement "balanced hours policies" that would expressly approve of associates working "80%, 70% or 60% of fulltime hours for proportional pay."[45]

Professors Marc Galanter and William Henderson raise concerns about complications of staffing projects and question whether such a proposal is economically realistic: "a lawyer who works 70% of the typical full-time load is unlikely to deliver a pro rata return on his or her time because fixed overhead for office space and support staff is not thereby proportionately reduced."[46] Given this concern, compensation for less than full-time workers probably needs to reflect something less than the proportional hours worked—say, 70 percent of full-time pay for working 80 percent of normal hours. Regardless of the specifics of the compensation scheme, firms need to make clear to the new generation of lawyers what work expectations are.

Craig Segall, a Stanford Law 3L at the time of the group's founding, expressed the hope that law students at "Tier 1" law schools such as his own had "the market power" to make law firms more humane. Segall recognized the forces his group was up against, forces which have only been exacerbated by the recent recession. "We are not so naïve to think the situation will change over night," Segall wrote. "Law students are hard to organize and this is a problem that's been developing for decades."[47]

Of course, not all law students and lawyers agree. In response to a *Wall Street Journal* article about BBLP, some law students wrote of their willingness to work for long hours even if members of the new organization chose not to. One student, who indicated that he or she was "dying to work hard," suggested to BBLP supporters: "Can't take the heat? Stay out of the kitchen. Go work your 1600 hours in some other industry." Another unsympathetic lawyer wrote, "Bottom line, they want the associational prestige of working at a brand name without having to put in the hours." Yet another lawyer suggested that the students consider working at smaller firms for "sane hours" but with less pay.[48]

The student-promoted revolution may not be taking hold among associates—particularly in tougher economic times. You are not likely to hear associates complaining as loudly as these law students about work-life balance issues, however unhappy they may be. As Segall noted, associates are poorly positioned to influence change: "Associates have very little market power and, due to the lousy conditions they work in, many plan to leave after a few years."[49]

Does this budding student revolt, centered at Tier 1 law schools, deserve a response from the nation's largest firms? Firms may conclude that the near constant availability of associates is critical to their clients, or that the economic efficiency that comes from assigning a single lawyer to work eighty hours instead of having two work forty hours each might seem irresistible. Firms could easily believe, and they might well be right, that their associational prestige will continue to attract a steady stream of top-flight legal talent from law schools despite a generation's growing concern with work–life balance. As one person commenting on the BBLP campaign saw it, the "social capital" of prestigious firms, with their "cool buildings" and "cool addresses" and "cool art collections" and especially high salaries, holds a huge appeal for graduates from national law schools.[50]

Stanford Law School Dean Larry Kramer recently bemoaned the "tendency of students from elite schools to go disproportionately to large firms"—a tendency which he said had grown "more pronounced in recent years."[51] Kramer worried that "too many of our graduates have gone to these firms for the wrong reason—and with predictable results, including boredom, frustration, and early lateral movement."[52] The desire to "add another prestigious line on a resume," says Kramer, proves irresistible to today's top students "who have been taught from an early age to collect gold stars."[53]

Even if a steady stream of stellar recruits continue to come through their doors, we believe that BBLP raises issues that law firms should address. There are obvious economic and other efficiencies that derive from the current structure, but the willingness of new hires to work for less suggests that compromises can be made that won't seriously harm the bottom line. Whether the group can live up to the billing of its title is an open question, but the legal profession has never seen a movement quite like this one—a grassroots organization, tapping the power of the labor market and using the capabilities of the internet to disseminate comparative data about law firms. More important, increasingly inhumane work environments have implications for how law is practiced, because harried, unhappy lawyers are undoubtedly more likely to be uncivil, cut corners, and engage in unethical practices. Moreover, weighing mightily for addressing some of BBLP's key concerns are all the advantages, laid out elsewhere in this book, that come to all members of a happy workplace.

Richard Thaler and Cass Sunstein, in their important bestseller *Nudge: Improving Decisions About Health, Wealth, and Happiness*, demonstrate how the architecture of choice shapes public and private decision-making. Their insights could be used by a firm seeking to maximize lawyer choice while moving towards a better work-life balance and overall level of happiness within a firm. Thaler and Sunstein note, for example, that people derive roughly twice as much unhappiness from losing a certain amount of money than they derive happiness from winning the same amount. A $50 loss causes the same value of negative feelings as a $100 win causes positive feelings. Most people, in other words, are "loss averse."[54] When people think about what they have lost, or what they didn't get that most people got, they are not happy campers. This would explain why most lawyers who are told "You can give up 20 percent of your pay in return for working proportionally fewer hours" might be unlikely to accept the offer, Instead, they will continue to grind away toward their unhappiness-producing 2,000 billable hours. However, if new hires are told, "We expect you to put in 1600 billable hours for $X (an amount equal to, say, 20 percent less than what is paid those who produce 2,000), but you have the option of working 2,000 hours and receiving a *bonus* (an amount that would bring pay up to the level currently paid for meeting the 2,000-hour expectation)," a much higher number of recruits might opt for the reduced pay and reduced hours, thus improving the overall psychological health of the firm. Why? Because the reduced hours for reduced pay, having become the default option, no longer is associated in the new lawyer's mind with "a loss."

Susan C. Robinson, dean of career services at Stanford Law School, offers another idea for producing "happy well-trained lawyers who not only stay in their firms, but in the profession."[55] Robinson suggests that firms drastically cut starting salaries, say to the $80,000 range, and use the savings to create a formal apprenticeship period during which new lawyers would have reduced-hour expectations and gain the ability "to cut their teeth on engaging legal work"—something they lost when clients began balking at paying "high-priced billable hours for untrained associates."[56] Several large law firms have already moved in the direction of apprenticeship-style programs. Howrey, a 600-plus lawyer firm, announced a pay cut for starting associates, coupled with training: "from $160,000 to $100,000 in base pay plus a $25,000 bonus to pay down law school loans—and they'll spend a good portion of their time attending classes with partners and shadowing them on client matters."[57] The firm will bill out new associates at half of prior billing rates, and has low billable hour expectations for the associates: 700 hours the first year and 1,000 hours the second year. Although the program will cost Howrey in terms of lost billable hours and partner time for training, the firm expects costs savings in starting salaries and larger gains down the road in associate loyalty and efficiency, as well as client public relations. As Robinson sees it, an apprenticeship period will bring relief to the new associates "burned out by the numbers of hours they are expected to clock and the tedium of the tasks they do."[58]

Structural Changes in Firms

Many large firms are making structural changes that allow their lawyers to find better work-life balance. These range from providing greater parenting leave to allowing workers to adopt flex-time schedules. *Working Mother* magazine and the national consulting group Flex-Time Lawyers compiled its second annual list of the fifty best law firms for women. Top ranking firms offer flexible work schedules and generous parenting leave. Among these top ranking firms, the average paid maternity leave is fourteen weeks; the average paid paternity leave is almost six weeks.[59] Larger firms tend to have written policies, while smaller firms tend toward more variation, allowing leave that builds on sick leave and accrued vacation time. Of course, the more some firms extend maternity, paternity, and parenting leave, the more that other firms will need to do so to remain competitive.

Various types of flexible arrangements have been tested in law firms. These approaches include flex time (no standard working hours, and individual lawyers arrange their own schedules); a compressed work week (say, four ten-hour days instead of five eight-hour days); staggering work hours (for instance, working five nine-hour days one week, and four the next week), telecommuting with computer access to the law firm's files; part-time work (simply a reduced number of hours expected); and job-sharing. Some firms employ new position categories (such as "of counsel" or "permanent associate"), while others adopt the target hours approach. Under the target hours method, firms publish the average billable and nonbillable hours worked by lawyers in different practice areas, according to years in practice and status level. Each attorney and his or her supervisor agree on a target number of hours for the upcoming year based on the firm's needs and the attorney's individual circumstances. Deborah Epstein Henry, president of Flex-Time Lawyers, a national work-life balance consulting firm, points out that "full-time" and "part-time" are concepts that tend to stigmatize and do not accurately reflect work done in different areas of specialization: "For associates at the same firm in the same year, a 'full-time' mergers and acquisitions lawyer may bill 2,300 hours and a 'full-time' trusts and estates lawyer may bill 1,800 hours, while a 'part-time' litigator may bill 1,800 hours and a 'part-time' family lawyer may bill 1,500 hours."[60]

Of Canadian lawyers who have used some type of flexible work arrangement, telecommuting (which eliminates commuting time and costs) was the most popular, with 77 percent of lawyers using it; flextime was chosen by 31 percent of lawyers, while a reduction in hours was used by 30 percent of lawyers.[61] Telecommuting can boost happiness of telecommuters because it allows them to gain a huge amount of control over when and where their work is performed. However, because relationships matter, firms might not be creating happier workplaces by taking workers (except the real sourpusses) out of the office. We will see this tension repeated with other dimensions of workplace happiness: some solutions that may give a satisfaction boost in one direction undermine it in another way.[62]

Underutilization of Existing Policies—A Public Relations Problem?

Although 98 percent of the 1,500 mostly larger law offices responding to a NALP survey in 2008 said that they permit part-time work schedules, only 5.6 percent of all lawyers work part-time.[63] Most of them are women. One feature limiting usage nationally is that more than one-half of firms offering part-time schedules precluded entry-level associates from using that option. Of those employees who are eligible, many may not be aware of part-time alternatives, and many more may be hesitant to pursue that career path. In one study, more than nine out of ten managing partners reported that their firms permitted attorneys to work less than full time, yet only six out of ten associates either knew of the policy or thought it was a realistic option.[64]

Gender stereotypes of various types can keep participation in flexible work arrangements low. Female attorneys may assume that they have to work harder than male attorneys to avoid being perceived as less capable or committed to their careers. Male attorneys may even be told that a "real man does not take parental leave."[65] Even if your firm supports attorney freedom or family commitments, lawyers perceive that using parenting leave time or flexible work arrangements will undermine their status in firms and have a negative impact on their careers. A majority of lawyers responding to one survey said that they did not think a lawyer who opted for either a full- or part-time flexible work arrangement could ever make partner.[66] Some research has shown that both men and women who use part-time or family-friendly policies in law firms are perceived as less competent than other full-time workers.[67] If firms really want to promote work satisfaction, they need to make it possible for associates to work reduced schedules and still become partner.

Despite the stigma and the problem of a part-time workload creeping into a full-time gig (while the attorney is still only paid for part-time work), lawyers who have these agreements are typically very satisfied with them. Consider the situation of Mary Jo Foster, then an associate at Streich Lang, who asked to work reduced hours when she adopted twin infants. She was expected to bill 80 percent of the usual billable hours target, and her compensation was reduced by 25 percent (the 5 percent difference went to overhead costs), but she kept full benefits. This arrangement eliminated most night and weekend work for her. She says, "'Most people in the firm didn't even realize that I was working a reduced-hours schedule.'"[68] Attorneys with variable-hour arrangements who litigate confess that depositions, trials, and travel require juggling of their commitments but that they still prefer the freedom of time.

One of the best ways to help your attorneys create work-life balance is to set realistic billable hour targets or eliminate billable hour minimums and convey average expectations. Although most law firms in America do precisely the reverse, the ABA's Law Practice Management Section suggests limiting the rewards attached to billable hours exceeding your firm's expectations.[69]

Although the movement toward individual schedules is slow to take off, the demand for individualization is increasing, and new work-hour arrangements are emerging. Managers may worry that these changes could cause workers to make comparisons between their arrangements. However, comparisons in the workplace are inevitable. The focus of comparative judgments in the workplace today is based primarily on salary: full-time fourth year Associate X contrasts his salary to that of full-time fourth year Associate Y. With a more flexible approach, these comparisons will include both compensation and workload. Individuated hourly plans offer flexibility and respond well to employees' desires for control of their work flow. They also respond to the specific attention that newer generations of workers crave. Although individualization undoubtedly swallows a significant amount of management time, the benefits to law firms—in attorney loyalty, firm morale, and economics—can be enormous.

Flexibility and Law Firm Productivity

James Sandman, the managing partner of Arnold & Porter, detailed the economic case for creating part-time programs. He observed that "an accessible part-time program enables firms to compete both in the market for talent and for clients: recruits appreciate the option to attempt to balance work and personal needs and clients appreciate committed attorneys who are sometimes better able to focus on their cases because they are assigned fewer of them."[70]

Although limited data directly relates to law firms, experiences in other industries show that job flexibility reduces attrition, and there is no reason to suspect law would be different.[71] One study of Washington, D.C., law firms showed that alternative scheduling arrangements were profitable for firms and helped them retain high performing attorneys. Michael Nannes of Dickstein, Shapiro, Morin & Oshinsky "discovered a startling fact: 'We were losing lawyers not to other law firms, but to other schedules.'"[72]

Law firm managers tend to think in terms of comparing the productivity of lawyers working full time with those working reduced hours and conclude that a full-time worker would be more productive. However, if the analysis is based on "productivity for the amount of time worked... lawyers working alternative work schedules are often more productive on a pro rata basis than their full-time colleagues. Because lawyers on alternative work schedules have a limited amount of time within which to complete their work, they are forced to be more organized and efficient."[73] Studies confirm this. They show that attorneys who work part time are more efficient than their full-time counterparts.[74] Anecdotal evidence indicates that attorneys who work part time typically work more than the agreed number of hours. One attorney who has worked in a job sharing arrangement for years comments, "Hiring two attorneys to job share often leads to the productivity of 1.5 attorneys working full time."[75]

4. Encouraging a Positive Attitude

As a managing partner, you may use emotional contagion—in the form of orientation lectures, pep talks, or training sessions—to foster a "can do" atmosphere. Associates fresh from law school may need to hear this message early on, because many have been trained as problem finders rather than problem solvers. (It may also be in the associate's interest to spot the difficulties with architecting a deal or pursuing an avenue of discovery, because the associate will probably be the one doing the work, even while it is usually in the firm's interest to do the additional work.)

Allen Rostron, now a law professor, tells a story about his first day as an associate at the prestigious New York firm of Cravath, Swaine & Moore. Much of the day was devoted to mundane orientation tasks, from filling out paperwork to being issued a coffee mug with the firm's name on it. The orientation also had a more serious side, as the new crop of nervous but eager associates gathered to hear several of the firm's partners talk about what the firm expected of its associates. The message was hardly a warm and fuzzy welcome. One of the partners, a very formal, somber lawyer from the corporate finance group, briefly welcomed everyone to the firm and then paused to look at each person around the table, as if to let anticipation build for a moment to underscore the importance of what he would say next. "There is one thing that it's important for you to know from the very start," he finally continued. "If anything goes wrong on any matter that you are working on, it is your fault. Nothing that happens is ever anybody else's fault. It's always your fault." "For goodness sakes, it's my first day, I haven't even done anything yet, and it's already all my fault," Rostron remembers thinking. As the partner elaborated on what he meant by this, the reaction of his audience slowly but dramatically shifted. The partner explained that the firm expected and needed excellence from each of its attorneys, from the top down to the most junior associates. "So when you get assigned to a deal, or a case," the partner said, "you've got to realize that it's yours. You've got to have the attitude that you're responsible for it, and you're going to make sure everything works. You can't sit back and wait for somebody to give you a list of tasks to do. You've got to own these things, and tell yourself that you're going to be on top of it." That's why, the partner explained, you should feel like anything that goes wrong is your fault. "You can't ever pass the buck," the partner said. "If there's an error in the document, you can't say, 'well, it was the secretary's fault.' Because you should have given more precise instructions, double checked it, or done whatever was necessary to make sure it got done right." As the associates listened, they realized that the partner's message was not what it had seemed at first. It wasn't about getting yelled at and blamed or being afraid of getting in trouble. It wasn't about what a partner or anybody else was going to think about you or say to you. It was about how you were going to think and what you were going to say to yourself. Ultimately, and ironically, believing "it's always my fault" was a positive message about taking control.

The partner later offered another example of the "can do" attitude that the firm demanded of its lawyers, even the newly minted associates. "Any time a client asks if the firm can do something," the partner said, "the first word out of your mouth should always be 'yes.' Always. The answer is never 'no.'" If the client calls one evening and asks if we can write a complex brief and file it the following morning, the answer should be "yes." If the client asks if we can restructure the deal at the last minute, the answer should be "yes." "Now, of course," the partner went on, "that 'yes' often will need to be followed by a lot more explanation. You may need to follow the 'yes' with a lot of serious warnings about the disadvantages and costs, the serious logistical difficulties that will have to be overcome, the alternative options, the corners that might have to be cut to file so quickly, the risks of making significant changes to what is already in place, and so on. But you always start with the 'yes.'" Finally cracking a smile, the partner said, "In fact, sometimes when a client asks if we can do something, you'll have to say 'yes—absolutely, we can do that—we can achieve your goal. . . . But of course we'll have to do it in a somewhat different manner, because what you just described is totally illegal." Again, the partner's point was that Cravath expected its associates to be problem solvers, not just problem spotters. "There are a lot of lawyers out there who are good at telling clients what they can't do," a tax partner said later in the meeting. "But that's not the sort of lawyer you want to be. You want to be the creative lawyer who figures out the way that it can be done."

The partners at Cravath spent time trying to shape a firm culture toward the positive. They made the points about the responsibility, control, and importance of each new associate—qualities that the literature indicates are associated with happiness—and emphasized that the new lawyers needed to be positive about achieving the goals the client wants. The danger of going too far in this direction is sometimes seen in business climates, where a "can do" attitude can become an Enron-like "we can do whatever we want" attitude, with excessive hubris and inappropriate attention to risks. But, as lawyers, we do not seem to have this dangerous unbounded optimism.

5. Valuing Employees

The happiness literature does not dictate any single right way to structure law firm compensation systems. There is no one-size-tickles-all model to recommend. Different systems will make various camps of people more or less satisfied. The one general statement than can be safely made is that lawyers are happiest when they think their work has been fairly valued.

Can't Buy Me Love: Partnership Structure, Firm Profits, and Satisfaction

Historically, law firms had two categories of lawyers—partners and associates—with many larger firms using a seniority-based lock-step compensation system for their associates in which all associates ratchet ahead yearly with their class.[76] Today your firm may have equity partners or shareholders, nonequity or income partners, associates, permanent associates, and a variety of "of counsel" positions, staff, and contract attorneys. Eighty percent of the country's two hundred largest firms have a two-tier partner structure.[77] According to a study of Am Law 200 firms, whether your firm has a single-tier partnership structure or a modified partnership structure does not have a statistically significant effect on associate satisfaction. Associates' reactions to the structure of the partnership seem to depend more upon individual risk preferences and perceptions of how the structure might affect them: "Some associates appreciate modified partnership structures' potential allowance for a stronger work-life balance. Others are angered by the additional structural barriers to election to equity partnership."[78]

A number of studies demonstrate an inverse correlation between law firm profits and the reported satisfaction levels of associates and partners. One study found negative correlations between both the profitability and prestige of law firms and lawyers' responses along various dimensions of satisfaction, such as family friendliness of the firm, desirability of working conditions, and firm openness regarding its finances.[79] A study of University of Michigan law school graduates showed that the "high-earning practitioners in large private practices report the lowest average job satisfaction."[80]

What accounts for this? One theory is that relentlessly profit-driven firms may not pay much attention to the personal satisfaction of their lawyers.[81] Focus on the bottom line might lead to neglect of relationship building or other well-established sources of worker happiness. A second theory is that the cases that yield the highest levels of firm income provide less satisfying work than less lucrative cases. Whatever the explanation, an increase in firms' profits will not provide a trickle-down of happiness.

Associate Compensation

Firms today typically compensate lawyers in one of two basic ways: lockstep (a ladder system with a base salary for each rung of the ladder, tweaked according to various performance measures) or some variation of a merit system, usually with an "eat what you kill" component (rewards tied in some way to the business the individual lawyer brings in).[82] Law firms often employ a bonus system, in which year-end bonuses are handed out to star performers (winners) without explicitly identifying less able performers (losers). If your law firm's primary objective is to make the *least* number of associates *unhappy*, you would do well to adopt lockstep compensation systems. However, the unhappiest associates under such a system might well be your hardest workers, and firms usually want to encourage productivity and reward excellent performance.

Compensation systems, which may seem dissimilar on the surface, actually share common features. Almost all compensation models consider some measure of status within the firm. Even most lockstep systems are not really lockstep, because firms find ways to compensate exceptional work or use wage incentives to keep people from leaving: rainmakers and rock stars are rewarded. Once those negotiable components enter the system, the differences between systems tend to dissipate.

Partner Compensation

The two primary factors in partner compensation are business origination and fees collected, although many firms have a formula or plan that also considers client and case responsibilities, contributions to management of the firm, pro bono work, and professional involvement enhancing the firm's reputation. Some formulas try to encompass ineffable qualities such as collegiality and cooperativeness. Other formulas incorporate measures of client satisfaction, skills, and contributions to the firm beyond simply the book of business and revenue production. Firms typically reserve some revenue for a bonus pool that can be divided pro rata or used to reward exceptional performance.

The recession has prompted some reconsideration of partner pay strategies. Because associates cost firms money, many of the larger firms are decreasing their associate numbers. Partners are hoarding work, and compensation compression is occurring, with incoming partners' compensation approaching that of more senior partners.[83] These factors may reintroduce rigidity, bean (and hour) counting, and competitiveness in partner relations, all of which steer away from job satisfaction. Compression will probably prompt people to engage in more salary comparisons. A central finding of happiness research is that people care about their standing or status in a social group—and law firms are no exception—so relative income matters much more than absolute income to life satisfaction.[84] Judge Patrick Schiltz tells the story of one lawyer who earned more than one million dollars a year who "came within a whisker of quitting his firm" when he learned that an income peer would received $10,000 more than he did as part of a year-end bonus.[85]

Do Some Compensation Systems Make Lawyers Happier Than Other Systems?

No study definitively proves one compensation system is superior to others in increasing lawyer satisfaction levels. Every compensation system will leave some lawyers in a firm unhappy. If relationships are key to life satisfaction, however, formulas that capture important contributions to firm life are more likely to promote a happier workplace. The ideal compensation system measures in some way an employee's overall contribution to the firm's well-being, satisfies the firm's key workers, is generally perceived to be fair, and is clearly explained up front to new members of the organization. The rub lies in the difficulty of measuring an employee's contribution to a firm's overall well-being. Based on happiness research, we know these contributions can come in many forms, including by supporting other employees, treating co-workers fairly, facilitating a transfer of more control to co-workers, and especially promoting trust within the office.[86] Noted British economist John Helliwell's research indicates that "among employed people, trust in management predicts life satisfaction more reliably than health, marital status, or income level."[87]

Retention

Firms make a mistake when they place too much reliance on compensation to keep lawyers on board. Firms think that salaries matter so much to people that they can buy off a little unhappiness on the job by paying attorneys more.[88] It works for a while. People overestimate how much happiness money will bring them. Over a relatively short time though, the happiness boost dissipates. "[T]he effect of an income increase after four years is only about 42% of the effect after one year: the majority of the short-term effect of income vanishes over time."[89] The hedonic treadmill begins to roll—as one earns a greater salary, expectations rise and people adapt to the higher income level. Both associates and partners clamor for something more than money: they want a better lifestyle, more communications from their firm, autonomy, fairness, trust, and to feel valued.[90]

Raising salaries is not the best retention lure. In exit interviews, associates mention numerous reasons for leaving firms. Although partners often speculate that money is a primary reason, that is not borne out by surveys of associates. The most common three reasons associates cite for leaving firms are 1) an absence of mentoring, training and development, whether formal or informal; 2) a lack of or problematic relationships with partners; and 3) workload demands and a need for better work–life balance.[91] Similarly, in a survey of more than one thousand lateral partners sponsored by *American Lawyer*, respondents said that anticipated compensation with their new firms was one of the *least* significant factors in their move. The most important reasons were their new firms' commitment to support or help expand their particular practice and the firms' ability to integrate them into the partnership.[92] Understanding that money is not the answer to their retention problems, some larger firms are investing in programs that are intended to "re-recruit" their mid-level associates. In Washington, D.C., Howrey offers five academies for associate development each year. The firm has also created a mentorship program that gives each associate an individual partner-mentor and trains the partners in leadership and coaching.[93] While rapport that evolves naturally might be more genuine, the firm is paying attention to key sources of satisfaction.

The main point here for managers is that, beyond certain base levels, relative income matters more to workers than actual income. A compensation system that promotes overall happiness should be perceived to be fair by as many of the valuable workers as possible. One way to create the fairness, even though it exposes the relative salary differentials, is by constructing a transparent compensation system.

Transparency

People's satisfaction with a job will be lower if they expect better rewards than they actually receive.[94] If expectations are key in determining satisfaction with compensation, keeping a close match between expectations and results minimizes feelings of dissatisfaction.

Consider the experiences of one large firm that revised its compensation and professional development practices. In 2001, the firm moved from a traditional lockstep system of pay and promotion to a level system of specifying competencies in seventeen areas, evaluating associates twice a year against these expectations, and adjusting compensation and associates' billing rates in accordance with those assessments.[95] Compensation, including bonuses, became individualized and tied to growth in competency areas. The partner in charge of recruiting and career development for the firm says one of the most difficult implementation features was getting his partners to ignore time served: "It is stunningly difficult for lawyers to let go of that because it is so deeply ingrained."[96] Another feature of the plan is an upward evaluation of partners by associates in categories of supervision, availability, respect for associate workload, offering a broad perspective on cases, providing adequate lead time to complete projects, openness to questions, constructive feedback, and career guidance. The competency-based compensation system thus does something that firms increasingly see as important: it assesses the mentorship performance of partners and rewards partners who are good mentors and managers. Although attributing causation is impossible, the firm has noticed a marked drop in associate attrition under the competencies system. In 2001, the associate attrition rate was 26 percent (32 percent for female attorneys); by 2006, the associate attrition rate was 11 percent (10 percent for female attorneys).

Transparency about the criteria used to evaluate performance and clear expectations seem to be two of the most important characteristics of a fair compensation plan. There is more than one good way to run a law firm. The important thing is to have a compensation scheme that is transparent so that people who are coming to the firm are those who would like whatever system the firm uses. Transparency lets people who have different objectives make a reasoned decision whether the firm fits their goals.

6. Promoting Social Interaction

Avoiding the Perils of Bigness

> The prevailing model of the large law firm is so shaky at this point that one of the things firms are going to have to do is rethink their basic organizational model and how they use their human resources. . . . We're in a moment where the large law firm model is under tremendous pressure and we're going to see whether people who organize the new models will take this into account and be more concerned about getting the maximum productivity and creativity out of their employees[97]

Something important is lost as organizations grow past a certain size. In his book *The Tipping Point*, Malcolm Gladwell makes the case that firms of over about 150 members lack the cohesiveness and collegiality to be a satisfying workplace—and generally become significantly less efficient at accomplishing their goals.

Drawing on the research of British anthropologist Robin Dunbar and others, Gladwell argues that once firms exceed about 150 members people cannot know their co-workers well enough that "what they think of you matters" and work becomes "a very different kind of experience."[98] Dunbar's research led him to conclude that the "'figure of 150 seems to represent the maximum number of individuals with whom we can have a genuinely social relationship, the kind of relationship that goes with knowing who they are and how they relate to us.'"[99] Up to a size of 150 or so, an organization can attain its goals informally, whereas larger firms are forced to rely on rules, regulations, and imposed hierarchies "to command loyalty and cohesion."[100] Firms of fewer than 150 members can have a sense of unity that comes from everyone knowing who to turn to for help in problem-solving. Each member knows what every other member brings to the table in terms of specialized knowledge—and they can all feel comfortable approaching each other for assistance. Gladwell compares the well-run firm of fewer than 150 members to the family in its "re-creation, on an organization-wide level, of the kind of intimacy and trust that exists in a family."[101]

What "The Rule of 150" suggests for law firms is that they should carefully weigh the social costs of expanding beyond that size. Most firms are highly unlikely to remake themselves into smaller firms, but Gladwell's point is to give consideration to other options once a firm approaches the 150 lawyer size: cap the firm size at 150, divide the firm into separate operations with distinct practice areas and distinct clients, or establish a satellite or branch office in a nearby city. While each of these options might, in certain cases, seem unrealistic, Gladwell suggests there will be significant costs to not taking one or the other step. Most large firms divide into separate practice groups for substantive areas. Being in a practice group helps, but doesn't really give you the *Cheers* benefit of working in a place where everybody knows your name. Gladwell notes that strict adherence to the Rule of 150 has been the key to the much-admired success of Gore Associates, the firm that manufactures a wide variety of articles ranging from Gore-Tex fabric to Glide dental floss to hospital equipment. He quotes founder Wilbert Gore who reports, "We found again and again that things get clumsy at a hundred and fifty."[102]

Having warned that the road to happiness might be harder at a behemoth firm, we should observe that not all lawyers at giant firms are unhappy. Many enjoy the type of work most likely found at larger firms: the intellectual challenge of particular kinds of cases—such as corporate restructurings, class actions, complex commercial litigation, or transnational work—as well as the benefits of a variety of practice areas, the economic strengths of diversified practice areas, the competitive advantages of size and resources (cutting edge technology and the ability to deploy attorneys into public service projects), the caliber of clients, and the prestige of the firm.

Large firms themselves are changing form. One of the net effects of the recession of 2009 may be some dismantling—or re-architecting—of giant firms. Douglas McCollam, a critic of large firm practice, offered this stark assessment:

> At bottom, what's in question is the whole economic edifice of the modern American law firm. Like the pharaohs of old, big firms are enamored of constructing pyramids with an ever-widening base of associates and nonequity partners toiling on behalf of a narrowing band of equity partners at the top. Increasing a firm's "leverage"—as expressed through the billable hour, one of the most pernicious creations in the annals of commerce—has been the key metric driving profitability at big law firms over the last generation. Numerous studies have documented the deleterious impact this model has had upon the legal profession and clients. To date, nothing has been able to kill it. It would be ironic indeed if the economic downturn that has cost lawyers so much ended up being the very thing that saved the legal profession from its own excess.[103]

Mentoring

Heading virtually any survey of associate dissatisfactions is a lack of mentoring. In one study, 43 percent of associates indicated that their supervising partners did not provide the mentorship the associates needed and wanted.[104] One of the largest national studies on associate attrition found that the availability or lack of mentoring and feedback frequently affected associates' decisions to stay with their firms or to leave them.[105] In a study of University Virginia law graduates, the aspect of the job setting with which men and women were the least satisfied was performance evaluation—and that could encompass the absence of evaluation, the quality of the evaluation that was given, or that the evaluation itself was negative.[106] People appreciate feedback that is phrased positively and gives a clear sense of expectations.

Mentoring can create profound social connections—and in numerous studies of helping behaviors, both benefactors and recipients show elevated levels of happiness from acts of kindness, counseling, and other supportive activities. Professor Sonja Lyubomirsky says that this is more than just a "helper's high"; assisting other people "can satisfy a basic human need for connecting with others, winning you smiles, thankfulness, and valued friendship."[107]

Those law firms rated among the nation's best are heralded for the training they provide. For example, the survey resulting in the fifty Best Law Firms for Women list found that "68 percent offer mentoring for senior female associates and 62 percent offer management training for women attorneys."[108]

Show Them the Love

> *What people seek from others, more than anything else, is attention and appreciation.*[109]

Beyond monetary valuation, in what ways can your law firm emphasize the importance of people as individuals? The various surveys of best companies and law firms—from Catalyst, Vault, and *Working Mother*—show a number of common features in firms' treatment of their employees that lead to satisfaction. Favored firms promote their employees' dreams and encourage innovation and risk-taking; they value their employee's opinions, listen to their ideas, and implement their suggestions. They give feedback and promote the social network at work. It is unsurprising that employees who think their company values workers as individuals report greater job satisfaction and organizational commitment than those who don't. Similarly, employees whose values match those of their colleagues are also more satisfied and committed to stay.[110] Successful law firms seem to have some sense of shared values or mission. Attorneys who are emotionally attached to their firms are the least likely to leave. On the other hand, "[w]hen individual practices merely exist under the same roof, internal competition, hoarding of work, jealousy and suspicion develop."[111]

To address a high level of associate attrition, Sullivan & Cromwell in 2006 held a training session for its partners on associate appreciation. This presentation encouraged partners to give associates feedback, to say "thank you," and "good job," and to [r]eturn associates' phone calls as quickly as you would a partner's or client's." The firm also arranged periodic associate lunches with the chairman of the firm and implemented a 360-degree review process—to give associates feedback from subordinates and peers as well as supervisors. In 2007, the firm's attrition rate dropped from 30-plus percent to 22 percent.[112]

Of course, all of these activities cost money. We are not suggesting endless feedback or parades of perks, but a balance. One thing to weigh in that balance is the costs, both economic and human, of attorney attrition. Another concern to weigh in your balancing is that an unhappy attorney is unlikely to be a good ambassador for your firm.

7. Giving the Pro Bono Bonus

> *It is one of the most beautiful compensations of this life that no man can sincerely try to help another without helping himself.*
>
> —Ralph Waldo Emerson

The opportunity to do pro bono work is tied to greater job satisfaction for lawyers. Happily, the concept that people who have a sense of civic engagement are more satisfied dovetails with pro bono obligations in law. A recent ABA survey reported that only 46 percent of surveyed lawyers met the ABA's goal of offering "50 hours of free pro bono services" each year.[113] Those who do provide pro bono legal services report a direct correlation between that form of giving back and their own satisfaction. Pro bono activities boost attorney morale.

The converse is also true: new lawyers identify the absence of pro bono opportunities as one of their largest areas of dissatisfaction with the practice of law. The ability to do pro bono work suffers from a lack of support from many firms and already-oppressive billable hour requirements.

Some things are changing in the public interest world. Law firms are beginning to see pro bono opportunities as good business, a method to help recruit talented law school graduates, valuable training ground for associates, and a way to engage with communities. Esther F. Lardent, president of the Pro Bono Institute at Georgetown University Law Center, says, "The nation's 150 largest law firms last year spent 4 million hours on pro bono, more than double what it was 10 years ago."[114] Gradually, larger firms are appointing directors of pro bono activities, although many cut back on their pro bono activities during the recent recession.

Attorneys gain a tremendous sense of personal meaning from representing people who are vulnerable and achieving some measure of justice for them—for making a difference in people's lives.

The range of possible pro bono possibilities is vast: representing detainees at Guantanamo Bay, death row inmates, or hurricane victims denied financial assistance; helping veterans obtain disability benefits; assisting with the legal needs of low income immigrants; or filing adoptions. Conservative or libertarian public interest lawyers promote the constitutional rights of crime victims, campaign against eminent domain and affirmative action, and defend individual economic liberties and property rights.

Lawyers can pursue the intersection of their hobbies or interests and law. For instance, lawyers interested in animal protection and animal rights have given time to the Humane Society and the American Society for the Prevention of Cruelty to Animals. One lawyer has successfully challenged black bear hunts; another has saved condemned dogs from execution (when the "client," a Rottweiler named Pookie, bit a child who stuck her foot through his fence).[115] Call it "pro bone" representation.

8. Creating a Playful Workplace

Law firms can look for inspiration from trendsetters in other industries. Law firms are behind the curve when it comes to creating workplaces where a sense of play is encouraged. Consider the workplace strategies and incentives of Google, rated the single best place to work in this country in both 2007 and 2008, according to a *Fortune* survey of more than 100,000 employees. While the compensation was top-notch (Google ranked 25th on the separate top-paying companies list in 2008), it was the attention to individuals, benefits, feel, and playfulness that rocketed Google to the number one spot on the best companies to work for list. Ninety-nine percent of employees receive stock options, and all of them can eat "free breakfast, lunch, and dinner at 17 gourmet cafes, [and receive] a subsidy for buying a fuel-efficient car and free shuttle service to and from work."[116] Part of the job satisfaction for Google employees may come from finding a workplace that prioritizes shared values, such as prizing tech wizardry, giving economic benefits for ecological acts, or sponsoring playfulness. Google's office in Zurich, for example, offers playrooms with pool tables and a huge slide from an upper floor into the lunchroom. Apart from all of the perks, employees gave Google the highest ratings for open communications, trust along various dimensions of respecting employees (such as caring for them as individuals and collaboration on relevant decisions), and camaraderie—a sense of family or team spirit about the workplace.

Google and other Silicon Valley firms are far ahead of anything most law firms have done to create a playful atmosphere at work. The exception may be boutique corporate defense firm Bartlit Beck in Chicago, which has a full-size mock courtroom in its offices and a basketball court in the middle of the firm—with courtside offices for several of the partners.[117] Its Denver office has a rock climbing wall in the lobby. Most law firms though have tended to be conservative, perhaps in part because of their image, but they are lagging dramatically in the workplace revolution. The new generation of workers in America places a much higher premium on play and creativity; allowing for these expressions can pay off in terms of revenue as well as morale.

Of course, law firms are rarely all work and no play. Your firm may be one that knows the value of having partners, associates, and staff engage in recreation together. Some firms make use of firm-purchased luxury boxes at concerts and sporting events, offer wine tastings and cooking classes, or sponsor firm-wide trivia contests.[118]

Pillsbury Winthrop Shaw Pittman, LLP, with fourteen offices and eight hundred lawyers, was one of only four law firms to earn a spot on *Working Mother*'s 100 Best Companies list. In addition to family-friendly flexible schedules and leave policies, the firm boasts an impressive roster of social events to help create personal relationships among its employees such as the following:

- In May the firm's Washington, D.C., office arranged a private screening of Pirates of the Caribbean: At World's End for attorneys, staff, and their families. All enjoyed pre-show appetizers in Pillsbury's first-floor conference rooms, which had been turned into pirate-themed hangouts complete with servers in costume.

- In July the firm's McLean, Virginia, office staged a "Smooth Operator Challenge," during which attorneys made their favorite nonalcoholic smoothies as part of a friendly competition. Employees were encouraged to "buy" a full-size smoothie for $5, which benefited the Medical Care for Children Partnership. The firm matched every dollar raised for the charity.

- Each office also holds an annual "Family Fun Day" at a popular amusement park or other fun venue.[119]

At this point, the evidence is anecdotal and it sifts through mostly in stories about firm recreational events, but it seems that firms that play together stay together.

9. DESIGNING LAW OFFICES TO PROMOTE LAWYER HAPPINESS

Beauty is . . . the promise of happiness.

—Krister Stendahl

Changing the physical design of a law office is a neglected tool in the search for greater lawyer happiness. Anyone who has ever spent much time in windowless cubicles or drab hotel rooms understands that interior spaces can affect moods. Some spaces rob us of optimism and a sense of purpose; other spaces make us happy and productive. Buildings can seem welcoming or forbidding, tranquil or exciting, harmonious or chaotic. A space that suits us just right at one time might not at another time.

Alain De Botton, author of *The Architecture of Happiness*, explains that buildings "speak of visions of happiness."[120] Not everyone shares the same vision of happiness, of course, so it is not surprising that two well-designed and happiness-promoting buildings might look very different from each other. One building might have an aristocratic feel while another seems more democratic. Anticipation of the future might be expressed in one building, while another communicates a fondness for the past. Nonetheless, there is growing agreement that certain design features tend to be associated with an increased sense of well-being in those who occupy the buildings fortunate enough to have them.

During the last several decades, the architectural community has become increasingly focused on the ways people interact with architecture. Christopher Alexander and his colleagues at the Center for Environmental Structure published, in 1977, a groundbreaking book called *A Pattern Language*, which identified and described 253 "patterns," or design features, of towns, communities, and buildings that tend to promote individual well-being and smoothly functioning communities.[121] A dozen or more of these 253 patterns are especially relevant to law office design and will be discussed below. The Academy of Neuroscience for Architecture, an organization founded in 2003, released data that supports our intuitions that natural light and natural air stimulate creativity at work. California architect Deborah Richmond agrees, arguing for "a democratic distribution of natural light and air, which is proven to increase productivity and reduce sick days."[122] The Academy of Neuroscience for Architecture has also published data showing that views of nature calm us and that low ceilings promote fine attention to detail while high ceilings facilitate more expansive thinking.

So what does the happy law office look like? To some extent, the answer depends on the personalities of the lawyers who occupy it (one person's thing of beauty is another person's bad and ugly), but architects and "environmental psychologists" are in general agreement that certain design features stand a good chance of making the smiles come easier.

Among the top recommendations is to rely as much as possible on natural light for illumination in every occupied office space. All the better if the natural light comes into the room from two sides. (There's a reason, other than prestige, why those corner offices are so sought after.) As Alexander notes, "When they have a choice, people will always gravitate to those rooms which have light on two sides, and leave the rooms which are lit only from one side unused and empty."[123] According to Alexander, "this pattern, more than any other single pattern, determines the success or failure of a room." This insight is hardly new, as "light on two sides" was a tenet of the old Beaux Arts design tradition. Alexander argues that rooms lit on two sides create a desirable social atmosphere because they have less glare and less disturbing light-dark contrast around the windows. The light distribution in a room lit on two or more sides allows occupants to better read the facial reactions of others in the room. In short, Alexander claims, "light on two sides allows people to understand each other"[124]—and understanding other people makes us happy.

There are compelling reasons to avoid the traditional model of one enclosed office per attorney, spread along a stretch of hallway. Closed-off offices discourage interaction. On the other hand, offices that are too exposed feel uncomfortable. Ideally, offices should strike a balance between enclosure and exposure. This can be accomplished in a variety of ways, many of which have the added benefit of increasing flexibility. If work areas or offices are too small, claustrophobia can be a problem: studies show that spaces less than sixty square feet in area make people feel cramped.

If a law office includes, as most do, separate offices for each lawyer, then each office should have a view overlooking life. Alexander contends, "Rooms without a view are prisons for people who have to stay in them."[125] Worse yet, they might be bad for your health. A study of hospital patients showed that patients with rooms overlooking trees had shorter hospital stays and fewer post-stay medical complaints than those with rooms overlooking brick walls.[126] The better the view, the freer one feels. A lawyer who can gaze out at a garden or pleasant street scene will be happier than one who looks out at a bulky air conditioner unit, the top of a parking garage, or an overgrown vacant lot. Obviously, not every law office can be located next to a botanical garden or an idyllic street, but in selecting a potential new office location, attention should be paid to the views it affords on all occupied sides. If staying put is the only viable option, well placed mirrors can sometimes be employed to create improved office views. You probably can't get the parking garage next door to move, but maybe you can peek around it.

Law firms, understandably, impose some limits on what individual lawyers can do with their own office space. *Playboy* pin-ups, black velvet Elvises, or lava lamps send messages to clients that many firms would prefer not be sent. But allowing attorneys to fill their offices with meaningful things from their own lives (not items chosen just to impress visitors) gives them a greater sense of control, an important component of a happy life. Moreover, a room that reflects the history and tastes of the occupant facilitates connections with those who might come to visit. ("Oh, I see you like to collect comic books—I loved Superman as a kid too.") Your office should tell your story. Unfortunately, as Alexander laments, too many are driven to "the artificial scene-making of 'modern décor'" that is "totally bankrupt."[127]

A law office designed to promote happiness should include a large, comfortable space for lawyers to gather together and socialize. Major pathways in the office should be tangent to this area. This plan brings lawyers close to the socializing space on a regular basis and, as an added benefit, eliminates the long sterile corridors that dampen spirits. A well-designed gathering place would include a variety of welcoming things, such as a fireplace, coffee pot, a variety of comfortable chairs, and newspapers. Lamps rather than uniform illumination should be used, as studies show people seek out pools of light even when overall illumination is adequate elsewhere. Warm colored light, produced by wall paint, natural wood, or light sources, should permeate the space.

Every law office should provide a place for communal eating. Thomas Merton, author of *The Living Bread*, writes, "The mere act of eating together . . . is by its very nature a sign of friendship and 'communion.'"[128] Just as the table can become the center of family life, it can bring office colleagues together through shared food, drink, stories, and laughter. Communal eating spaces in a large firm can serve another function: they allow lawyers to meet and find colleagues who have mutual affinities that they might otherwise never get to know. In the well-designed eating space, lights directly over tables serve to focus attention on the communal activity and help bind groups.

Large undifferentiated spaces are not comfortable places for groups of lawyers to work. According to one large study of office workers, large spaces make workers "feel unimportant" and give the "uncomfortable feeling of being watched all the time."[129] For a legal team to do its best work—and be happiest—it needs a smaller work area or meeting room, preferably one that provides partial views out into a larger common area.

Our affinity for certain features, such as natural plants and moving water, may trace back to our origins as a species. Plants of varying shapes and sizes should be scattered throughout the office. Moving water, most likely produced by a fountain, is associated with an increased sense of well-being and should be featured in a place where as many lawyers as possible might benefit from it.

When it comes to law office design, there are indications that some firms are moving in the right direction. Firms are "adding more communal spaces, from coffee bars to visitor lounges."[130] San Francisco-based architect Barbara Gunn says law firms are "looking for opportunities to encourage collegiality and chance encounters" between lawyers.[131] A New York lawyer overseeing the remodeling of his firm's offices agrees, saying that the goal is not "to impress clients," but to create "a work environment that really encourages and supports building collegiality and communication and teamwork." The new look in law firm architecture is a trend toward the building of "teaming rooms where people from different practice groups can work together."[132]

It is unrealistic to expect any office to offer all of the happiness-promoting design features described above, but the more that are part of the office landscape, the happier the lawyers who work (and sometimes play) in it are likely to be.

10. ASKING FOR FEEDBACK

Keep in mind that mattering matters to people. People like feedback from their firm; they also like to be asked what they think about their working conditions.

Why not conduct an anonymous survey of your lawyers and staff to assess the dimensions of their job satisfaction? Using a survey questionnaire and scale of agreement (ranging from "strongly agree" to "strongly disagree"), you can ask whether your employees are satisfied with such measures as communication, feedback, training, mentoring, expected hours, ability to maintain a reasonable balance between work and personal life, collegiality, the physical structure of the workplace, and compensation. Assure anonymity, and add an open-ended area for comments on things that would enhance their satisfaction with the firm, the best aspects of working for the firm, and what bothers them the most. Merely asking for opinions provides a happiness boost.[133]

Is Your Law Firm a Happy Place?

This list is not intended as a one-size-fits-all checklist. The purpose of the enumerated questions is to translate those characteristics the happiness literature identifies as correlating with job satisfaction into pragmatic advice for law firm managers.

1. In what ways do you tell valued players what they mean to the firm and that the firm wants them to be happy? Are all attorneys given rewards, recognition, emotional support, and encouragement to take risks and pursue dreams? What opportunities do you provide for career advancement? Do partners relay to associates good things clients say about them, and do they remember to give associates credit for the heavy lifting in front of clients? Are all attorneys trained in how to respect and work with staff?

2. Does your work assignment system allow attorneys any flexibility to choose the projects or cases on which they would like to work? Are more junior attorneys given responsibility to manage cases independently? Are they given training in how to manage cases and develop business? Do partners frequently take associates with them to meet with clients? Do they routinely take associates out for social occasions?

3. What proactive efforts does the firm take toward creating flexible schedules and compensation plans for attorneys and staff? Is your compensation structure transparent, and are new hires informed about it? What percent of your employees actually take advantage of flex- or part-time

policies? Do you have policies offering generous maternity and paternity leave?

4. Do you have a mentoring program for more junior associates that matches mentors and mentees based on the associates' developmental needs and allows participants to designate mentor characteristics they would prefer (such as practice area, gender, or family status) or select their own mentors? Does the program provide training for mentors that stresses understanding each associate's individual goals, creating a career roadmap, and promoting career development? Is an evaluation mechanism in place for associates to give confidential upward feedback on the quality of the mentoring they have been receiving? Is mentoring valued enough to factor into partner or senior associate compensation? Is the mentor also a guardian who can help resolve unreasonable conflicting demands on associates or run interference for them?

5. Do attorney performance appraisals include benchmarks for skills and knowledge expected of associates? Are the criteria communicated so associates understand the expectations? Does the firm offer strategies for working on identified weaknesses? Does the firm provide regular and constructive feedback?

6. To avoid surprises that make people feel insecure ("Before you hear this from someone else..."), does your firm have an established policy for the release of information about firm events and plans? Or do you rely on information leaking out and trickling down?

7. Does your firm have regular opportunities to socialize (wine and cheese on the last Friday of the month, a co-ed softball game, or a group charitable project)? How often do your

attorneys get together for lunch? What ties does your firm have to the community?

8. Does the physical layout of your offices promote interaction and opportunities for the exchange of ideas? Does your firm offer places where attorneys can congregate and talk? Are you tolerant of water cooler time—downtime where attorneys can share insights?

9. Do you pay attention to indicators of attorney and staff satisfaction? What are your attrition rates for lawyers and staff at various levels? Are all attorneys, including those on alternate career paths, and staff asked about how firm policies affect their work? Are they asked for their ideas and input on innovations, efficiency, and firm practices?

CHAPTER 7

Lawyers' Stories

THE BEST WAY TO PREDICT WHAT EXPERIENCES WILL make us happy, or unhappy, is to look at how other people have reacted to those experiences. We think we are unique—and, yes, we are—but people are far more alike than they are different, and the reactions of others who have gone before us turn out to be the very best guide to our own possible futures. When we let our own imaginations, rather than the reports of others, predict our reactions to future experiences, we tend to miss the mark rather badly. There are many reasons why our imaginations fail us but chief among them are that we let our present attitudes and interests overly color our imagined futures, and we fail to appreciate how rapidly we adapt to both good and bad events.

Daniel Gilbert says it is better that we rely on even "a single randomly selected individual" than our own imaginations when it comes to predicting how we will experience the future.[1] Gilbert's suggestion is certainly open to a validity critique: "Of course, relying on a sample of one is probably not going to tell you too much, especially when the sample is intrinsically biased. (Instead of talking to a yodeler, why not talk to someone who dropped out of yodeling class?)"[2] A better method of collecting information about career satisfaction in law—better than relying on your own imagination or selecting the single yodeler—is to talk to a variety of people in the profession.

In this chapter, we invite you to let other lawyers be your guide. In their stories they will warn you of missteps they have taken, identify the peaks and valleys of their experiences as lawyers, and point to various paths that lead in the direction of satisfying careers in law. We offer stories from happy lawyers, unhappy lawyers, and lawyers whose career satisfaction falls somewhere in between.[3] Finally, we provide a few thoughts of our own on what these stories, and many others we haven't room to include, tell us about the pluses and minuses of practicing law and what you might expect as your career arcs from law school to retirement.

ABOUT BALANCING WORK AND THE REST OF YOUR LIFE

When we asked hundreds of lawyers, in nearly every state and in a wide variety of practice areas, to identify what they've found in their careers to be the biggest obstacle to personal happiness, they most frequently cited their difficulty in achieving a satisfactory balance between the demands of their career and their other personal goals and responsibilities. "The law is a jealous mistress and requires a long and constant courtship," noted U.S. Supreme Court Justice Joseph Story in 1829. Justice Story's observation seems as true today as it did nearly two centuries ago. Lawyers continue to make personal sacrifices to further their legal careers, but they are often not very happy about it.

A typical complaint comes from an Atlanta attorney who says she "felt a great deal of pressure to work longer rather than smarter" and found that career satisfaction sank "in an environment that rewarded people for the number of hours they spent away from their families." A Kansas City attorney says, "It is very easy to get in a job and then find yourself looking around one day wondering where the last five years and all your friends went."

A California attorney reports she is "frustrated by the lack of time to develop my personal life—to make new friends, to find a romantic partner, and to be my best self physically." "There are only 24 hours in day," a hard-working New York tax attorney writes, "so I can't do a lot of things that I would otherwise do, and that's tough." Another New York City lawyer notes that it is not just the long hours of practice that are tough but also the anxiety associated with always being on call: "Having to stay in the office all night to review and comment on an unexpected series of documents sent from lawyers on the other side of a transaction was certainly not ideal, but the nights when I left at 5 or 6 and spent the evening worrying that I had left too early because something unexpected might arise were probably even worse." An Illinois attorney who is in-house counsel for a large corporation agrees, writing, "It is difficult to completely separate myself from my job. Too many people and the success of my company depend upon me and my colleagues."

The large firm focus on billable hours is a source of much lawyer unhappiness, in part because it seemingly de-emphasizes work quality in favor of work quantity. A Missouri lawyer who "takes pride in being efficient and cost-effective" finds billable hours to be a source of frustration: "I am being punished for being efficient, a perverse consequence of hourly billing," and, as a result, "lose time with family and friends." Another attorney complains, "At the end of the day, it seems my only value to the firm is based on billable hours." A California attorney finds that basing value on billable hours breeds resentment by associates against other associates who fail to work the same unreasonably long hours that they do. She quotes a colleague who once told her, "All the galley slaves need to row at the same pace."[4]

The long hours associated with law firm practice are especially tough on attorneys who have children. A marketing consultant for law firms puts it this way: "'The law firm is probably the most family unfriendly place you can go…It's difficult to recruit women because they feel that somewhere down the line, they are going to have to choose between having a family and having a job, which is not a fair choice.'"[5] One attorney and mom tells this story about her difficulties in balancing work life and family life:

> It was a Friday afternoon and my three-year-old son had a pre-school Mother's Day program.... After the program, I checked my voicemail and was treated to a rant [from a partner for whom I worked] including curse words I hadn't heard before on how I was needed that afternoon, how my priorities were screwed up, and how I had left him in a lurch. I returned with my son to the office to find that some discovery had been hand-delivered and I wasn't there for him to give it to. Discovery! We had thirty days to respond to it! The real problem was that he was going on a canoe trip the next Monday for a week and wanted me to work on it before he left. As I left his office, I heard him yell at his secretary while I was in earshot that the firm needed to stop hiring mothers. The kicker is that this attorney had been appointed by the bar association to serve on a committee to improve the status of women in the profession.

What can be done to restore a better balance between work and personal life? One approach is to change jobs. A lawyer who, as a litigator, found himself "consistently at the mercy of deadlines" decided he "needed a change because of the demands of the job." His new position as a compliance officer for the athletics department at the University of Oklahoma has more regular work hours. Another lawyer (and mother) reports that her move from a large private firm to a three-day-per-week in-house counsel job restored the connections she needed to have with her young family. A lawyer who left private practice for a position with the federal public defender's office appreciates that as a federal employee, his number of vacation days increases each year and that he has a new-found flexibility for scheduling his dream trips.

Short of changing jobs, lawyers offer other advice for achieving a better work-life balance. An attorney in a large private firm finds more hours for personal life this way:

> Train clients not to call you at the last minute or on your cell phone unless it is an emergency. Don't schedule conference calls at lunch time. Don't schedule plane flights at 6:00 A.M. Take time to go to your kid's events, but take turns with your spouse. Go home in time to have dinner with your family regardless of the looks you get from your partners. Be happy with your compensation, regardless of others who are making more because they have different priorities than you do.

An attorney in a small town in the Midwest adds this: "Know when to go home. And don't be a lawyer when you are with your family."

Some lucky lawyers are able to find an appropriate work–play balance even within the confines of their law firm. One happy lawyer in a small workers' compensation firm enjoys his office foosball table, dartboard, and bar, where firm members gather regularly after work to toast the day and discuss sports, music, and other things on their minds. Because clients rarely meet at the law firm, he comes in jeans and regularly tosses a Frisbee around the office with his partner.

Another solo practitioner in Virginia echoes this concept of playfulness:

> I would tell students not to be afraid to try unusual places or ways in which to practice law. I would never have pictured myself as a solo practitioner in a poor area of rural Virginia, but overall I am extremely satisfied in life and practice here. . . . I can raise show dogs, go to my office in shorts, and still face exciting challenges and intellectual stimulation in my practice.[6]

Some firms help lawyers achieve a better work-life balance by adopting flexible work policies or by allowing lawyers to bring family members to the office. For example, a senior in-house counsel for a national association praises her organization's policy that offers a compressed schedule option. Attorneys in her company are able to take one paid day off for every two weeks so that they work eighty hours in nine days instead of ten. The lawyer is also grateful for the association's infants-in-the-workplace program that allows mothers and fathers to bring their infants with them to work until the children reach six months of age. The baby stays with the parent while the parent is working in the office, and there are two or three designated individuals who can stay with the baby when the parent needs to be away.

ABOUT WORKING WITH PEOPLE YOU LIKE AND TRUST

When asked what about their job makes them most happy, lawyers often come up with the same answer: people. Lawyers who regularly interact with colleagues and clients that they like and trust tend to report high levels of career satisfaction. On the other hand, those who must frequently deal with ungrateful clients, unsympathetic supervisors, or unethical and unscrupulous opposing attorneys tend to be much less happy.

A number of lawyers surveyed identify good relationships as their greatest source of happiness. "Surround yourself with people you enjoy working with and make work fun," advises the managing partner of a small plaintiff's personal injury firm. This sentiment is echoed by the chair of a practice area at one of the country's largest law firms, who suggests, "Learn to relate to your clients and colleagues as people—you will not have much time for friends outside your practice and it is a blessing to have colleagues and clients who are friends."

An equally large number of lawyers see bad relationships as the cause of great career dissatisfaction. One managing partner who has practiced for more than twenty-five years complains about "the lack of civility" in the profession and the "demoralizing" willingness of some lawyers to compromise the truth in their "incessant quest for money." Another lawyer from the Midwest believes, "I have probably cut my life short by a matter of months stressing over unethical litigation tactics that certain adversarial attorneys have used against me and my clients." A Los Angeles attorney observes, "I began to wake up every morning wondering what sort of dirty trick opposing counsel would pull that day." The director of the California Bar's Lawyer Assistance Project says, "I've never seen such a lonely profession—there's an inability to connect with other people at a deep level because there's so much of an adversarial relationship. The profession in a lot of ways makes it difficult to build trust."[7] An unhappy big firm lawyer in the Southwest writes to complain about fellow lawyers who "procrastinated and then shoved work onto others at the last minute," lawyers who "took credit for other people's work," and about the "general smugness" that he found "ubiquitous in large firms." A government lawyer complains about being frustrated by "mid-level government bureaucrats who were shameless toadies to anyone above them and petty tyrants to those below them." Another attorney simply states his complaint about the practice: "I have always said that the practice of law would be a happy profession if it wasn't for opposing counsel, clients and judges."

An East Coast lawyer recalls the morning he was taking a deposition in Connecticut when the receptionist mentioned that a plane had just crashed into the World Trade Center. As the morning went on, and the terrible fact of the twin towers' collapse became known, the deposition proceeded:

> We didn't really know what else to do, and figured that it was going to be hard for people to get back to their homes anyway, so we just carried on with the deposition all that day and the

next. And the striking thing to me was that everybody carried on pretty much as normal, bickering and squabbling over every little thing. And it just seemed very petty, given the events going on that day.

Just as there are lawyers who report good and bad experiences with other lawyers, reports about client relationships are also a mixed bag. One attorney says "rarely are any of my clients happy to see me, because if they need to see me, they are going through some sort of life crisis." A Kansas lawyer came to realize suddenly that clients were at times her "greatest obstacle to happiness as a lawyer":

> I was working late one night to get ready for a big and important trial where millions of dollars and jobs were at stake. In the middle of going over very technical, mind-numbing budget numbers, my client looked at me and said, "You don't do any 'happy law,' do you?" I was floored. Until then, despite the grueling hours, the lack of recognition, the abuse by clients, partners, and staff, the impact on my family, my health, and my sleep, I still loved my job as a bankruptcy lawyer. But I had never thought about it that way before. I realized that almost everything we do as lawyers involves unhappy people who are asking us to solve their unhappy problems, and many times there is no good solution that will make the client happy. And, I have found out, misery loves company and unhappy people want to make YOU unhappy.

Clients can be a source of unhappiness, a source of joy, and a source of the deepest anguish you can imagine in practicing law. Death penalty lawyer Sean O'Brien relates his worst experience practicing law:

> On October 20, 1992, I had to break the news to Ricky Grubbs, a mentally retarded man, that the U.S. Supreme Court had declined to hear his case, and that he was going to be executed

forthwith. I tried to break the news gently, "The Court decided not to hear your case....your appeals are over...Governor Ashcroft is not going to intervene....there is nowhere else to go...." He kept asking "What's that mean?" until I finally had to tell him that he was going to be executed right away, tonight. While I was talking to Ricky the guards came for him with the gurney, took him off the phone, strapped him down and killed him.

That case, O'Brien says, "sent me to a dark, angry place for a long time."

While some lawyers' darkest moments come from their clients, or what happens to their clients, other lawyers find them their greatest source of professional joy. A public defender from New Jersey says, "My best experiences revolved around showing my clients that someone in the criminal justice system cared for them and their well-being. Some clients came to trust me after I was able to show them that I was completely on their side, no matter what they had done. That type of trust, which has to be first earned and then maintained, gave me the greatest satisfaction." An experienced attorney in Ohio, after having represented some of the same clients for over three decades, is of the same mind. He reports that several clients have "become some of my closest friends" and are the people he turns to when it is time to put away the briefcase and have fun.

If relationships are central to happiness, then it is hard to fault the advice of a South Carolina lawyer who writes, "Try to avoid working with angry, nasty people. Try to find work with people who treat you with a basic level of dignity and respect. Try hard to treat the people around you, especially those down the food chain from you, the same way." Conflict, mistrust, and ungratefulness are, unfortunately, always going to be part of a lawyer's job. But how big a part they are will depend upon the job you choose.

ABOUT FINDING THE FLOW

You didn't need to buy this book to know that interesting work makes us happier than boring or anxiety-producing work. The challenge, of course, is identifying the work that interests you and then finding a way to get paid for it. The luckiest lawyers in the world are those who each morning can't wait to head into the office and find themselves asking, from time to time, "How is it that I actually get paid for doing work that I love so much?" Does that describe you? It probably does not. Law practice typically mixes interesting work with the not-so-interesting, includes fun cases and the not-fun cases, and offers both absorbing and tedious problems.

There is something appealing about the nature of law practice that got you to law school in the first place. Perhaps you always enjoyed puzzle-solving and recognized that law practice provides an opportunity to solve challenging real-world problems. What facts can I develop that will present my client's case most favorably? What case out there in Westlaw's or LexisNexis's cyberspace of cases best furthers my client's cause? What set of questions will best serve to weaken the power of an opposing lawyer's witness? Puzzles such as these, for the right person, can soak up time and attention.

We all know law practice is not just a bowl of cherries. There are humdrum cases, lengthy forms to fill out, footnotes to put in order, and billing documentation, in its six or ten or fifteen-minute increments, to complete. There are many times when law doesn't flow like a mountain stream in spring. Admit it: sometimes law practice is boring. Consider Catherine Kersh's description of a "no flow" experience when she worked as litigator at a big firm on the West Coast. Kersh, who now works for a nonprofit group administering scholarships, remembered spending a period of weeks in which she and many other associates were stuck in a room reviewing endless boxes of documents: "Every day, for 12 hours, [we] fastened Post-it notes to legal briefs. 'You look around at the other associates, trying to remind ourselves, why did we go to law school?'"[8]

The goal is to improve the ratio of enjoyable work to tedious work. To some extent, this happens naturally over the course of a career, as your firm hires younger associates to do the more routine bottom-of-the-totem-pole work that almost every firm has. Also, in many cases, as your career progresses you will gravitate to the type of work you find most interesting.

In our survey, lawyers identify a number of tasks they find especially tedious or unpleasant. A New York tax associate says, "A lot of what I do—poring over contracts, in particular, can be pretty dry. But I knew this before I signed up, so fair warning." A real estate attorney complains bitterly about recording billable hours: "Time keeping is the worst part of being a lawyer and it is a drudge. It's a pain and you have to plow through it and I hate every second of it."

Most lawyers, however, find their work to be generally satisfying. An Indiana lawyer suggests that you "remember that the best part of being a lawyer is the intellectual challenges that face you every day. You get paid to creatively solve problems—and the vast majority of workers don't get that luxury." An Alabama lawyer finds satisfaction in "looking at chaos and imposing order on it, either in the form of telling a coherent story about it for a statement of facts or in the form of synthesizing a set of rules from it (legal research)." A lawyer from the middle of the United States says, "I enjoy writing and working with words tremendously. I usually do about seven drafts of everything I write and I convince myself that each draft is better than the previous one." A Chicago employment lawyer finds flow "the moment when I sit down to ask the first question in an important deposition," and on "jury trial days." A happy Vermont lawyer describes how flow comes "all the time":

> I absolutely love writing a brief or legal memorandum or motion for a client; I enjoy the research and especially the challenge of

putting all the pieces of the puzzle together in a way that is persuasive. I also love working on Excel spreadsheets and doing child support calculations and examining tax issues for a client, to see what the best financial solution might be for a client.

A patent lawyer in New York agrees:

> One of the things I love about practicing law is that it is so engaging that 'clock-watching' is rarely a problem. I often felt that way as a patent prosecutor: I loved the initial stages of patent prosecution: working with the inventors and writing a patent application. I could put in 17 hour days with barely a break, and go home happy, and start in early the next day again.

A commercial lawyer from Nevada finds time passes quickly when he has the opportunity to work with colleagues on a meaningful case:

> I experienced flow regularly when working on team projects with two or more colleagues, putting together filings and strategizing. The solitary work of research and writing has never generated flow for me, but working in concert with others on a time deadline has almost been sublime, even when there was ostensible pressure and should have been anxiety.

Experienced trial attorneys, unsurprisingly, report finding flow in trials. Noted criminal defense lawyer James Brosnahan says, "Nothing compares to the electricity of an actual trial, and it is magnified when it is a jury trial." According to Brosnahan, there's great satisfaction in representing criminal defendants who feel the whole world is against them. He recalls his first meeting with John Lindh, the young California man who was the first American to face terrorism-related charges after 9–11. Lindh greeted him with the words, "'Boy, am I glad to see you.'" "That's why I became a trial lawyer," says Brosnahan.[9] Also finding flow in trials is an attorney who writes that the "first few minutes in an opening statement is magic. The world belongs to me. Nothing matters but the words coming out of my mouth."[10]

When the flow is not there, consider changing jobs. A former New York tax attorney, who felt anxiety from having "a lot of work dumped on me without explanation or guidance" finds greater satisfaction in public interest litigation:

> I started to get the chance to feel like I knew what I was doing. I'd be the one who knew the most about the case, from reviewing all the documents and doing the legal research, and it's a good feeling to feel like you're on top of things and contributing. It's just like when you're a child—it feels good to master things, and it's unpleasant when you don't know what you're doing and no one is helping you.

A civil rights lawyer offers perhaps the best advice on finding happiness in the actual practice of law:

> Every day, you're going to get up and do something (interview people, go through documents to find facts, negotiate, write persuasive arguments, draft documents, or something else), so make sure that it is something that you enjoy doing.

ABOUT ALIGNING WORK AND YOUR VALUES

You are happiest when you think your work matters. Like everyone else, you want to make a positive difference in the world. When work aligns with your values you feel good about what you're doing. It's a simple fact, an obvious fact, but one that often spells the difference between careers that are satisfying and those that are not.

When a lawyer feels his or her efforts don't matter and aren't valued, even good pay and good colleagues are not enough to produce happiness. Sometimes unhappiness stems from projects that seem to be a waste of time. A Florida attorney writes:

I did not enjoy working on matters that were not meaningful to me. Once I was working on a matter that required me to travel around a state to interview members within an industry. After toiling over a month on the interviews and the report, it landed in a pile of bureaucratic paper wastage and probably wasn't read. A nice income doesn't deaden that kind of suck from one's life-force.

For some attorneys, the problem is not that their work is of no account but rather that they sense they've joined the wrong side. They're working for the Empire, and no Force will ever be with them. A lawyer in Tennessee tells this story:

My firm represented a couple of slimy real estate developers. My managing partner assigned me to clean up all their dirty work. They were being sued by just about everyone with whom they had ever dealt. I was taking a deposition of a woman who was suing them over a landlord/tenant dispute and she interrupted the deposition saying, "You seem like a nice person. How do you sleep at night representing these scumbags?" For one of the only times in my life, I was speechless! The truth hurts.

If some of lawyers' darkest moments come when their work is either unvalued or undermines their own sense of justice, it is also true that some of their brightest days come when they believe that their work made a positive difference in their clients' lives. Attorney Jim Husen, a family law lawyer in South Carolina, observes that "people come to us when they are caught up in the vortexes of institutional power or face insurmountable obstacles or feel like they have been wronged." He says that to help clients, lawyers must "draw on everything in our lives." In identifying so deeply with the causes of his clients, Husen finds satisfaction: "I can think of almost no other job where that kind of commitment is called for."[11]

Time and time again, when asked to relate their peak experiences as lawyers, respondents in our survey point to cases in which they contributed to just outcomes that affected individual lives. Typical is the response of a Pennsylvania lawyer who says, "When a client left court with the child custody she so desperately wanted, that made me happy." A Massachusetts attorney reports, "I filed suit against a non-profit student study abroad organization for having placed my client in a home in Chile where she was repeatedly raped by her host brother. I settled the case with just filing the complaint. It's what I went to law school to do."

A family law lawyer from North Carolina tells of "a precious moment" in her career that "still brings tears to my eyes":

> I was finishing a very contentious collaborative divorce. The husband and wife had been married almost 20 years and the marriage ended badly with a lot of discord but they shared a commitment to co-parenting their children. It was not the lovey-dovey case that most people imagine collaborative divorces to be, but they worked very hard and we came up with a deal that suited both of them. We gathered for the signing ceremony and were waiting for the notary to arrive. Someone suggested that we ought to sit and have a beer while we waited and our host happened to have some in the fridge. The husband and wife decided they didn't want a whole beer and decided to share one. It was an intimate moment that seemed to bring back memories of many times shared. The notary arrived, the papers were signed. As we stood up to leave, the husband and wife looked at each other and hugged. As they held each other, he tenderly petted her hair and each thanked the other for everything that had worked in their marriage and for working so hard to come to agreement.

For a Springfield, Missouri, lawyer a peak experience that came to mind was at the conclusion of a guardianship proceeding involving a female patient in the adult psychiatric unit in a hospital that she represented:

Her partner was unable to care for her any longer, as he was very ill. Our patient was not safe to leave the hospital without a guardian, as she was severely mentally ill, and could not be relied upon to take her prescribed medications on her own. Thankfully, the court appointed the public administrator to serve as this patient's guardian. As I was leaving the courthouse that day, the patient's long-term partner approached me with tears in his eyes. He was frail and very thin, and was coughing up blood into his handkerchief. He told me that he was dying of AIDS and that he could no longer take care of his beloved. He had managed her medications for many years, but his doctor told him that he would die very soon, so he decided it was time to find someone else to take care of her. He took my hand, looked into my eyes, and thanked me for obtaining a guardian for his one true love. He explained that he could now die in peace because he knew she would be taken care of.

Several estate lawyers tell us they find great satisfaction in their work. For example, an estate lawyer from Arizona says:

I absolutely LOVE helping clients maneuver through two of the inevitable aspects of life: Death and Taxes. From the time I was a first year attorney, I knew I could provide great assistance to my clients by providing clear guidance to them which would ultimately make the transition of their assets after they die to the people and charities that mattered the most to them. I have always enjoyed teaching my clients about estate planning and dispelling the myths that others tell about probate or taxes. When a client dies and the estate plan "matures," I feel it is an honor to be the person that the surviving loved ones turn to for help in handling the deceased client's affairs. It always gave me pride in being able to take the burden off those left behind so that I can focus on the paperwork, while they are able to focus on grieving as they need to and getting stronger emotionally day after day.

Alignment of work with values comes naturally for lawyers who obtain positions with public interest firms that match their values and politics. For a New Jersey American Civil Liberties Union (ACLU) lawyer, satisfaction comes from working on a daily basis for a cause he strongly supports:

> Every day that I go to work at the ACLU, I strive to advance values that make this country great: freedom, democracy, and equality. I work on a wide range of constitutional rights issues, including freedom of speech, freedom of assembly, freedom of the press, religious liberty, privacy, the right to be free from unwarranted police intrusion, the right to counsel, racial justice, gender equality, student rights, reproductive freedom, lesbian and gay rights, voting rights, and prisoner rights.... Those who work at the ACLU and other public interest organizations are not motivated by the desire to get rich, but rather by the desire to achieve the greater good. I believe that this difference helps to create a wonderful, collaborative, and supportive atmosphere in the office. Though we often work long hours, we do so because we want to and without resentment. Our work to preserve civil liberties and civil rights is a labor of love.

Some lawyers find satisfaction in making things possible that tangibly improve their communities. For example, a large-firm real estate developer had this to say about what he found most satisfying in his practice:

> The fun part of practicing revolves around feeling like you've accomplished something that's significant. Whether that's helping someone save a building and turn it into a hotel or helping the guys at a struggling shopping mall that's a liability to the city turn it into a useful asset.

The votes are in, and it is clear that aligning your work and your values contributes to lawyer happiness. But how do you do that? You have to pay the bills after all—and sometimes the most satisfying cases are neither ones that pay well or do much to advance your career. A lawyer in our survey bemoans the day he chose prestige over principles:

> I went to law school intent on becoming a civil rights lawyer. My hero was Clarence Darrow because he was my mother's hero. Before I even knew what a lawyer was, she would tell me tales of this great man who took on unpopular causes, always championing the underdog. I ended up a victim of my own success. High grades and law review, followed by a federal judicial clerkship, opened doors to the highest-paying, most prestigious job opportunities. People I respected, my judge and my brother (a successful lawyer), told me no one in their right minds would turn down an offer from the [Biggest & Best] law firm. But it was never for me. I knew that at the interview. The partners were stuffy, arrogant, and conservative. It was not a good fit. But instead of following my own heart, I did what other people thought I should do. Bad mistake.

Many lawyers do find themselves stuck in jobs they don't want. Don't wait too long to make your move, suggests a New Orleans environmental lawyer:

> I know so many people who feel stuck in jobs they don't want. In the beginning, they knew it was not for them, but said, I'll work here, advocating positions I don't like and working 2000+ hours a year for just a while. Once I make lots of money, I will move on. They get in it and find themselves vested and unable or unwilling to take the risk. Years of their lives will get by them with little reward except perhaps money, and that does not compensate them for having no life. I say, take a job that satisfies you and allows you to embrace your interests now, not later.... Working for people, and undertaking causes and cases, you believe in. I call that Tikkun Olam, leaving the world a better place.

If you get it wrong, don't be afraid to change course. You'll have company. Eighty-five percent of lawyers change jobs at least once during their careers.[12] A lawyer who practiced in the state of Washington offers this advice on how to keep your values and work relatively aligned as your career progresses:

> Write a letter to yourself explaining why you went to law school and what you hope to accomplish in your life with your law degree, for yourself, for your family, and for others. Put that letter in a safe place and look at it at least once a year. You can edit that letter from time to time. Circumstances and dreams change, after all. But if you change course, do it consciously and for good reasons. Be in charge.

ABOUT CAREER PATHS AND HAPPINESS

Humans are happiness-seeking animals. When a choice, including a career choice, fails to bring the expected level of happiness and another opportunity arises, we usually leap to grab it. In the case of lawyers, the most striking trend over the course of a career is the number of lawyers who leave private practice for other law jobs. As the American Bar Association reports, "As lawyers move deeper into their careers, fewer and fewer work in private practice."[13] Nationally, eight out of ten lawyers depart from large law firms by their fifth year of practice.[14] Unsurprisingly, most move to other law jobs, but a significant number of lawyers eventually find their way into nonlaw jobs. Among graduates of Stanford Law School, to take one example, 2 percent of the class of 2005 held nonlaw positions within three years of graduation from law school, but among graduates fifteen to twenty-five years out, more than 20 percent had shifted out of law practice entirely.[15]

Many who leave law practice have law to thank for their new careers. For example, one lawyer who worked at law firms representing musicians jumped to a nonlegal management position in a music company. For lawyers with the right credentials, this type of move is not unusual. Companies recognize that well-trained lawyers bring a lot to the corporate table. One entertainment industry executive observed, "When you hire a lawyer, you're getting someone really smart and open to learning."[16]

Other former practitioners apply their knowledge of the law in new fields. Legal journalism is one example. Dahlia Lithwick is a former divorce attorney in Reno who became a popular commentator and reporter on cases at the U.S. Supreme Court for the online magazine *Slate*. She describes how she fell into her new job and found happiness. Working on divorces, Lithwick discovered, "was not my thing." On a trip to Washington, D.C., to visit a friend, good fortune came from a chance phone call. *Slate* called her friend, a professional writer, to see if she could cover a trial. After saying she couldn't, she handed the phone to Lithwick, who took the job. She found *Slate* to be the "perfect forum in which to write—this instant, slightly quirky humor, kind of 'law as theater.'" Lithwick says:

> I really do feel that I might be one of those lucky people who stumbled into the perfect job when she was 30 years old...I wake up every morning, and I'm so happy...I can't quite fathom what would be as wonderful as this.[17]

Most law school graduates do not leave the practice of law, but they still tend to get happier over time, even those who stay in practice. As time marches on, lawyers gain competence and new responsibilities and achieve a greater sense of control. One partner, reflecting back on his days as an associate, observes:

> When I was an associate, there were times when I would wake up and dread the day. . . . Having to answer to so many people was frustrating. . . . Associates don't normally get to see the project the whole way through which makes lack of control an issue for them.

Some litigators conclude they would rather be transactional lawyers. The roller-coaster life of a litigator has great rewards, but it isn't for everyone. As one litigator tells us, "The highs are higher and the lows are lower compared to the experiences of a typical transactional lawyer." Sometimes the ups and downs occur while working with the same case: a trial victory can quickly turn into an appellate loss, or vice versa.

The fact is you might be wrong about what kind of practice best suits your skill set and your personality. A federal district judge has these words of advice:

> Many new lawyers know exactly the law they would like to practice and they are right. Many think they know what kind of law they would like to practice and they are wrong. Others, like me, had no idea what type of practice will lead to the greatest job satisfaction. Of course, there is no way to know in advance what field of law will be most personally rewarding. All one can do is begin, discover and adjust.... I began my career representing banks, corporations and insurance companies. I concluded it representing people. I found that representing people was far more gratifying professionally. Coincidentally, it was more remunerative as well. If you think you know what you want to do, do it. If you do not know, engage in a general practice until you gravitate to that field.

A sports law attorney regrets that legal education doesn't provide a systematic means for experimenting with career options:

> I wish the legal system had a 'residency requirement' similar to the practice of medicine. A young lawyer could work various 'rotations' to experience various practice areas to determine what they like/don't like.

The type of practice you develop may not be one that you envision when you start out. When Bill Colby was a young lawyer and took on a pro bono probate matter, he never envisioned it would become the first right-to-die case to reach the U.S. Supreme Court. It was a guardianship for the parents of Nancy

Cruzan, a young woman who had been in a persistent vegetative state for four years following a single-car accident. Her family was united in their belief that Nancy would not have wanted to live that way and they desired to remove her feeding tube. The Missouri attorney general opposed removal of medically supplied nutrition and hydration and the case wended its way to the U.S. Supreme Court.

The Court held that competent people have a constitutional due process right to refuse life-sustaining treatment. For an incompetent patient like Nancy, the Court ruled that the state of Missouri could require her parents to produce clear and convincing evidence of their daughter's wishes. Colby assembled that evidence when friends of Nancy came forward after hearing about the case in the firestorm of media coverage. A number of years after the Supreme Court decision in *Cruzan v. Director, Missouri Department of Health*, Colby relinquished his partnership at the firm to write *Long Goodbye: The Deaths of Nancy Cruzan*. He later became a senior fellow with the Center for Practical Bioethics. In that capacity he was able to give lectures at medical schools, hospitals, and hospices about end of life issues. Part of his life's work has been dedicated to making sure other families will not have to suffer anguishing legal battles at the end of their loved ones' lives. Today, he is the general counsel at a large, inner city safety net hospital system.

Colby cautions that not every pro bono case will be like *Cruzan*—they are not all of national importance or life-altering for the lawyer. He tells law students "that a lot of them get ungrateful clients, and witnesses that lie to you; and you don't feel that you're still helping to solve society's problems, which is what lawyers do." But many cases you take will be life-altering for your clients: "I feel lucky that I got to know that family and had the chance to help them, and that I was involved in an issue that is important to society. But for me it was always about the family and getting to their end—as bad as that end was."

In addition to not being afraid to take a new path, a large part of Colby's happiness may have to do with how he looks back at the path he has taken. If *you* are fortunate—and Colby's "luck" may relate to his general outlook on the world as much as the circumstances of that little pro bono probate matter he agreed to handle—you may take away life lessons. The *Cruzan* case, he says, "was a great blessing for me, because it always gave me and still today gives me the ability (when I start to get the grump-its even a little bit) to say my life's pretty good—which is nice to have."

If there is one consistent piece of career advice that experienced lawyers seem to give law graduates it is to follow their bliss. One former lawyer, now a teacher, has this to say:

> Follow your heart in choosing your career path. It's the most important advice I give my students each year. Such simple advice, yet so hard to follow. If you get it wrong the first time, which you are likely to do, don't be afraid to change course.

His sentiments are echoed by another attorney from the nation's capital:

> My advice to a recent graduate is: find something that you love to do, something that will motivate you to get out of bed when you are tired, something that you will try to work on when you are sick, something that you would want to do even if you didn't have to earn a living, and then see if someone will pay you to do that work. And, understand that even when you're in the right job, doing the right thing, and happy, there will still be bad days, there will still be things that you don't like. There will be moments when you don't think you can do what needs to be done. Take a breath, take some chocolate, triage, prioritize, get something done, cross it off your list and move on to the next thing. Don't let the best be the enemy of the good.

What Happiness Research Predicts About Your Career

1. You are more likely to be happy with your career if you work in solo practice or a small firm than in a large firm.
2. You are more likely to be happy if you work for the government than for a private firm.
3. You are more likely to be happy if your compensation is above $70,000 per year than if it is below that amount.[18]
4. You are more likely to be happy if you have been a lawyer for ten years or more than if you recently graduated from law school.
5. You are more likely to be happy if you've always wanted to be a lawyer since a young age.[19]
6. You are likely happy with the intellectual challenge that your law career affords.
7. If you are a woman, you are more likely to be dissatisfied with your work-life balance than if you are a man.
8. You are more likely to be happy if you like and trust the people you work with.
9. You are somewhat less likely to be happy with your career if you graduated from a top national law school than if you graduated from a "fourth-tier" law school.[20]
10. You are more likely to be happy if you believe that your work aligns with your values.
11. You are most likely to complain about lack of feedback, lack of work-life balance, unethical attorneys and ungrateful clients, and meaningless work.
12. You are likely to change jobs three or more times before your career ends.
13. You are likely, at the end of your career, not to regret your decision to become a lawyer (although there will have been days when you questioned your decision).

CHAPTER 8

Seeking Happier Ground

To everything there is a season, and a time to every purpose under heaven...A time to weep, and a time to laugh; a time to mourn, and a time to dance...

—*Ecclessiates* 3:1–3:4

How we spend our days is, of course, how we spend our lives.

—Annie Dillard, *The Writing Life*

THE BOOKS OF OUR CHILDHOOD TOLD OF LIVES LIVED happily ever after. As adults, we know that real lives are never like that. There is no kingdom of happiness that we cross into and then dwell within forever. Happiness is a shifting landscape on which no person ever becomes a permanent resident. The best we can hope for is to grab our share of visits. We also recognize that what brings us happiness at one time might not the next. If someone offers a surefire recipe for happiness, be skeptical. What happiness we experience is the result of a mix of genetics, circumstances, and our own thoughts and actions. The complexities of our emotions are beyond capture in a formula. We can, however, as this book has sought to demonstrate, increase the likelihood that we will experience more happiness in our legal careers. We do what we can, and we hope that it is enough. Sometimes, as songwriter Townes Van Zandt says, "the blue wind blows our dreams away." But on other days, the gentle breeze comes, the clouds part, and the sun begins to shine.

How do we position ourselves to best capture that kind breeze when it comes along? That's really what this book has been about. But we need to understand that sometimes skies stay gray for longer stretches than we'd like; we need to appreciate our emotional lows as well as our highs.

MAKING THE BEST OF IT: THE USEFULNESS OF BOREDOM AND MELANCHOLY

We'll be the first to admit that you could act on every piece of advice offered in this book and still not be happy. Perfect happiness was not part of the plan. (Whether it's God's or Evolution's, we'll leave for you to decide.) Sometimes our genetic makeup, in the form of a low happiness set point or a predisposition to depression, keeps us tethered to unhappy ground. At other times, adverse circumstances—ranging from marital or health problems to a bad slump for our favorite sports team—block our path to happiness. Be patient. Those less-than-happy times of our lives are inevitable and it's important that we make the best of them.

Martin Seligman, probably the most prominent voice in the positive psychology movement, admitted that he once believed that he could make a person happy just by ridding them of their sadness. He found, however, that he couldn't. When he simply focused on ridding a patient of his sadness what he got was not a happy person but an empty one.[1]

Happiness and sadness are not opposite sides of the same coin; they are sides of different coins.[2] Both are necessary in any complete life. If you're feeling sad, sometimes you just have to accept that sadness is part of life. Would you value your happiness as much if you've never been sad? Could you say you really *knew* happiness if you'd never met unhappiness? Carl Jung, founder of analytical psychiatry, noted that the "word 'happy' would lose its meaning if it were not compensated by some sadness."[3] Of all the many conversations Eric Weiner had during his worldwide exploration of "the geography of bliss," none stuck with him more than the comment of a musician in the happy city of Reykjavik, Iceland: "'I'm happy, but I cherish my melancholia.'"[4]

Nurture your melancholy and use it as an opportunity for personal growth or better self-understanding. Melancholy is critical to an understanding of what it means to be human. It leads, as Eric G. Wilson argued in *Against Happiness: In Praise of Melancholy*, to an awareness of things passing, and from that awareness we gain a deeper sense of our own mortality and, it is hoped, a better grasp of the world's fragile beauty.[5] Or, as Alan Wolfe recently contended, "[A]n unhappy consciousness may take us further toward understanding than a Bovary-like contentment."[6]

The notion that melancholy might have its beneficial aspects is not new. Aristotle contended that "all men who have attained excellence in poetry, in art and politics, even Socrates and Plato, had a melancholic habitus." Charles Darwin, a rather melancholic soul himself, suspected that sadness serves an evolutionary purpose in that it is "well adapted to make a creature guard against any great or sudden evil."

Neuroscience research supports Aristotle's and Darwin's ideas that melancholy promotes creativity and helps focus the mind on problems. Negative moods increase activity in the prefrontal cortex and make "it easier to pay continuous attention to a difficult dilemma." Persistence, a side-benefit of melancholy, is a trait associated with people who achieve success in creative fields; authors and artists often walk on the dark side. Also, research shows, sadness correlates with a "more successful communication style," higher scores on intelligence tests, a better ability to judge the accuracy of rumors, and enhanced recall. In one study, shoppers remembered four times as many trinkets stacked near a check-out counter on rainy days than they did on sunny days. Jonah Lehrer, in a *New York Times Magazine* article summarizing the recent research, concludes that sadness "draws us toward our proplems, like a magnet to metal."[7] When sadness enters your day at the office, tackle that complicated legal question that you've put on the back burner. There is, as Ecclesiates reminds us, "a time to mourn and a time to dance." Accept what both times can offer you.

Boredom is the pale hint of sadness. Just as into every life a little rain must fall, into every career a little boredom must creep. Not every task in a lawyer's day can produce flow. There will be repetitious tasks and tedious tasks. In a 1994 commencement address, poet Joseph Brodsky told Dartmouth College graduates, "A substantial part of what lies ahead of you is going to be claimed by boredom."[8] He warned that "even unusually gifted individuals must endure boredom."[9] Boredom compels us to invent means to escape its clutches. In the context of careers, your avenue of escape might entail looking for a more satisfying job. Although this search might keep you entertained for a while, Brodsky warned that "before long this quest turns into a full-time occupation, with your need for an alternative coming to match a drug addict's daily fix." Instead, he urged that we learn from boredom one of life's most central lessons: Boredom "is your window on time's infinity. . . . It puts your existence in proper perspective, the net result of which is precision and humility. . . . And the more finite a thing is, the more it is charged with life, emotions, joy, fears, compassion."[10]

Do not try to be happy 100 percent of the time. You will fail. More than that, you will not realize your potential. Comedian Conan O'Brien, being serious for a moment, ended his 2000 commencement address to Harvard University students with a wish that they experience both times of happiness and times of sadness: "So that's what I wish for all of you. The bad as well as the good. Fall down, make a mess, break something occasionally, and remember the story is never over."[11]

Do not run from sadness and boredom. The path to happiness often runs through, not around, those often unappreciated emotional states.

THE WELL-LIVED LIFE

We've saved for this last chapter one of the most important messages we want to convey: happiness isn't everything. In fact, as odd as it may seem for the authors of a book called *The Happy Lawyer* to say, happiness isn't even—for everybody—the most important thing.

For most of human history, happiness wasn't the issue, survival was. And when philosophers began their serious pondering, they by and large ignored the question of happiness and focused on other values such as virtue and honor and loyalty. The primary message of our central religious texts, the Bible, the Koran, and others, is not "Be happy!" In a world of war and woe, who could question the words of Thomas Jefferson: "Perfect happiness... was never intended by the Deity to be the lot of his creatures."[12]

History shows us that obsession with happiness is a modern development made possible by the high standard of living now enjoyed by many occupants of the planet. Our expectations for achieving happiness—at least in *this* life—outstrip our capacity to achieve it. Setting realistic goals about our own future happiness, including happiness in our careers, is the first step toward getting there. Your brain, unable to comprehend life's messy reality, has constructed an abstract and nearly perfect model of the ideal job. Your real job, in contrast to the ideal job lodged in your brain, will always fall short, given the sometimes triviality of day-to-day work in the office and a law career's inevitable disappointments.

As you stumble into dissatisfaction from time to time, remember that those other high values of old still matter. A single-minded striving for personal happiness can damage the fabric of society if it leads to neglect of family or community.

Fortunately, as we've suggested, the best path to happiness lies *in the direction* of family and community. The point here is that the search for happiness, properly undertaken, can lead to a life well-lived. Being true to the noblest values of our profession will almost never hinder your quest for career satisfaction. If you turn out to be one of those persons constitutionally unable to find true happiness, find consolation in knowing that you have served your values and done well by others.

But, hey, you bought this book because you wanted a happier career as a lawyer, not because you want to be told that it's okay if that doesn't happen. And, of course, happier is better than not. We'll end this exploration of lawyer happiness by reminding ourselves of what we consider most central to satisfying careers in law.

GETTING READY FOR HAPPINESS

You move toward happier ground when you first open yourself up to the possibility of becoming a happier lawyer. Lawyers are purposeful people. You might be inclined to tell yourself, "I'm going to become happier, damn it, and I'm going to become happier right now!" In fact, such an attitude more likely will prolong your unhappiness than lead you out of it. As John Stuart Mill once noted, "'Happiness should be approached sideways like a crab.'"[13]

Happiness is experienced mainly in the present. Obsessing about your unhappiness, or overanalyzing your condition, takes you out of the present and into your past or future. To quote Mill again, "Ask yourself if you are happy and you cease to be so."[14] With that caveat in mind, what attitudes or steps get us heading toward a more satisfying career? Let's review what we consider to be the five factors most closely tied to lawyer happiness.

1. Find Work That Interests You

Let's consider the nature of your work. Does it interest you? Do you feel challenged by your work, yet not so much so as to be constantly anxious about your ability to meet the expectations of clients or supervisors? If the answer to either of these questions is "no"—if you are bored by your work, or tired of filling out the same forms or making the same simple arguments—it's time to explore whether you can change departments, clients, or the way you tackle your assignments. The field of law is not perfect, but it is, in many of its manifestations, challenging. If you don't feel challenged, look around, discover where the challenges are, and rise to meet them. A good first step to finding interesting work is to gain an understanding of your own competencies. Once you have identified your strengths, try to find a way to use them.

Good work is challenging, but it also affords variety. As humans, we crave novelty. Performing the same task for the hundredth time will afford you little of the satisfaction that it once did. If you're lucky to find a job with not only content variety but also variety in work settings and colleagues so much the better. Novelty enhances the intensity of experience.

2. ALIGN YOUR WORK WITH YOUR VALUES

The closer your values align with your work, the happier you feel about your work. Even boring or anxiety-producing work has its benefits if it is consistent with your values. When asked to identify peak experiences, lawyer after lawyer in our study turned to cases where they believed that their work made a difference. There's a very important lesson here. Absorb it. Think about your deepest beliefs and, when there is a conflict between what your heart and what your head is telling you to do, listen to your heart.

When you find work that you can love, commit to it. Commitment is a word associated most commonly with relationships, but it is no less central to a successful career than a successful marriage. Take that foot out of the door and you'll begin to build better workplace relationships and find greater career fulfillment.

3. Balance Your Work and the Rest of Your Life

Another large theme in this book has been the importance of control. We've explained that control has many aspects, all of which are associated with increased career satisfaction. Still, for lawyers at least, one aspect stands above the others. If you feel good about the balance you have between your work obligations and your obligations to others (including family, friends, and self), you're likely to feel a lot better about your job.

Of course, achieving a work-life balance is easier said than done. If your job makes such a balance impossible—well, *do something.* If you are in a large firm, you might try to convince the powers-that-be that more concern about work-life balance issues is in the firm's long-term interest. If you are in solo practice or a small firm, perhaps you can learn to say "no" to some potential new clients, even if it means a loss of income.

Kids grow up quickly; your athletic prowess slips away; friendships die without attention. Don't keep postponing your happiness. You might just postpone it all the way to your graveyard.

4. Deepen Workplace Relationships

"Social embeddedness"[15] is the single best predictor of happiness. Consider the people with whom your work hours are spent. If you are to become happier, in large part it will be because of them. If our exploration of happy lawyering has convinced us of anything, it is that relationships with other human beings are the greatest source of happiness. People who feel connected in meaningful ways with people they love and trust are best positioned to find happier ground. Trust: it's a small word with big meaning. The inability to trust will undermine happiness as surely as the capacity and willingness to trust will promote happiness—in you and in those around you.

Psychiatrist George Valliant devoted his lifetime to a seventy-year longitudinal study of Harvard University graduates of the late

'30s and early '40s. When asked recently what the study taught him, he replied, "That the only thing that really matters in life [is] your relationships to other people."[16] Happiness is built above all on love, trust, and a sense of feeling valued. Should you not feel valued in your present workplace, should your present workplace not offer opportunities for deepening relationships, get out. There has to be some other job that would serve you better.

5. SAVOR THE SMALL PLEASURES

Ben Franklin urged people to find happiness in "the little advantages" of their daily lives. Almost all lawyers have some aspects of their jobs that give them pleasure. For you, it might be strategizing with colleagues about litigation, outlining an appellate brief, or just experiencing the sense of satisfaction that comes from clearing a few headaches out of your inbox. Whatever those moments are, recognize them. This requires some self-study: we are not all naturally attuned to what gives us genuine pleasure. The warm glow from achieving a good settlement, the buzz of excitement from brainstorming about an interesting case, the feeling of satisfaction from writing a well-turned phrase: Happiness is found in such moments. Savor them. Try to find ways to experience more of them. You might never experience the ecstasy of a winning a victory in the U.S. Supreme Court, but you will feel the pleasure of a client's compliment.

WHAT WILL BEING A HAPPY LAWYER DO FOR THE REST OF MY LIFE?

As nice as increased career satisfaction is, don't expect it to change your overall happiness level dramatically. As one career advisor pointed out, "Asking a job to solve our unhappiness problem is asking too much of a job."[17] She offered this analogy: It's "like asking an exercycle to solve your weight problems without giving up doughnuts." Our overall happiness levels are more affected by our close personal relationships than they are by our career satisfaction.[18] Developing a close set of nonwork friends, finding your true love, or making up with your estranged teenage daughter is the better bet for making life as a whole look sunny.

Still, careers are important. In addition to meeting the innate need of humans to be competitive, a career adds to your "self-complexity." Your career as a lawyer adds another dimension to your life. You may be, for example, a mother, a friend, a member of the P.T.A, a Presbyterian, and an Ohioan, but you are also a member of the legal profession. When things go sour in one or more of the other dimensions of your life, law can be a refuge or a source of pride. Your practice can be a buffer against setbacks in other domains of life.[19] In general, the more self-complex we are, the more resilient we are—and resilience in the face of difficulty is one of the best measures of a successful life.[20]

You didn't need us to tell you that life is not one smile after another. You probably have realistic expectations as to how much more satisfying your law career can be. Even professional chocolate tasters have bad days at the office. We sincerely believe, however, that by taking some of the steps identified in this book you can have a happier career. The level of improvement is dependent upon such things as your happiness set point, what's going on in the rest of your life, the range of career options open to you, and how much you open yourself up to the possibility of greater career satisfaction.

A FINAL WORD

In the course of researching this book, we read a great many opinions about what makes us happy. Every author, it seems, uses the last page to identify the most important "take away" they want the reader to have. In our opinion, the best of these authors tended to circle around the same point: love makes us happier than anything. By this, we do not necessarily mean romantic love. Rather, it is the love inherent in *being attentive*—caring deeply about somebody or something. It could as well be love for justice or a cause or the life of the mind. British scholar Avner Offer puts the point concisely: "Attention is the universal currency of well-being."[21]

We generally think of love as it relates to our feelings for another human being. But it is also possible to love your job—to pay attention to your work and to respect its traditions and noble goals. Like any marriage, your relationship with your work will have its tensions. There may be days when you wish you were doing something else. But as long as your work holds your attention, there's more than just hope for being a happy lawyer.

Acknowledgments

WE ARE INDEBTED TO THE MORE THAN TWO HUNDRED lawyers across the country who took the (nonbillable) time to give thoughtful answers to our survey and share their stories.

We thank our colleagues and friends who brought so many different facets of their expertise to this project: Jasmine Abdel-khalik, David Achtenberg, Terri Beiner, Mark Berger, Bill Black, Paul Callister, Julie Cheslik, Bill Colby, Richard Delgado, Bob Downs, Alice Eakin, Jerald Enslein, Kathy Hall, Bob Hayman, Peter Huang, Mary Kay Kisthardt, Tony Luppino, Mira Mdivani, Lynda Moore, Sean O'Brien, Colin Picker, Judy Popper, Ortrie Smith, Barb Snell, Ellen Suni, Rob Verchick, Wanda Temm, Kevin Travis, and Dan Weddle. Special thanks to Lara Krigel Pabst, Andrew Schermerhorn, and Katie Woods for research assistance, to Elizabeth Johnson for administrative assistance, and to librarian Lawrence MacLachlan for research guidance. We also thank the University of Missouri-Kansas City Law Foundation for its research grant and the *Syracuse Law Review* for permission to include a portion of our earlier article, *Happy Law Students, Happy Lawyers*, 58 SYRACUSE L. REV. 351 (2008), in this book. We are especially grateful to Naomi Cahn, June Carbone,

Barb Glesner Fines, Aaron Geary, Andrew McClurg, and Allen Rostron for their thoughtful advice, constructive criticism, editing wizardry, playfulness, and unflagging support.

Our greatest thanks are for our families, to whom this book is dedicated.

Our gratitude is also an acknowledgement, that can't really be captured in words, of how important all of you are in our lives. You make us so happy.

Notes

Foreword

1. *Fax Poll: It Becomes a Miserable Profession*, CAL. LAW., Mar. 1992, 3; Alex Williams, *The Falling Down Professions*, N.Y. TIMES, Jan. 6, 2008, at 91.

2. Stephanie Francis Ward, *Pulse of the Legal Profession*, A.B.A. J., Oct. 2007, 29, 32 (noting that only 44 percent of eight hundred survey respondents say "I would recommend a legal career to a young person").

3. Ashby Jones, *The Third Year Dilemma: Why Firms Lose Associates*, WALL ST. J., Jan. 4, 2006, *available at* http://208.144.115.173/salarydata/law/20060105-jones.html.

Chapter 1

1. Robert Biswas-Diener et al., *Most People Are Pretty Happy, But There Is Cultural Variation: The Inughuit, the Amish, and the Maasai*, 6 J. HAPPINESS STUD. 205 (Sept. 2005).

2. Sue M. Halpern, *Are You Happy?*, 55 N.Y. REV. BOOKS 24 (Apr. 3, 2008), *available at* http://www.nybooks.com/articles/21197.

3. John Monahan & Jeffrey Swanson, *Lawyers at Mid-Career: A 20-Year Longitudinal Study of Job and Life Satisfaction*, 5 J. EMPIRICAL LEGAL STUD. 1, 3 (forthcoming 2009).

4. RONIT DINOVITZER ET AL., AFTER THE J.D.: FIRST RESULTS OF A NATIONAL STUDY OF LEGAL CAREERS 19 (2004); AMERICAN BAR ASSOCIATION, 2009 NATIONAL LAWYER POPULATION SURVEY, http://www.abanet.org/market research/2009_NATL_LAWYER_by_State.pdf.

5. Tom W. Smith, National Opinion Research Center/University of Chicago, Job Satisfaction in the United States (Apr. 17, 2007) [hereinafter "NORC Study"]. The NORC Study surveyed more than 27,500 randomly selected people concerning their job satisfaction and happiness in 198 occupations. Clergy reported the highest levels of both job satisfaction (87.2 percent very satisfied) and general happiness (67.2 percent very happy). Roofers had the lowest mean score (only 25.3 percent very satisfied) for job satisfaction, and service station attendants the lowest mean score for general happiness (only 13.2 percent were very happy); 52.4 percent of lawyers said they were very satisfied with their jobs, and 43 percent said they were generally happy in life.

6. Peter H. Huang & Rick Swedloff, *Authentic Happiness & Meaning at Law Firms*, 58 Syracuse L. Rev. 335, 343 (2008).

7. Stephanie Francis Ward, *Pulse of the Legal Profession*, A.B.A. J., Oct. 2007, at 30, 32.

8. American Bar Association Young Lawyers Division, ABA Young Lawyers Division Survey: Career Satisfaction 17 (2001), http://www.abanet. org/yld/satisfaction_800.doc. The survey of 2,136 members of the Young Lawyers Division yielded 842 responses. "Most young lawyers are at least somewhat satisfied both with their current job and with the practice of law generally." *Id.* at 1. These numbers match up with an American Bar Foundation study of Chicago lawyers in the mid-1990s, in which 84 percent reported being either satisfied or very satisfied with their work. John P. Heinz et al., *Content With Their Calling? Work Satisfaction in the Chicago Bar*, 9 Am. B. Found. Pub. 1 (1998).

9. Susan Daicoff, *Lawyer, Be Thyself: An Empirical Investigation of the Relationship Between the Ethic of Care, the Feeling Decisionmaking Preference, and Lawyer Wellbeing*, 16 Va. J. Soc. Pol'y & L. 87 (2008).

10. American Bar Association Young Lawyers Division, *supra* note 8, at 17.

11. For every report showing generally happy lawyers, fulfilled by their work, there's another with glum numbers suggesting the opposite. Is there an explanation for the contradictory results? One possibility—and this is true for all the survey data—may have to do with the different populations sampled. For instance, those who responded to the ABA Young Lawyers Division job satisfaction survey might disproportionately be people who like to belong—joiners. Is it possible that ABA Young Lawyers are more gregarious and upbeat—happier—than the average lawyer? Sure, it is.

Another variable that can compromise the validity of studies is how they are phrased. If survey headings telegraph the results the researchers are seeking, respondents will be inclined to self-select either toward or away from participating and even give answers they think will please the researchers. As one example, "the American Bar Association surveys conducted in 1984 and 1990 consisted of a mail-back questionnaire titled 'National Survey of Lawyer Satisfaction/Dissatisfaction.' Although response rates for these surveys were fairly high, there is no way to know for sure whether disgruntled lawyers were disproportionately willing to participate." Kathleen E. Hull, *Cross-Examining the Myth of Lawyer Misery*, 52 VAND. L. REV. 971, 972 (1999).

Survey results also depend heavily on the questions asked. If the question asked is "Are you happy right now?," that will elicit a different set of responses than if the questions are about plans to leave a job within five years. Attorney satisfaction scores often stem from surveys that ask a domain-specific happiness question: "Are you happy with your job?" The reported domain-specific happiness scores can be affected by other life satisfaction variables or recent life events.

12. *Fax Poll: It Becomes a Miserable Profession*, CAL. LAW., Mar. 1992, at 3; Alex Williams, *The Falling Down Professions*, N.Y. TIMES, Jan. 6, 2008, at 91.

13. Heinz et al., *supra* note 8, at 1.

14. Hull, *supra* note 11, at 972. The *California Lawyer* poll is discussed in the text *supra* note 12.

15. Monahan & Swanson, *supra* note 3, at 2.

16. Ronit Dinovitzer & Bryant G. Garth, *Lawyer Satisfaction in the Process of Structuring Legal Careers*, 41 LAW & SOC'Y REV. 1 (2007).

17. Ward, *supra* note 7, at 34.

18. Ashby Jones, *The Third Year Dilemma: Why Firms Lose Associates*, WALL ST. J., Jan. 4, 2006, *available at* http://208.144.115.173/salarydata/law/20060105-jones.html.

19. Williams, *supra* note 12, at 91.

20. DOUGLAS LITOWITZ, THE DESTRUCTION OF YOUNG LAWYERS: BEYOND ONE L 9 (2006).

21. Martin E.P. Seligman et al., *Why Lawyers Are Unhappy*, 23 CARDOZO L. REV. 33, 52 (2001).

22. Robert Kurson, *Who's Killing the Great Lawyers of Harvard?*, ESQUIRE, Aug. 2000, at 84.

23. William W. Eaton et al., *Occupations and the Prevalence of Major Depressive Disorder*, 32 J. OCCUPATIONAL MED. 1079, 1083 (1990); G. Andrew H. Benjamin et al., *The Prevalence of Depression, Alcohol Abuse, and Cocaine Abuse Among United States Lawyers*, 13 INT'L J.L. & PSYCHIATRY 233, 240 (1990), *available at* http://www.lawyerswithdepression.com/uploads/dep2.pdf. Other studies do not show that law is the occupational category with the very highest rate of suicide but still show that lawyers are in higher risk jobs. Steven Stack, *Occupation and Suicide*, 82 SOC. SCI. Q. 384, 392 (June 2001).

24. Stack, *supra* note 23, at 391.

25. In chapter 3 we explore further the question of whether the practice of law makes people unhappy or whether people prone to unhappiness are drawn to law.

26. *See* Seligman et al., *supra* note 21, at 45–49.

27. Hull, supra note 11, at 971.

28. *See, e.g.,* Monahan & Swanson, *supra* note 3, at 2.

29. AMERICAN BAR ASSOCIATION, LAWYER DEMOGRAPHICS, 2008, http://www.abanet.org/marketresearch/Lawyer_Demographics_2008.pdf.

30. Dinovitzer & Garth, *supra* note 16, at 7; Ward, *supra* note 7 at 32.

31. *Study Reveals Conflicts in Attorneys' Personal Lives*, MO. LAW. WKLY. Feb. 20, 2006, *available at* 2006 WLNR 9004939; Ward, *supra* note 7, at 34.

32. David G. Blanchflower & Andrew Oswald, *Is Well-Being U-Shaped Over the Life Cycle?*, J. SOC. SCI. & MED. (Aug. 14, 2006), *available at* http://www.nd.edu/~adutt/activities/documents/BlanchOsUshapeCohorts14Aug2006.pdf (thirty-five-year longitudinal study); Mark Killian, *TV Advertising Dilutes Public Confidence in the Profession*, 30 FLA. B. NEWS 1 (July 15, 2003).

33. Ward, *supra* note 7, at 32.

34. BUREAU OF LABOR STATISTICS, U.S. DEP'T OF LABOR, OCCUPATIONAL OUTLOOK HANDBOOK 2008–09, LAWYERS, http://www.bls.gov/oco/ocos053.htm (last visited July 20, 2009). The median salary for associates who have at least three years of experience in Houston is $86,300; $89,200 in Philadelphia; $93,500 in Washington D.C.; and $105,800 in San Francisco, with a national average of $79,500. For mid-career attorneys (ten to fifteen years of experience), salaries range from $128,600 in Houston to $134,700 in Washington, D.C., and $143,700 in San Francisco, with a national average of $120,500. Justin Rebello, *Pay Scale: Who Makes What Where?*, *in* TWENTY THINGS LAWYERS NEED TO KNOW 20–22 (Nov. 2008). The median salaries of all lawyers nine months after graduation in 2005 was $60,000; for those who entered private practice, it was $85,000; for those entering government work, $46,158; for those in academics or judicial clerkships, $45,000. BUREAU OF LABOR STATISTICS, *supra*.

35. *See* David Leonhardt, *Money Doesn't Buy Happiness…Well, On Second Thought…*, N.Y. TIMES, Apr. 16, 2008, at C1 ("In the United States, about 90 percent of people in households making at least $250,000 called themselves 'very happy' in a recent Gallup Poll. In households with income below $30,000, only 42 percent of people gave that answer.").

36. Daniel Kahneman et al., *Would You Be Happier If You Were Richer? A Focusing Illusion*, SCIENCE, June 30, 2006, at 1908, 1909.

37. Daniel Gilbert, *What You Don't Know Makes You Nervous*, N.Y. TIMES, May 20, 2009, at A35.

38. Betsey Johnson & Justin Wolfers, *The Paradox of Declining Female Happiness*, 1 Am. Econ. J: Econ. Pol'y 190, 217–224 (2009).

39. Nearly as many women as men enter the practice of law, although there is a decreasing entry rate into the profession for women. In 1980 slightly more than one-third of law students (34.2 percent) were women. This number peaked to almost half (49 percent) in 2002 and 2003, but it has dropped to just under 47 percent in the past five years. American Bar Association, First Year and Total J.D. Enrollment by Gender, 1947–2008, http://www.abanet.org/legaled/statistics/charts/stats%20-%206.pdf (last visited Feb. 23, 2008).

40. American Bar Association Commission on Women, The 2008 Goal IX Report Card—An Annual Report on Women's Advancement into Leadership Positions in the ABA, Feb. 2008, at 4.

41. Dinovitzer et al., *supra* note 4, at 58.

42. Mona Harrington & Helen Hsi, Women Lawyers and Obstacles to Leadership 12 (2007), http://web.mit.edu/workplacecenter/docs/law-report_4–07.pdf. *See also* Theresa M. Beiner, *Not All Lawyers Are Equal: Difficulties That Plague Women and Women of Color*, 58 Syracuse L. Rev. 317, 326 (2008).

43. Monahan & Swanson, *supra* note 3, at 20, 24, 2.

44. Kenneth G. Dau-Schmidt et al., *Men and Women of the Bar: The Impact of Gender on Legal Careers*, 16 Mich. J. Gender & L. 49 (2009).

45. *Gender or Childcare? Study Sheds Light on Career Roadblocks*, Indiana L., Fall 2009, at 3.

46. *Id.* (quoting Ken Dau-Schmidt).

47. Dau-Schmidt et al., *supra* note 44, at 72.

48. In 2009, 31 percent of all lawyers were women. American Bar Association, 2009 National Lawyer Population Survey, *supra* note 4. This compares to 30.2 percent in 2006–7, and 29.4 percent in 2005–6. These percentages were up from 1990 when women comprised 22 percent of the profession and from 2000 when women were 27 percent of lawyers. *See also* Malaika Costello-Dougherty, *We're Outta Here: Why Women Are Leaving Big Firms*, Cal. Law., Feb. 2007, at 20.

49. Danielle M. Evans, Note, *Non-equity Partnership: A Flawed Solution to the Disproportionate Advancement of Women in Private Law Firms*, 28 Women's Rts. L. Rep. 93, 94 (2007). "By 2000, 'only [sixty-one] percent of the female partners in the National Law Journal's 250 firms [had] equity status, as opposed to almost [seventy-five] percent of the male partners.'" *Id.* at 94.

50. Laura T. Kessler, *Keeping Discrimination Theory Front and Center in the Discourse Over Work and Family Conflict*, 34 Pepp. L. Rev. 313, 316 n.17 (2007).

51. *See* AMERICAN BAR ASSOCIATION, VISIBLE INVISIBILITY: WOMEN OF COLOR IN LAW FIRMS 8–10 (2006); Jill Schachner Chanen, *Early Exits: Women of Color at Law Firms Tell ABA Researchers They Are Being Overlooked and Under-valued—Maybe That's Why They Are Leaving in Droves,* 92 A.B.A. J 32, 33, 35 (Aug. 2006).

52. Eric Swedlund, *Choose Law! Event Targets Would-be Lawyers,* ARIZ. DAILY STAR, Mar. 3, 2007, at B5 (noting that 3.9 percent are African American, 3.3 percent are Hispanic, 2.3 percent are Asian American, and 0.2 percent are Native American).

53. DINOVITZER ET AL., *supra* note 4, at 64.

54. *Id.* at 64–65.

55. More than half of all minorities—male and female—leave within three years. *See* Wayne J. Lee, Brown v. Board, *Are We There Yet?,* 51 LA. B.J. 404, 405 (Apr./May 2004).; Charles Toutant, *Women, Minorities Make Strides at Firms, But ABA Study Casts Pall,* 185 N.J.L.J. 653, Aug. 21, 2006, at 3; Debra Cassens Weiss, *Survey Reveals the Unhappiest Associates,* A.B.A. J., Nov. 7, 2007, http://www.abajournal.com/news/survey_reveals_the_unhappiest_associates/ (last visited Jan. 4, 2008).

56. Charles Toutant, *Women, Minorities Make Strides at Firms, But ABA Study Casts Pall,* 185 N.J.L.J. 653, Aug. 21, 2006, at 3.

57. Dinovitzer & Garth, *supra* note 16, at 12.

Chapter 2

1. Carlin Flora, *The Pursuit of Happiness,* PSYCH. TODAY, Jan./Feb. 2009, at 62.

2. Ruut Veenhoven, World Database of Happiness, http://worlddatabaseofhappiness.eur.nl/ (last visited July 8, 2009).

3. Thinkers in numerous other disciplines, from economists and sociologists to epidemiologists and linguists, are drawing on and adding to these works in science and psychology. *See, e.g.,* BRUNO S. FREY & ALOIS STUTZER, HAPPINESS & ECONOMICS: HOW THE ECONOMY AND INSTITUTIONS AFFECT WELL-BEING (2001); Benedict Carey, *Does a Nation's Mood Lurk in Its Songs and Blogs,* N.Y. TIMES, Aug. 3, 2009, *available at* http://www.nytimes.com/2009/08/04/health/04mind.html. Our focus is on the fields we think will be most instrumental in leading to happiness for lawyers.

4. David M. Buss, *The Evolution of Happiness,* 55 AM. PSYCHOLOGIST, Jan. 2000, at 15.

5. EDUARDO PUNSET, THE HAPPINESS TRIP: A SCIENTIFIC JOURNEY 1 (2007).

6. *Id.* at 16–17.

7. *Id.* at 16.

8. Susan Viebrock, *World-Renowned Scientist Delves Into Happiness Research*, TELLURIDE DAILY PLANET, Mar. 27, 2007, http://www.telluridegateway.com/articles/2007/03/28/news/news03.txt.

9. RICHARD LAYARD, HAPPINESS: LESSONS FROM A NEW SCIENCE 17–18 (2005).

10. JEROME KAGAN, WHAT IS EMOTION? (2007), quoted in Sue M. Halpern, *Are You Happy?*, 55 N.Y. REV. BOOKS 24 (Apr. 3, 2008), *available at* http://www.nybooks.com/articles/21197.

11. Viebrock, *supra* note 8.

12. Natalie Angier, *A Molecule of Motivation, Dopamine Excels at Its Task*, N.Y. TIMES, Oct. 27, 2009, at D1, D3.

13. LAYARD, *supra* note 9, at 15.

14. Marnia Robinson, *Your Brain on Sex, Reuniting: Healing With Sexual Relationships*, June 25, 2005, www.reuniting.info/science/sex_in_the_brain.

15. Angier, *supra* note 12, at D3.

16. PUNSET, *supra* note 5, at 126.

17. Natalie Angier, *The Biology Behind the Milk of Human Kindness*, N.Y. TIMES, Nov. 24, 2009, at D2.

18. Viebrock, *supra* note 8. Viebrock quotes researcher Richard Davidson:

> We discovered that when expert practitioners meditated—and our subjects had between 12,000—62,000 hours of meditation each over the course of their lives—there were major, observable changes in the brain, some quite unusual. We saw the production of certain rhythms over extended periods of time, minutes, even hours. In normal individuals, these patterns occur very episodically and last only seconds. What we observed is the brain getting reorganized. We are using these findings to identify long-term end points achievable through intense practice.

> *Id.*

19. Gretchen Reynolds, *Stress Relief: Why Exercise Makes You Less Anxious*, N.Y. TIMES MAG., Nov. 22, 2009, at 16.

20. Of 178 nations ranked for happiness in 2006 by Adrian White, an analytic social psychologist at the University of Leicester in England, Japan came in as the 90th happiest nation, while Canada ranked 10th and the United States 23d. *Canada Scores High on World Happiness Map*, TORONTO'S CITY NEWS, July 28, 2006, www.citynews.ca/news/news_2279.aspx .

21. ERIC WEINER, THE GEOGRAPHY OF BLISS 310 (2008).

22. Sue M. Halpern, *Are You Happy?*, 55 N.Y. REV. BOOKS, Apr. 3, 2008, *available at* http://www.nybooks.com/articles/21197.

23. DANIEL NETTLE, HAPPINESS: THE SCIENCE BEHIND YOUR SMILE 49, 53 (2005).

24. Alan Wolfe, *Hedonic Man*, NEW REPUBLIC, July 9, 2008, at 47.

25. David Lykken & Auke Tellegen, *Happiness Is a Stochastic Phenomenon*, 7 PSY-CHOL. SCI. 186 (May 1996), *available at* http://www.psych.umn.edu/psylabs/happness/happy.htm ("From 44% to 53% of the variance in [wellbeing], however, is associated with genetic variation. Based on the retest of smaller samples of twins after intervals of 4.5 and 10 years, we estimate that the heritability of the stable component of subjective wellbeing approaches 80%.").

26. *See* Thomas J. Bouchard, Jr. et al., *Sources of Human Psychological Differences: The Minnesota Study of Twins Reared Apart*, 250 SCIENCE 223, 250 (Oct. 12, 1990); Auke Tellegen et al., *Personality Similarity in Twins Reared Apart and Together*, 54 J. PERSONALITY & SOC. PSYCHOL. 1031, 1036 (1988).

27. SONJA LYUBOMIRSKY, THE HOW OF HAPPINESS: A NEW APPROACH TO GETTING THE LIFE YOU WANT 21 (2007).

28. MICHAEL F. MELCHER, THE CREATIVE LAWYER: A PRACTICAL GUIDE TO AUTHENTIC PROFESSIONAL SATISFACTION 78 (2007).

29. *Id.*

30. Martin E.P. Seligman et al., *Why Lawyers Are Unhappy*, 23 CARDOZO L. REV. 33, 40 (2001).

31. WEINER, *supra* note 21, at 14.

32. LYUBOMIRSKY, *supra* note 27, at 21.

33. Jonathan Rottenberg, *State Happiness Rankings Reveal Americans' Happiness Insecurity*, Psychology Today Blog: Charting the Depths, http://www.psychologytoday.com/blog/charting-the-depths/200912/state-happiness-rankings-reveal-americans-happiness-insecurity (last visited Dec. 29, 2009).

34. Lewis Diuguid, *Survey Says We Can Be in a Happier State, Like Utah*, K.C. STAR, Dec. 28, 2009, at A13.

35. Carl Bialik, *The Drag of Devising a State-by-State Mirth Meter*, WALL ST. J., Dec. 23, 2009, at A8. *See* Andrew J. Oswald & Stephen Wu, *Objective Confirmation of Subjective Measures of Human Well-Being: Evidence from the U.S.A.*, SCIENCE ONLINE, Dec. 17, 2009. http://www.sciencemag.org/cgi/content/abstract/sci;science.1180606v1?maxtoshow=&HITS=10&hits=10&RESULTFORMAT=&fulltext=andrew+oswald&searchid=1&FIRSTINDEX=0&resourcetype=HWCIT.

36. Rottenberg, *supra* note 33.

37. Forty-three percent of people who attend religious services weekly say they are "very happy" compared to 26 percent of people who never attend religious services. PEW RESEARCH CENTER PUBLICATIONS, ARE WE HAPPY YET?, Feb. 13, 2006, http://pewresearch.org/pubs/301/are-we-happy-yet.

38. Ruut Veenhoven, *Hedonism and Happiness*, 4 J. HAPPINESS STUD. 437, 452 (2003).

39. LAYARD, *supra* note 9, at 15–17.

40. *See* James H. Fowler & Nicholas A. Christakis, *Dynamic Spread of Happiness in a Large Social Network: Longitudinal Analysis Over 20 Years in the Framingham Heart Study*, 337 BRITISH MED. J. 2338 (Dec. 4, 2008).

41. LYUBOMIRSKY, *supra* note 27, at 44.

42. *Id.* at 17, quoting Daniel Gilbert.

43. LAYARD, *supra* note 9, at 30.

44. Adrian White, *A Global Projection of Subjective Well-Being: The First Published Map of World Happiness*, 2006, http://news.bbc.co.uk/2/shared/bsp/hi/pdfs/28_07_06_happiness_map.pdf. *See also Psychologist Produces the First-Ever "World Map of Happiness*, SCIENCE DAILY, Nov. 14, 2006, http://www.sciencedaily.com/releases/2006/11/061113093726.htm.

45. LAYARD, *supra* note 9, at 69.

46. *Id.* at 64.

47. *Happiness. What Is It To You?*, http://www.esearch.com/member/quiz/results/happiness.shtml (last visited July 12, 2009).

48. LYUBOMIRSKY, *supra* note 27, at 6.

49. *Id.* at 20.

50. Lawrence S. Krieger, *Psychological Insights: Why Our Students and Graduates Suffer, and What We Might Do About It*, 1 J. ASSOC. LEGAL WRITING DIRECTORS 265 (2002).

51. BARRY SCHWARTZ, THE PARADOX OF CHOICE: WHY LESS IS MORE 88 (2004).

52. *See* Jane S. Schacter, *The Gay Civil Rights Debate in the States: Decoding the Discourse of Equivalents*, 29 HARV. C.R.-C.L. L. REV. 283, 299 (1994).

53. DANIEL GILBERT, STUMBLING ON HAPPINESS 33 (2006).

54. LYUBOMIRSKY, *supra* note 27, at 25.

Chapter 3

1. TOM W. SMITH, NATIONAL OPINION RESEARCH CENTER/UNIVERSITY OF CHICAGO, JOB SATISFACTION IN THE UNITED STATES (Apr. 17, 2007).

2. Sonja Lyubomirsky et al., *The Benefits of Frequent Positive Affect: Does Happiness Lead to Success?*, 131 PSYCHOL. BULL. 803, 826 (2005).

3. *See* SONJA LYUBOMIRSKY, THE HOW OF HAPPINESS: A NEW APPROACH TO GETTING THE LIFE YOU WANT 128–32 (2007); AMERICAN BAR ASSOCIATION YOUNG LAWYERS DIVISION, ABA YOUNG LAWYERS DIVISION SURVEY: CAREER SATISFACTION 20 (2001), http://www.abanet.org/yld/satisfaction_800.doc.

4. ABA YOUNG LAWYERS DIVISION SURVEY, *supra* note 3, at 17.

5. Stephanie Francis Ward, *Pulse of the Legal Profession*, A.B.A. J., Oct. 2007, at 31–32.

6. ABA Young Lawyers Division Survey, *supra* note 3, at 31, Table 23.

7. Jonathan Foreman, *My Life as an Associate*, City J., Winter 1997, *available at* http://www.city-journal.org/html/7_1_a2.html.

8. The practice of law presents other pressures as well. In a "satisfaction survey" of Oregon bar members, 54 percent identified time and workload pressures as among the most frustrating aspects of their work, and 47 percent said they worried about making mistakes. Janine Robben, *Burnout*, 69 Or. St. B. Bull. 17, 18–19 (Oct. 2008).

9. *See* National Association for Law Placement, *How Much Do Associates Work?*, Table 3. Billable Hours Requirements per Year by Firm Size, NALP Bull., Apr. 2009, http://www.nalp.org/may07billablehrs; Julie A. Oseid, *When Big Brother Is Watching [Out For] You: Mentoring Lawyers, Choosing a Mentor, and Sharing Ten Virtues From My Mentor*, 59 S.C. L. Rev. 393, 409 n.84 (2008). *See generally* Jean Stefancic & Richard Delgado, How Lawyers Lose Their Way: A Profession Fails Its Creative Minds 53 (2005).

10. Ronit Dinovitzer et al., After the J.D.: First Results of a National Study of Legal Careers 33 (2004). One study offered estimates of the average number of hours that lawyers spent at work, varying from a high of fifty-three hours per week at a large private law firm to forty-seven for a small private firm, forty-nine for lawyers working in business or finance, and forty-four for government lawyers. John Monahan & Jeffrey Swanson, *Lawyers at Mid-Career: A 20-Year Longitudinal Study of Job and Life Satisfaction*, 5 J. Empirical Legal Stud. 1, 35 (forthcoming 2009).

11. National Association for Law Placement, *supra* note 9.

12. Douglas Litowitz, The Destruction of Young Lawyers: Beyond One L 15 (2005).

13. National Association for Law Placement, *Salaries at Largest Firms Up Again*, Aug. 21, 2008, http://www.nalp.org/salariesatlargestfirmsupagain.

14. Susan Saab Fortney, *The Billable Hours Derby: Empirical Data on the Problems and Pressure Points*, 33 Fordham Urb. L.J. 171, 177 (2005).

15. William G. Ross, The Honest Hour: The Ethics of Time-Based Billing by Attorneys 3–4 (1996) (quoting Paul Reidinger, *Confessions of The Rodent*, A.B.A. J., Aug. 1995, at 82, 83).

16. Michael Asimow, *Embodiment of Evil: Law Firms in the Movies*, 48 UCLA L. Rev. 1339, 1377 (2001).

17. Amy Kolz, *Don't Call Them Slackers*, Am. Law., Oct. 3, 2005, *available at* http://www.law.com/jsp.article.jsp?id=1127898311339 (last visited Jan. 3, 2008).

18. Patrick J. Schiltz, *On Being a Happy, Healthy and Ethical Member of an Unhappy, Unhealthy, and Unethical Profession*, 52 Vand. L. Rev. 872, 903 (1999).

19. *Retaining the Winners*, Nat'l L.J. 18, Mar. 17, 2008, at 18.

20. National Association for Law Placement, Keeping the Keepers: Strategies for Associate Retention in Times of Attrition (1998), http://

www.nalpfoundation.org/webmodules/articles/anmviewer.asp?a=61. For an elaboration of generational differences, see chapter 6 at notes 10–18.

21. In response to surveys, "[j]udges and lawyers both agreed there has been 'a significant increase in instances of incivility/unprofessionalism in civil litigation in the last decade.'" Jeffrey A. Parness, Civility Initiatives: The 2009 Allerton House Conference, 96 ILL. B.J. 636, 637 (Dec. 2008). Other evidence of growing incivility documents increased discovery abuses, competition for clients concerns, and disciplinary actions against lawyers. See Melissa S. Hung, A Non-Trivial Pursuit: The California Attorney Guidelines of Civility and Professionalism, 48 SANTA CLARA L. REV. 1127, 1133 (2008).

22. Kenneth A. Sprang, Holistic Jurisprudence: Law Shaped by People of Faith, 74 ST. JOHN'S L. REV. 753, 758 n.30 (2000).

23. Lilia M. Cortina et al., What's Gender Got To Do With It? Incivility in the Federal Courts, 27 LAW & SOC. INQUIRY 235, 235 (2002).

24. Christopher J. Piazzola, Comment, Ethical Versus Procedural Approaches to Civility: Why Ethics 2000 Should Have Adopted a Civility Rule, 74 U. COLO. L. REV. 1197, 1199 n.14 (2003); Ward, supra note 5, at 31.

25. Thomas M. Reavley, Rambo Litigators: Pitting Aggressive Tactics Against Legal Ethics, 17 PEPP. L. REV. 637, 638 (1990).

26. Joseph J. Ortego & Lindsay Maleson, Under Attack: Professionalism in the Practice of Law, Mar. 20, 2003, available at http://www.nixonpeabody.com/ publications_detail3.asp?ID=303#ref19.

27. http://www.youtube.com/watch?v=td-KKmcYtrM.

28. Marc S. Galanter & Thomas M. Palay, Large Law Firm Misery: It's the Tournament, Not the Money, 52 VAND. L. REV. 953, 960 (1999).

29. David Guenther, To Be or Not Be a Lawyer, That Is the Question, 2001, http:// www.100megsfree3.com/wordsmith/2bornot1.html.

30. Douglas R. Richmond, Law Firm Partners as Their Brothers' Keepers, 96 KY. L.J. 231, 263 (2007–08).

31. THE GALLUP POLL, HONESTY/ETHICS IN PROFESSIONS (2007), available at http://www.galluppoll.com/content/? ci=1654&pg=1.

32. AMERICAN BAR ASSOCIATION SECTION OF LITIGATION, PUBLIC PERCEPTIONS OF LAWYERS: CONSUMER RESEARCH FINDINGS 7–8 (2002), http:// www.abanet.org/litigation/lawyers/publicperceptions.pdf.

33. Michael Asimow, Bad Lawyers in the Movies, 24 NOVA L. REV. 533, 537 (2000).

34. ANDREW MCCLURG, FIGHT CLUB: DOCTORS VS. LAWYERS—THE RIVALRY BETWEEN AMERICA'S MOST REVERED, REVILED, AND MISUNDERSTOOD PROFESSIONS (forthcoming 2011, manuscript on file with authors).

35. Margaret Raymond, On Legalistic Behavior, the Advocacy Privilege, and Why People Hate Lawyers, 55 BUFF. L. REV. 929, 930 (2007).

36. ANTHONY J. LUPPINO, CAN DO: TRAINING LAWYERS TO BE EFFECTIVE COUNSELORS TO ENTREPRENEURS, REPORT TO THE EWING MARION KAUFFMAN

FOUNDATION, Jan. 30, 2008, at 6, http://papers.ssrn.com/sol3/papers.
cfm?abstract_id=1157065.

37. *Id.*

38. Arthur Gross Schaefer & Leland Swenson, *Contrasting the Vision and the Reality: Core Ethical Values, Ethics Audit and Ethics Decision Models for Attorneys*, 32 PEPP. L. REV. 459, 459 (2005).

39. Stephen D. Easton, *My Last Lecture: Unsolicited Advice for Future and Current Lawyers*, 56 S.C. L. REV. 229, 244 (2004).

40. Charles Silver & Frank B. Cross, *What's Not to Like About Being a Lawyer?*, 109 YALE L.J. 1443, 1476–77 (2000).

41. Frank B. Cross, *The First Thing We Do, Let's Kill All the Economists: An Empirical Evaluation of the Effect of Lawyers on the United States Economy and Political System*, 70 TEX. L. REV. 645, 678 (1992).

42. Legal Underground, Feb. 14, 2005, http://www.legalunderground.com/2005/02/what_do_you_lik.html.

43. Andrew Schepard & Theo Liebmann, *Law and Children*, 235 N.Y.L.J., Jan. 18, 2006, at 3.

44. Guenther, *supra* note 29.

45. Martin Luther King, *Where Do We Go From Here?*, Aug. 16, 1967, http://www.indiana.edu/~ivieweb/mlkwhere.html.

46. Ward, *supra* note 5, at 32.

47. Joshua Wolf Shenk, *What Makes Us Happy?*, ATLANTIC, June 2009, *available at* http://www.theatlantic.com/doc/200906/happiness.

48. Monahan & Swanson, *supra* note 10, at 2.

49. *Id.* at 22.

50. BARRY SCHWARTZ, THE PARADOX OF CHOICE: WHY LESS IS MORE 104, 111 (2004).

51. Pew Research Center, *Are We Happy Yet?*, Feb. 13, 2006, http://pewresearch.org/pubs/301/are-we-happy-yet.

52. DANIEL NETTLE, HAPPINESS: THE SCIENCE BEHIND YOUR SMILE 73–74 (2005).

53. Patrick Radden Keefe, *White Shoe, Black Hat: Michael Clayton's Devastating Critique of the Legal Profession*, SLATE, Feb. 19, 2008, http://www.slate.com/id/2184068/.

54. *See* SUSAN SWAIM DAICOFF, LAWYER, KNOW THYSELF, A PSYCHOLOGICAL ANALYSIS OF PERSONALITY STRENGTHS AND WEAKNESSES 41 (2004).

55. *See, e.g.*, Don Peters & Martha M. Peters, *Maybe That's Why I Do That: Psychological Type Theory, the Myers-Briggs Type Indicator, and Learning Legal Interviewing*, 35 N.Y.L. SCH. L. REV. 169, 169 (1990).

56. Susan Daicoff, *Asking Leopards to Change Their Spots: Should Lawyers Change? A Critique of Solutions to Problems with Professionalism by Reference*

to Empirically-Derived Attorney Personality Attributes, 11 Geo. J. Legal Ethics 547, 587–88, 595 (1998).

57. The "lawyer personality" is itself a category in the Myers-Briggs personality inventory. Based on the standard categorization of personality types, lawyers are much more inclined that the general public to be "Thinkers" (versus "Feelers"), "Introverts" (versus "Extroverts"), and "Intuiting" types (versus "Sensing" types). For example, 66 percent of all female lawyers are "Thinking" types compared to only 35 percent of women generally. (Male lawyers are even more likely to be "Thinking" types, with 81 percent getting that label, based on survey results.) On the Extroversion-Introversion scale, a full three-quarters of the general population turn out to be "Extroverts" compared to just 43 percent of lawyers. Finally, on the Sensing-Intuiting scale, 70 percent of lawyers score as "Intuiting" types, while in the general population, the percentages are exactly the reverse. (Intuiting types are considered to be past or future-oriented, impatient with the routine, doubt-ridden, and attracted more to the theoretical than the practical.) On only one of the standard personality scales, "Perceiving" types versus "Judging" types, do lawyers generally reflect percentages found in the population as a whole. Michael Melcher, The Creative Lawyer: A Practical Guide to Authentic Professional Satisfaction 76–79 (American Bar Association, 2007).

58. Martin E.P. Seligman et al., *Why Lawyers Are Unhappy*, 23 Cardozo L. Rev. 33, 34 (2001).

59. Catherine Gage O'Grady, *Cognitive Optimism and Professional Pessimism in the Large-Firm Practice of Law: The Optimistic Associate*, 30 Law & Psychol. Rev. 23, 37–38 (2006).

60. Seligman et al., *supra* note 58, at 41.

61. Lawrence S. Krieger, *The Inseparability of Professionalism and Personal Satisfaction: Perspectives on Values, Integrity and Happiness*, 11 Clinical L. Rev. 425, 433, 434 (2005).

62. Douglas O. Linder, *Who Is Clarence Darrow?*, http://www.law.umkc.edu/faculty/projects/ftrials/DARESY.htm (last visited Aug. 11, 2009).

63. Alice Park, *A Primer for Pessimists*, Time, Apr. 6, 2009, at W1 (quoting Martin Seligman).

Chapter 4

1. Eduardo Punset, The Happiness Trip: A Scientific Journey 55 (2007).

2. *Id.* at 56.

3. William W. Eaton et al., *Occupations and the Prevalence of Major Depressive Disorder*, 32 J. Occupational Med. 1079, 1083 (1990).

4. American Bar Association Young Lawyers Division, Table 23, ABA Young Lawyers Division Survey: Career Satisfaction 31 (2001), http://www.abanet.org/yld/satisfaction_800.doc.

5. *Id.* at 22.

6. Peter Warr, *Jobs and Happiness*, SOCIETY FOR INDUSTRIAL & ORGANIZATIONAL PSYCHOLOGY, INC., Jan. 2007, http://www.siop.org/tip/Current/04warr. aspx.

7. DANIEL GILBERT, STUMBLING ON HAPPINESS 23 (2006).

8. PUNSET, *supra* note 1, at 78.

9. Stephanie Francis Ward, *Pulse of the Legal Profession: 800 Lawyers Reveal What They Think About Their Lives, Their Careers and the State of the Legal Profession*, 93 A.B.A. J. 30, 34 (Oct. 2007).

10. Ross Gittins, *Happiness Is the Job You Like*, SYDNEY MORNING HERALD, Mar. 10, 2004, *available at* http://www.smh.com.au/articles/2004/03/09/ 1078594359806.html?from=storyrhs.

11. INTERNATIONAL LABOUR ORGANIZATION, KEY INDICATORS OF THE LABOUR MARKET PROGRAMME 6, 10, http://www.ilo.org/public/english/employ-ment/strat/kilm/download/kilm06.pdf (last visited July 9, 2009).

12. JEROME KAGAN, WHAT IS EMOTION? (2007), quoted in Sue M. Halpern, *Are You Happy?*, 55 N.Y. REV. BOOKS 24 (Apr. 3, 2008), *available at* http://www. nybooks.com/articles/21197.

13. DANIEL NETTLE, HAPPINESS: THE SCIENCE BEHIND YOUR SMILE 38 (2005).

14. American Public Media, *Bhutan's Falling Happiness Index*, Nov. 14, 2007, http://marketplace.publicradio.org/display/web/2007/11/14/consumed5_ mmr_1/.

15. According to a recent study, 96 percent of people in the highest social class report being in control of their lives, compared to 81 percent in the lowest social class. NETTLE, *supra* note 13, at 73–74.

16. ERIC WEINER, THE GEOGRAPHY OF BLISS 251 (2008).

17. RICHARD LAYARD, HAPPINESS: LESSONS FROM A NEW SCIENCE 40 (2005). Richard Wilkinson and Kate Pickett amass substantial evidence that societ-ies with greater economic and political equality have healthier and happier citizens. RICHARD WILKINSON & KATE PICKETT, THE SPIRIT LEVEL: WHY MORE EQUAL SOCIETIES ALMOST ALWAYS DO BETTER (2009).

18. SONJA LYUBOMIRSKY, THE HOW OF HAPPINESS: A NEW APPROACH TO GETTING THE LIFE YOU WANT 116 (2007).

19. WEINER, *supra* note 16, at 114.

20. LAYARD, *supra* note 17, at 16.

21. Warr, *supra* note 6.

22. *Id.* at 15.

23. TOM W. SMITH, JOB SATISFACTION IN THE UNITED STATES (Apr. 17, 2007) (National Opinion Research Center, University of Chicago study).

24. Barbara Rose, *Money Can't Buy Happiness, Study Finds*, CHI. TRIB., Apr. 17, 2007.

25. GILBERT, *supra* note 7, at 166.

26. ROBERT PUTNAM, BOWLING ALONE: THE COLLAPSE AND REVIVAL OF AMERICAN COMMUNITY (2001).

27. LYUBOMIRSKY, *supra* note 18, at 64, 89–101.

28. Ward, *supra* note 9, at 33.

29. Physorg.com, *First Ever World Map of Happiness Produced*, http://www.physorg.com/news73321785.html, July 28, 2006. Austria ranked third, followed by Iceland. The United States ranked 23d.

30. WEINER, *supra* note 16, at 318.

31. Leslie A. Gordon, *Mid-Career Malaise: How to Find a New Path for Your 40s*, A.B.A. J., Sept. 2008, at 38, 40.

32. *Id.*

33. Debra Cassens Weiss, *Long Hours and Hard Work Took a Toll on Sotomayor's Relationships*, A.B.A. J., July 10, 2009, *available at* http://abajournal.com/news/long_hours_and_hard_work_took_a_toll_on_sotomayors_relationships.

34. TAL BEN SHAHAR, THE QUESTION OF HAPPINESS: ON FINDING MEANING, PLEASURE, AND THE ULTIMATE CURRENCY 46 (2002) (quoting Csikszentmihalyi).

35. MIHALYI CSIKSZENTMIHALYI, FINDING FLOW: THE PSYCHOLOGY OF ENGAGEMENT WITH EVERYDAY LIFE 29 (1997).

36. David Achtenberg, interview, Jan. 29, 2009.

37. *See generally* CSIKSZENTMIHALYI, *supra* note 35; MIHALYI CSIKSZENTMIHALYI, FLOW: THE PSYCHOLOGY OF OPTIMAL EXPERIENCE (1990).

38. GILBERT, *supra* note 7, at 111–71, 212–33.

39. LAYARD, *supra* note 17, at 48–49.

40. WEINER, *supra* note 16, at 310.

41. Penelope Trunk, Brazen Careerist, http://blog.penelopetrunk.com/2006/05/15/forget-the-soul-search-just-do-something (May 15, 2006).

42. Daniel T. Gilbert et al., *The Surprising Power of Neighborly Advice*, 323 SCIENCE 1617, 1618 (Mar. 20, 2009).

43. Trunk, *supra* note 41, citing Daniel Gilbert.

44. *See* Michael A. Cohn et al., *Happiness Unpacked: Positive Emotions Increase Life Satisfaction by Building Resilience*, 9 J. EMOTION 361 (2009); *Smallest Joys Add Up to a Lot*, K.C. STAR, July 12, 2009, at A11.

45. LYUBOMIRSKY, *supra* note 18, at 194.

46. BEN SHAHAR, *supra* note 34, at 54–57.

47. *See* MARTIN E.P. SELIGMAN, AUTHENTIC HAPPINESS: USING THE NEW POSITIVE PSYCHOLOGY TO REALIZE YOUR POTENTIAL FOR LASTING FULFILLMENT (2002).

48. Jean Stefancic & Richard Delgado, How Lawyers Lose Their Way: A Profession Fails Its Creative Minds 14–15 (2005).

49. Deborah Rhode, *Foreword: Personal Satisfaction in Professional Practice*, 58 Syracuse L. Rev. 217, 224 (2008).

50. Ward, *supra* note 9, at 33 (68 percent of public sector lawyers polled said they "were satisfied with their professional lives.").

51. Punset, *supra* note 1, at 41.

52. Unfortunately, however, pro bono opportunities in most workplaces are very limited these days. One half of all attorneys report being dissatisfied with pro bono opportunities offered by their firms, and actual pro bono work averages less than thirty minutes per week. Rhode, *supra* note 49, at 225. Only a quarter of lawyers say that their firms fully count pro bono work toward billable hours and about two-thirds believe that pro bono work will not help, or is more likely to hurt, their prospects for promotion or increased compensation. *Id.* at 226. Profits rule at most firms—and the drive for ever higher profits (to pay ever higher salaries) has taken its toll on pro bono activity. The failure of firms to place a high priority on pro bono work is unfortunate.

53. *Id.* at 233.

54. *Id.*

55. Penelope Trunk, Brazen Careerist, http://blog.penelopetrunk.com/2007/01/16/the-connection-between-a-good-job-and-happiness-is-overrated (Jan. 16, 2007).

56. Erica Goode, *Exploring Life at the Top of the Happiness Scale*, N.Y. Times, Jan. 29, 2002, at F6.

Chapter 5

1. *See, e.g.,* Andrew McClurg, 1L of a Ride: A Well-Traveled Professor's Roadmap to Success in the First Year of Law School (2008); Helene Shapo & Marshall Shapo, Law School Without Fear: Strategies for Success (2d ed. 2002).

2. American Bar Association, Enrollment and Degrees Awarded 1963–2008, http://www.abanet.org/legaled/statistics/charts/statspercent20-percent201.pdf. In that same time frame about 5,000 first year students left law school each year; approximately 1,400 left law school during their second year, and about 300 left during their third year. American Bar Association, Total J.D. Attrition 1981–2006, http://www.abanet.org/legaled/statistics/charts/stats%20-%2017.pdf. These attrition rates include students who left voluntarily, flunked out, and transferred to another school. The numbers may say more about a school's admissions and retention

practices than individuals' choices. In 2005 six law schools had attrition rates for first years above 30 percent. Debra Cassens Weiss, *1L Attrition Topped 30 Percent at Six Law Schools*, A.B.A. J., Apr. 25, 2008, *available at* http://www.abajournal.com/news/1l_attrition_topped_30_percent_at_six_law_schools.

3. Deborah Rhode, *Personal Satisfaction in Professional Practice*, 58 SYRACUSE L. REV. 217, 223 (2008).

4. Allen K. Rostron, *Lawyers, Law & the Movies: The Hitchcock Cases*, 86 CAL. L. REV. 211, 214 (1998).

5. People who engage with and care about other people report greater satisfaction over their life span. Nisha C. Gottfredson et al., *Identifying Predictors of Law Student Life Satisfaction*, 58 J. LEGAL EDUC. 520 (Dec. 2008).

6. *Id.*

7. Barbara Glesner Fines, interview, Apr. 21, 2009.

8. GARY A. MUNNEKE ET AL., NONLEGAL CAREERS FOR LAWYERS 3–4 (5th ed. 2006).

9. GARY A. MUNNEKE, THE LEGAL CAREER GUIDE: FROM LAW STUDENT TO LAWYER 5 (4th ed. 2002).

10. NICHOLAS A. CHRISTAKIS & JAMES H. FOWLER, CONNECTED: THE SURPRISING POWER OF OUR SOCIAL NETWORKS AND HOW THEY SHAPE OUR LIVES (2009).

11. Graduates of fourth-tier law schools are happier (43 percent are extremely satisfied) than graduates of elite law schools "working in the most prestigious settings"—who are the least likely to report being extremely satisfied (24 percent) "with their decision to become a lawyer." Ronit Dinovitzer & Bryant G. Garth, *Lawyer Satisfaction in the Process of Structuring Legal Careers*, 41 LAW & SOC'Y REV. 1, 25 (2007).

12. LAW SCHOOL SURVEY OF STUDENT ENGAGEMENT, STUDENT ENGAGEMENT IN LAW SCHOOL: PREPARING 21ST CENTURY LAWYERS (2008), http://lssse.iub.edu/2008_Annual_Report/pdf/j4u5h7e9/LSSSE_2008_Annual_Report.pdf [hereinafter LSSSE].

13. *Princeton Review's Best 174 Law Schools*, Tax Prof Blog, http://taxprof.typepad.com/taxprof_blog/2008/10/princeton-revie.html (Oct. 20, 2008).

14. *See* LSSSE, *supra* note 12, at 11–14.

15. *See* Lawrence S. Krieger, *Human Nature as a New Guiding Philosophy for Legal Education and the Profession*, 47 WASHBURN L.J. 247, 264 (2008).

16. Susan Sturm & Lani Guinier, *The Law School Matrix: Reforming Legal Education in a Culture of Competition and Conformity*, 60 VAND. L. REV. 515, 532–33 (2007).

17. *See* Patrick J. Schiltz, *Making Ethical Lawyers*, 45 S. TEX. L. REV. 875, 879–85 (2004).

18. LAW SCHOOL SURVEY OF STUDENT ENGAGEMENT, ENGAGING LEGAL EDUCATION: MOVING BEYOND THE STATUS QUO 8, 13 (2006), http://lssse.iub. edu/2006_Annual_Report/pdf/LSSSE_2006_Annual_Report.pdf.

19. Denise Riebe, *A Bar Review for Law Schools: Getting Students on Board to Pass Their Bar Exams*, 45 BRANDEIS L.J. 269, 331 (2007).

20. *See* Brigette LuAnn Willauer, Comment, *The Law School Honor Code and Collaborative Learning: Can They Coexist?*, 73 UMKC L. REV. 513, 525–34 (2004).

21. Anthony J. Luppino, *Minding More Than Our Own Business: Educating Entrepreneurial Lawyers Through Law School-Business School Collaborations*, 30 W. NEW ENG. L. REV. 151, 166 (2007).

22. *See, e.g.*, Janet Weinstein & Linda Morton, *Interdisciplinary Problem Solving Courses as a Context for Nurturing Intrinsic Values*, 13 CLINICAL L. REV. 839, 846 (2007).

23. Luppino, *supra* note 21, at 178–86.

24. *The Endangered Trial Lawyer*, 95 A.B.A. J. 63 (Mar. 2009).

25. PAULINE H. TESLER, COLLABORATIVE LAW: ACHIEVING EFFECTIVE RESOLUTION IN DIVORCE WITHOUT LITIGATION xx–xxi (2001).

26. Susan Grover, *Personal Integration and Outsider Status as Factors in Law Student Well-Being*, 47 WASHBURN L.J. 419, 427 (2008).

27. Paula Lustbader, *You Are Not in Kansas Anymore: Orientation Programs Can Help Students Fly Over the Rainbow*, 47 WASHBURN L.J. 327, 350 (2008).

28. Christine Hurt, *No Harm Intended*, CHRON. HIGHER EDUC., May 25, 2005, *available at* http://chronicle.com/jobs/news/2005/05/2005052501c.htm.

29. *See* Michael Hunter Schwartz, *Humanizing Legal Education: An Introduction to a Symposium Whose Time Has Come*, 47 WASHBURN L.J. 235 (2008).

30. American Bar Association, *Alphabetical School List*, http://www.abanet.org/legaled/approvedlawschools/alpha.html (last visited Mar. 25, 2009). We are indebted to Lawrence MacLachlan for conducting this survey.

31. Lewis & Clark's "Lawyering in Society," Temple's "Law, Happiness, & Subjective Well-Being," the University of California at Berkeley's "Effective and Sustainable Law Practice: the Meditative Perspective," the University of Missouri-Kansas City's "Quest for a Satisfying Career in Law," the University of Virginia's "Legal Careers and Life Satisfaction, and Yale's "Happiness and Morality." *See* Peter H. Huang & Rick Swedloff, *Authentic Happiness & Meaning at Law Firms*, 58 SYRACUSE L. REV. 335, 346–47 (2008).

32. *See, e.g.*, DANIEL GILBERT, STUMBLING ON HAPPINESS (2006); Daniel Kahneman et al., *Would You Be Happier If You Were Richer? A Focusing Illusion*, 312 SCIENCE 1908 (June 30, 2006); Barry Schwartz & Andrew Ward et al., *Maximizing Versus Satisficing: Happiness Is a Matter of Choice*, 83 J. PERSONALITY & SOC. PSYCHOL. 1178 (2002).

33. Doug Linder & Nancy Levit, *The Quest for a Satisfying Career in Law*, Spring 2009, http://www.law.umkc.edu/faculty/projects/ftrials/happylawyers/Questions.html.

34. Doug Linder, *Searching for Law's Heroes*, 2001, http://www.law.umkc.edu/faculty/projects/ftrials/trialheroes/HEROSEARCH1.html.

35. Doug Linder, *Does the Law Have Heroes?*, 2001, http://www.law.umkc.edu/faculty/projects/ftrials/trialheroes/HEROSEARCH4.html.

36. Boston College, *Law School Personal Statement*, http://www.bc.edu/offices/careers/gradschool/law/lawstatement.html (last visited Mar. 3, 2010).

37. William H. Colby, Unplugged: Reclaiming Our Right to Die in America 109, 114 (2006). Lawyer Bill Colby created this term in another context, but it refers to a phenomenon of institutions creating structures that route people in prescribed directions.

38. Daisy Hurst Floyd, *Lost Opportunity: Legal Education and the Development of Professional Identity*, 30 Hamline L. Rev. 555, 562 (2007).

39. Harry Lewis, Excellence Without a Soul: How a Great University Forgot Education 12–14, 140 (2005).

40. *See* Luppino, *supra* note 21, at 194.

41. Lawrence S. Krieger, The Hidden Sources of Law School Stress: Avoiding the Mistakes That Create Unhappy and Unprofessional Lawyers 5 (2006), *available at* http://www.law.fsu.edu/academic_programs/humanizing_lawschool/images/EP.pdf.

42. Pierre Schlag, *Hiding the Ball*, 71 N.Y.U. L. Rev. 1681, 1683 (1996).

43. Paul J. Zak & Ahlam Fakhar, *Neuroactive Hormones and Interpersonal Trust: International Evidence*, 4 Econ. & Hum. Biology 412 (Dec. 2006).

44. Schwartz, *supra* note 29, at 241 n.43 (This game "involves assigning bingo squares to students who engage themselves in classroom discussions and then playing according to the normal bingo rules as those students participate in class.").

45. Jess M. Krannich et al., *Beyond "Thinking Like a Lawyer" and the Traditional Legal Paradigm: Toward a Comprehensive View of Legal Education*, 86 Denv. U.L. Rev. 381, 385 (2009).

46. Barbara Glesner Fines, Law School and Stress (1999), http://www.law.umkc.edu/faculty/profiles/glesnerfines/bgf-strs.htm.

47. Gerald F. Hess, *Heads and Hearts: The Teaching and Learning Environment in Law School*, 52 J. Legal Educ. 75, 77 (2002).

48. A 1993 Association of American Law Schools survey of almost 3,400 students at nineteen law schools showed that 8.2 percent had used marijuana in the previous month, 8.8 percent had used some form of illicit drug, and 14 percent had drunk alcohol ten or more times in the previous month;

during the previous year, 20.8 percent reported use of marijuana and 4.8 percent had used cocaine. *Report of the AALS Special Committee on Problems of Substance Abuse in the Law Schools*, 44 J. LEGAL EDUC. 35, 41 (1994).

49. Intriguingly, while medical students suffered some similar symptoms of depression and anxiety, they did so at about half the rate of law students. Connie J.A. Beck et al., *Lawyer Distress: Alcohol-Related Problems and Other Psychological Concerns Among a Sample of Practicing Lawyers*, 10 J.L. & HEALTH 1 (1995–96).

50. Susan Daicoff, *Lawyer, Know Thyself: A Review of Empirical Research on Attorney Attributes Bearing on Professionalism*, 46 AM. U. L. REV. 1337, 1341–50 (1997).

51. Kennon M. Sheldon & Lawrence S. Krieger, *Does Legal Education Have Undermining Effects on Law Students? Evaluating Changes in Motivation, Values, and Well-Being*, 22 BEHAV. SCI. L. 261, 264 (2004).

52. KRIEGER, *supra* note 41, at 3 (emphasis in original).

53. INDIANA UNIVERSITY CENTER FOR POSTSECONDARY RESEARCH, LAW SCHOOL SURVEY OF STUDENT ENGAGEMENT: LAW SCHOOL REPORT 2007, OVERVIEW 7 (2007), *available at* http://lssse.iub.edu/pdf/LSSSE%202007%20Overview_FINAL%20(PDF).pdf.

54. Peter F. Lake, *When Fear Knocks: The Myths and Realities of Law School*, 29 STETSON L. REV. 1015, 1034 (2000).

55. James H. Backman, *Practical Examples for Establishing an Externship Program Available to Every Student*, 14 CLINICAL L. REV. 1, 4 n.16 (2007) (listing only eight law schools that do not have an in-house clinic).

56. Mitu Gulati et al., *The Happy Charade: An Empirical Examination of the Third Year of Law School*, 51 J. LEGAL EDUC. 235, 249 (2001).

57. Jonathan D. Rowe, *"It Gets Late Early Out There": Yogi Berra Tours the Law Schools*, 77 MICH. B.J. 664, 666 (1998).

58. KRIEGER, *supra* note 41, at 4.

59. Nisha C. Gottfredson et al., *Identifying Predictors of Law Student Life Satisfaction*, 58 J. LEGAL EDUC. 520, 527 (2008). *See also* Dinovitzer & Garth, *supra* note 11, at 25.

60. *Id.*

61. *See* Sheldon & Krieger, *supra* note 51.

62. *See* Susan Daicoff, *Lawyer, Be Thyself: An Empirical Investigation of the Relationship Between the Ethic of Care, the Feeling Decisionmaking Preference, and Lawyer Wellbeing*, 16 VA. J. SOC. POL'Y & L. 87, 133 (2008).

63. Michael Hunter Schwartz, *Teaching Law Students to Be Self-Regulated Learners*, 2003 MICH. ST. DCL L. REV. 447, 481–83.

64. *See, e.g.,* Edwin S. Shneidman, *Personality and "Success" Among a Selected Group of Lawyers*, 48 J. PERSONALITY ASSESSMENT 609, 613–15 (1984).

65. Celestial S.D. Cassman & Lisa R. Pruitt, *A Kinder, Gentler Law School? Race, Ethnicity, Gender, and Legal Education at King Hall*, 38 U.C. DAVIS L. REV. 1209, 1263–64 (2005).

66. Gregory Bowman, *The Comparative and Absolute Advantages of Junior Law Faculty: Implications for Teaching and the Future of American Law Schools*, 2008 B.Y.U. EDUC. & L.J. 171, 188.

67. Tan N. Nguyen, *An Affair to Forget: Law School's Deleterious Effect on Students' Public Interest Aspirations*, 7 CONN. PUB. INT. L.J. 251, 252–52 (2008).

68. *Id.* at 257, 259–60.

69. AMERICAN BAR ASSOCIATION, LAW SCHOOL TUITION, http://www.abanet. org/legaled/statistics/charts/stats%20-%205.pdf (last visited Aug. 8, 2008).

70. Kathy Kristof, *The Great College Hoax*, FORBES, Feb. 2, 2009, *available at* http://www.forbes.com/magazines/forbes/2009/0202/060.html

71. *The End of an Era: The Bi-Modal Distribution for the Class of 2008*, Empirical Legal Studies, at http://www.elsblog.org/the_empirical_legal_studi/2009/06/the-end-of-an-era-the-bimodal-distribution-for-the-class-of-2008.html (June 29, 2009) (based on more than 22,300 recent graduates—"over half of all 2008 graduates"—who reported their starting salaries). This chart is copyrighted by the National Association for Law Placement (NALP) and reprinted with permission.

72. *Id.* You can easily find websites to research the starting salaries at individual firms in various locations. http://www.infirmation.com/shared/search/scored-search.

73. National Association for Law Placement, *How Much Do Law Firms Pay New Associates? A 12-Year Retrospective as Reported by Firms,* Oct. 2007, Table 1. Median Starting Salaries for First-Year Associates by Firm Size, Table 3, Median Starting Salaries for Selected Non-Firm Lawyer Jobs, http://www. nalp.org/2007octnewassocpay.

74. The states are: Arizona, Florida, Indiana, Kentucky, Maine, Maryland, Massachusetts, Minnesota, Missouri, Montana, New Hampshire, New Mexico, New York, North Carolina, Texas, and Washington.

75. Equal Justice Works, *State LRAPs,* http://www.equaljusticeworks.org/node/71. Three states, Kentucky, Maine, and New Hampshire, have no income cap.

76. Equal Justice Works, *Law Schools With LRAPS,* http://www.equaljustice-works.org/node/66

77. One provides state and local prosecutors and public defenders with $10,000 per year for a three year commitment. Another offers civil legal aid lawyers $6,000 for each year of a renewable three-year commitment (up to a maximum of $40,000). The third will give $2,000 per year (up to a maximum of $10,000) to public interest lawyers (including prosecutors, public defenders,

and lawyers in low-income communities who work at nonprofit organizations). The fourth is a loan cancellation program which offers partial loan forgiveness for certain public service jobs. Equal Justice Works, *New Resource: Higher Education Reauthorization and College Opportunity Act of 2008*, http://www.equaljusticeworks.org/node/421

78. IBRinfo, *What Are These New Programs?*, http://www.ibrinfo.org/what. vp.html (last visited Jan. 26, 2009).

79. DANIEL NETTLE, HAPPINESS: THE SCIENCE BEHIND YOUR SMILE 152 (2005).

80. MUNNEKE, *supra* note 8, at 4.

81. EDUARDO PUNSET, THE HAPPINESS TRIP: A SCIENTIFIC JOURNEY 54 (2007).

82. Nguyen, *supra* note 67, at 257–60.

83. David Hricik & Victoria S. Salzmann, *Why There Should Be Fewer Articles Like This One: Law Professors Should Write More for Legal Decision-Makers and Less for Themselves*, 38 SUFFOLK U. L. REV. 761, 769 (2005).

84. Joshua J.A. Henderson & Trevor C.W. Farrow, *The Ethical Development of Law Students: An Empirical Study*, 72 SASK. L. REV. 75, 98 n.80 (2009).

85. Michael Sauder & Wendy Nelson Espeland, *Strength in Numbers? The Advantages of Multiple Rankings*, 81 IND. L.J. 205, 211 (2006).

86. Dinovitzer & Garth, *supra* note 11, at 4.

87. One survey of almost 19,000 associates asked them to rank firms along various dimensions, such as prestige, diversity, and quality of life (including measures such as hours and compensation, but also formal and informal training, and treatment by partners). Vault, *Top 100 Law Firms, 2009 Rankings*, http://www.vault.com/nr/lawrankings.jsp?law2009=1&ch_id=242.

88. Judged, http://www.judged.com/jdfirmrankings.php (last visited July 21, 2009).

89. *See* BARRY NALEBUFF & IAN AYRES, WHY NOT? HOW TO USE EVERYDAY INGENUITY TO SOLVE PROBLEMS BIG AND SMALL (2003).

90. BARRY SCHWARTZ, THE PARADOX OF CHOICE: WHY LESS IS MORE 77–96 (2004).

91. *Id.* at 104.

92. *Id.* at 25.

93. *Id.* at 4.

94. *Id.* at 62; Barry Schwartz & Andrew Ward et al., *Maximizing Versus Satisficing: Happiness Is a Matter of Choice*, 83 J. PERSONALITY & SOC. PSYCHOL. 1178, 1179 (2002).

95. Michael Melcher, *Why Thinking Like a Lawyer Is Bad for Your Career*, A.B.A. J., Apr. 15, 2009, http://www.abajournal.com/weekly/why_thinking_like_a_lawyer_is_bad_for_your_career.

96. *Id.*

97. *Id.*

98. Tal Ben-Shahar, The Question of Happiness: On Finding Meaning, Pleasure, and the Ultimate Currency 54 (2002).

99. Christopher Peterson & Martin E.P. Seligman, Values in Action (VIA) Classification of Strengths, Jan. 4, 2003, http://www.ppc.sas.upenn.edu/ viamanualintro.pdf, at 4. Character Strengths and Virtues: A Handbook and Classification (Christopher Peterson & Martin E.P. Seligman eds. 2004). The twenty-four strengths are the positive character traits that are components of the virtues. Courage encompasses bravery, industry (perseverance and diligence), honesty (authenticity, sincerity, and integrity), and vitality. Humanity includes strength in the areas of intimate attachment, kindness, and intelligence. Justice includes citizenship and teamwork, fairness, and leadership. Temperance consists of forgiveness and mercy, modesty and humility, prudence, and regulation of oneself. Transcendence is comprised of an appreciation of beauty and excellence (awe and wonder), gratitude, hope (optimism, future-mindedness, future orientation), playfulness and humor, and spirituality. Wisdom contains creativity (originality and ingenuity), curiosity, active open-mindedness, love of learning, and perspective.

100. Martin Seligman, *Authentic Happiness,* http://www.authentichappiness.sas. upenn.edu/Default.aspx (last visited July 4, 2009).

101. Peter H. Huang, *Authentic Happiness, Self-Knowledge and Legal Policy,* 9 Minn. J.L. Sci. & Tech. 755, 766 (2008).

102. Christopher K. Hsee & Reid Hastie, *Decision and Experience: Why Don't We Choose What Makes Us Happy?,* http://papers.ssrn.com/sol3/papers. cfm?abstract_id=929914&rec=1&srcabs=935470.

103. Gilbert, *supra* note 32, at 137.

104. *Id.* at 143.

105. Hsee & Hastie, *supra* note 102, at 3.

106. *Id.*

107. François de La Rochefoucauld, quoted in Daniel T. Gilbert et al., *The Surprising Power of Neighborly Advice,* 323 Science 1617 (Mar. 20, 2009).

108. Gilbert, *supra* note 32, at 223.

109. Penelope Trunk, *The Connection Between a Good Job and Happiness Is Overrated,* Brazen Careerist, http://blog.penelopetrunk.com/2007/01/16/ the-connection-between-a-good-job-and-happiness-is-overrated (Jan. 16, 2007) (citing Daniel Gilbert).

110. Heather Brewer, *Snap Judgments,* 9 Bus. L. Today 4 (Nov./Dec. 1999).

111. Lawrence S. Krieger, *The Inseparability of Professionalism and Personal Satisfaction: Perspectives on Values, Integrity, and Happiness,* 11 Clinical L. Rev. 425, 435–36 (2005).

112. *Id.* at 436–37.

Chapter 6

1. JEREMY BLACHMAN, ANONYMOUS LAWYER 3 (2006).

2. Susan Deutschle, *Law Firm Retention Strategies Useful in Combating Attorney Turnover*, COLUMBUS BUSINESS FIRST, Feb. 9, 2007, *available at* http://columbus.bizjournals.com/columbus/stories/2007/02/12/focus3.html?jst=s_cn_hl.

3. Michael Renetzky, *The Smart Choice for Large Law Firms*, http://westlegaledcenter.com/prm/prmJSF.jsf?id=5085614 (last visited July 11, 2009).

4. ELLEN FREEDMAN, CALCULATING THE TRUE COST OF TURNOVER, 2005, http://www.pa-lawfirmconsulting.com/pdfs/hr/CALCULATING_THE_TRUE_COST_OF_TURNOVER.pdf.

5. Peter Huang & Rick Swedloff, *Authentic Happiness & Meaning at Law Firms*, 58 SYRACUSE L. REV. 335, 337 (2008) (citing studies).

6. *See* Carol Graham, *Does Happiness Pay? An Exploration Based on Panel Data from Russia*, Center on Social and Economic Dynamics Working Paper No. 28, May 2002, *available at* http://ssrn.com/abstract=1028319.

7. J.R. Minkel, *Happiness: Good for Creativity, Bad for Single-Minded Focus*, SCI. AM., Dec. 18, 2006, *available at* http://www.scientificamerican.com/article.cfm?id=happiness-good-for-creati.

8. While numerous researchers have found effects in the populations they studied of co-workers spreading happiness, *see* KIM S. CAMERON ET AL., POSITIVE ORGANIZATIONAL SCHOLARSHIP: FOUNDATIONS OF A NEW DISCIPLINE (2003); Sigal G. Barsade, *The Ripple Effect: Emotional Contagion in Groups*, Oct. 2000, http://papers.ssrn.com/sol3/papers.cfm?abstract_id=250894; Joanne H. Gavin & Richard O. Mason, *The Virtuous Organization: The Value of Happiness in the Workplace*, 33 ORG. DYNAMICS 379 (2004); Marisa Salanova et al., *Flow at Work: Evidence for an Upward Spiral of Personal and Organizational Resources*, 7 J. HAPPINESS STUD. 1 (2006), other researchers have not found such workplace effects. *See* James H. Fowler & Nicholas A. Christakis, *Dynamic Spread of Happiness in a Large Social Network: Longitudinal Analysis Over 20 Years in the Framingham Heart Study*, 337 BRITISH MED. J. 2338 (Dec. 4, 2008).

9. *See* ELAINE HATFIELD ET AL., EMOTIONAL CONTAGION (1994).

10. Leslie A. Gordon, *Mid-Career Malaise*, 94 A.B.A. J. 38, 42 (Sept. 2008) (attorney career coach Debra Bruce).

11. *What Makes a Law Firm a Good Place to Work?*, 26 PA. LAW. 14 (Dec. 2004).

12. Marc Galanter & William Henderson, *The Elastic Tournament: A Second Transformation of the Big Law Firm*, 60 STAN. L. REV. 1867, 1922 n.235 (2008).

13. Diane Stafford, *Gen Y Reshaping the Workplace*, K.C. STAR, July 6, 2008, at C1.

14. Peggy Blake Gleeson, Managing and Motivating the Generations: Implications for the Student and the Employee 7, Feb. 12–16, 2003, http://www.uwsp.edu/Education/facets/links_resources/4413.pdf.

15. Neil Howe & William Strauss, *Characteristics of the Millennial Generation*, *in* Millennials Go to College (2003), *available at* http://www.d.umn.edu/advising/MillennialTraits.doc.

16. Shannon Henson, *Senior Partners Not LOLing at Gen Y's Perceptions*, Oct. 9, 2008. http://securities.law360.com/articles/71585.

17. Gleeson, *supra* note 14, at 7.

18. M. Diane Vogt & Lori-Ann Rickard, Keeping Good Lawyers: Best Practices to Create Career Satisfaction 84 (2000).

19. Lisa B. Bingham et al., *Exploring the Role of Representation in Employment Mediation at the USPS*, 17 Ohio St. J. on Disp. Resol. 341, 350 (2002).

20. *See* Lisa G. Lerman, *The Slippery Slope From Ambition to Greed to Dishonesty: Lawyers, Money and Professional Integrity*, 30 Hofstra L. Rev. 879 (2002).

21. Gina Passarella, *Keeping a Legal Department Effective on a Smaller Budget*, Legal Intelligencer, Dec. 17, 2008, at 7.

22. Aric Press, *In-House at the American Lawyer*, Am. Law., Dec. 2008, at 11.

23. Call to Action: Diversity in the Legal Profession, *Corporate Signatories*, http://www.clocalltoaction.com/ (last visited Dec. 1, 2008).

24. *See* Angela Brouse, Comment, *The Latest Call for Diversity in Law Firms: Is It Legal?*, 75 UMKC L. Rev. 847 (2007).

25. *First Ever World Map of Happiness Produced*, July 28, 2006, http://www.physorg.com/news73321785.html.

26. Robert Putnam, *E Pluribus Unum: Diversity and Community in the Twenty-first Century*, 30 Scandinavian Political Stud. 137, 149–50 (2007).

27. Martin L. Hoffman, Empathy and Moral Development: Implications for Caring and Justice 62 (2000).

28. *See, e.g.,* Michael E. Murphy, *The Nominating Process for Corporate Boards of Directors: A Decision-Making Analysis*, 5 Berkeley Bus. L.J. 131, 158 (2008) ("While individuals value the strong relationships found in cohesive groups, they are most likely to find new ideas in social links that put them in contact with other social worlds or ways of thinking.") (citing studies).

29. *See also* Galanter & Henderson, *supra* note 12, at 1922 (noting that Gen Y'ers "demand a high level of racial and gender diversity within the firm's workforce").

30. Malcolm Gladwell, http://www.ted.com/index.php/talks/lang/eng/malcolm_gladwell_on_spaghetti_sauce.html.

31. *See* Muriel Goode-Trufant, *Beyond Diversity 2009: The Next Generation*, 1722 PLI/Corp 53, Feb. 25, 2009; David B. Wilkins, *From "Separate Is Inherently*

Unequal" to "Diversity Is Good for Business": The Rise of Market-Based Diversity Arguments and the Fate of the Black Corporate Bar, 117 HARV. L. REV. 1548, 1557 (2004).

32. Putnam, *supra* note 26, at 165.

33. Sunil J. Ramlall, *Enhancing Employee Performance Through Positive Organizational Behavior*, 38 J. APP. SOC. PSYCHOL. 1580 (2008).

34. Peter Warr, *Jobs and Happiness*, SOCIETY FOR INDUSTRIAL & ORGANIZATIONAL PSYCHOLOGY, INC., Jan. 2007, http://www.siop.org/tip/Current/04warr.aspx.

35. CATALYST, WOMEN IN THE LAW: MAKING THE CASE 34 (2001), *available at* http://www.catalyst.org/file/165/women_in_law_making_the_case.pdf.

36. In the After the J.D. study, the measures on which lawyers expressed the highest degree of job satisfaction (on a scale of 1–7) were relationships with colleagues (5.7), level of responsibility (5.6), control over work methods (5.4), and intellectual challenge (5.4). Ronit Dinovitzer & Bryant G. Garth, *Lawyer Satisfaction in the Process of Structuring Legal Careers*, 41 LAW & SOC'Y REV. 1, 9 (2007).

37. Martin Seligman et al., *Why Lawyers Are Unhappy*, 23 CARDOZO L. REV. 33, 42 (2001).

38. Bruce A. Green, *Professional Challenges in Large Firm Practices*, 33 FORDHAM URB. L.J. 7, 16–17 (2005).

39. *Id.* at 14.

40. SUSAN SAAB FORTNEY, IN PURSUIT OF ATTORNEY WORK-LIFE BALANCE: BEST PRACTICES IN MANAGEMENT 95–96 (Paula Patton ed. 2005).

41. Stephanie Ward, *The Ultimate Time-Money Trade-Off*, A.B.A. J., Feb. 2, 2007, at 2.

42. ABA COMMISSION ON BILLABLE HOURS, ABA COMMISSION ON BILLABLE HOURS REPORT ix n.iii (2002), http://www.abanet.org/careercounsel/billable.html; Francesca Jarosz, *Tipping Back the Scales*, 16 BUS. L. TODAY 13, 18 (Mar./Apr. 2007).

43. CATALYST, BEYOND A REASONABLE DOUBT: LAWYERS STATE THEIR CASE ON JOB FLEXIBILITY 3 (Nov. 2006), http://www.catalyst.org/publication/40/beyond-a-reasonable-doubt-lawyers-state-their-case-on-job-flexibility.

44. Joan C. Williams et al., *Law Firms as Defendants: Family Responsibilities Discrimination in Legal Workplaces*, 34 PEPP. L. REV. 393, 411 (2007).

45. Building a Better Legal Profession, http://www.betterlegalprofession.org/principles.php (last visited July 5, 2009).

46. Galanter & Henderson, *supra* note 12, at 1924.

47. Peter Lattman, *You Say You Want a Big-Law Revolution*, WALL ST. J., Apr. 3, 2007, *available at* http://blogs.wsj.com/law/2007/04/03/you-say-you-want-a-big-law-revolution.

48. *Id.*

49. *Id.*

50. *Id.*

51. Larry Kramer, *From the Dean*, 81 STAN. LAW. 1 (Fall 2009).

52. *Id.*

53. *Id.*

54. RICHARD H. THALER & CASS R. SUNSTEIN, NUDGE: IMPROVING DECISIONS ABOUT HEALTH, WEALTH, AND HAPPINESS 33–34 (2009).

55. Sharon Driscoll, *Law Firm Hiring: Time for a Change?*, 81 STAN. LAW. 9, 11 (Fall 2009).

56. *Id.*

57. Jeff Jeffrey, *Apprentice Programs Give First Years Extra Training*, MIAMI DAILY BUS. REV., July 2, 2009, at A3.

58. Driscoll, *supra* note 55, at 11.

59. Thomas Adcock, *10 N.Y. Firms Listed as Best for Women*, N.Y.L.J., Aug. 15, 2008, at 24; Working Mother, *2008 50 Best Law Firms for Women*, 2008, http://www.workingmother.com/web?service=vpage/2907.

60. Deborah Epstein Henry, *Facing the FACTS: Introducing Work/Life Choices for All Firm Lawyers Within the Billable Hours Model*, http://www.flextimelawyers.com/pdf/art10.pdf (last visited Feb. 3, 2009).

61. CATALYST, *supra* note 43, at 12.

62. For example, individualized work schedules may prompt lawyers to make relative comparisons.

63. Maria Vogel-Short, *Part-Time Lawyers Still a Rarity and Three-Quarters Are Women, Survey Says*, N.J. L.J., Jan. 2, 2009, *available at* http://www.law.com/jsp/article.jsp?id=1202427138453.

64. Michael A. Scaperlanda, *Lawyering in the Little Way of St. Therese of Lisieux With Complete Abandonment and Love*, 46 J. CATH. LEGAL STUD. 43, 48 (2007).

65. Joan Williams, *Our Economy of Mothers and Others: Women and Economics Revisited*, 5 J. GENDER RACE & JUST. 411, 426 (2002).

66. CATALYST, *supra* note 43, at 12.

67. Joan C. Williams & Stephanie Bornstein, *The Evolution of "FRED": Family Responsibilities Discrimination and Developments in the Law of Stereotyping and Implicit Bias*, 59 HASTINGS L.J. 1311, 1329–30 (2008).

68. Ann A. Scott Timmer & Maureen Beyers, *Alternative Work Arrangements*, 37 ARIZ. ATT'Y 40 (May 2001).

69. VOGT & RICKARD, *supra* note 18, at 61. The idea is that firms should not pay bonuses for hours worked over a set amount. Instead, it is better to allow

some carryover of hours into the next year or simply insist that your lawyers take the time off.

70. Audrey J. Lee, *Negotiating Part-Time Work: An Examination of How Attorneys Negotiate Part-Time Arrangements at Elite Law Firms*, 6 PEPP. DISP. RESOL. L.J. 405, 414 (2006).

71. In 2004 IBM conducted a global work-life satisfaction survey of more than 42,000 of its employees in seventy-nine countries after implementation of flexible work options. It showed that 94 percent of all managers reported a strong link between those arrangements and the "company's 'ability to retain talented professionals.'" ARLENE JOHNSON ET AL., BUSINESS IMPACTS OF FLEXIBILITY: AN IMPERATIVE FOR EXPANSION 10 (2005), *available at* www.cvworkingfamilies.org/downloads/BusinessImpactsofFlexibility.pdf?CFID=54713857&CFTOKEN=52379382. This experience echoed that of Deloitte in the 1990s when it undertook an initiative to reduce the high turnover rate for women. Surveys of its workers showed that flexibility was "the factor most likely to improve retention of women," so "the firm implemented flexibility as a key component of its women's initiative. Since then the turnover of women has dropped significantly, to the point that men's and women's turnover rates are now nearly equal." *Id.*

72. Linda Bray Chanow, *The Business Case for Reduced Hours, Project for Attorney Retention*, http://www.pardc.org/Publications/business_case.shtml (last visited June 20, 2009).

73. Law Society of Alberta, Alternative Work Schedules: Guidelines for Law Firms, http://www.lawsocietyalberta.com/resources/modelEquityPolicies/alternativeschedules.cfm (last visited June 29, 2009).

74. DEBORAH L. RHODE, BALANCED LIVES: CHANGING THE CULTURE OF LEGAL PRACTICE 41 (2001).

75. Kira Dale Pfisterer, *When Three Fill Two: Part-Time Strategies for Full-Time Jobs*, 51 ADVOCATE (Idaho) 15, 17 (Feb. 2008).

76. MILTON C. REGAN, JR., EAT WHAT YOU KILL: THE FALL OF A WALL STREET LAWYER 37 (2004).

77. William D. Henderson, An Empirical Study of Single-Tier Versus Two-Tier Partnerships in the Am Law 200, 84 N.C. L. REV. (2006), http://papers.ssrn.com/sol3/papers.cfm?abstract_id=871094.

78. Ian J. Silverbrand, Note, *Modified Partnership Structures and Their Effects on Associate Satisfaction*, 21 GEO. J. LEGAL ETHICS 165, 195 (2008).

79. William D. Henderson & David Zaring, *Young Associates in Trouble*, 105 MICH. L. REV. 1087, 1096 (2007).

80. Kenneth G. Dau-Schmidt & Kaushik Mukhopadhaya, *The Fruits of Our Labors: An Empirical Study of the Distribution of Income and Job Satisfaction Across the Legal Profession*, 49 J. LEGAL EDUC. 342, 346 (1999).

81. *See* Silverbrand, *supra* note 78. This might also be a function of the greater competition for partnership positions at the studied firms.

82. *Redefining How Your Law Firm Splits the Pie: What Works Now?*, 06–8 LAW OFF. MGMT. & ADMIN. REP. 2 (Aug. 2006) ("56.1% of law firms with 100 or more attorneys use a lockstep system by class for associate compensation. The same is true for 45.4% of firms with 50 to 99 lawyers, but only 21.4% of smaller firms.").

83. Joel A. Rose, *Firms Rethink Partners' Pay as Leverage Declines*, 09–04 COMP. & BENEFITS FOR LAW OFFICES 1, 2–3 (Apr. 2009), *available at* www.ioma.com/law.

84. Maarten Vendrick & Geert Woltjer, *Happiness and Loss Aversion: When Social Participation Dominates Comparison*, July 2006, http://papers.ssrn.com/sol3/papers.cfm?abstract_id=921067.

85. Patrick J. Schiltz, *On Being a Happy, Healthy, and Ethical Member of an Unhappy, Unhealthy, and Unethical Profession*, 52 VAND. L. REV. 871, 906 (1999).

86. Stephen Overell, *A Working Recipe for the Quality of Life*, FINANCIAL TIMES (London), Jan. 24, 2002, at 13.

87. Steve Crabtree, *The Economics of Happiness*, GALLUP MGMT. J., Jan. 10, 2008, http://gmj.gallup.com/content/103549/Economics-Happiness.aspx.

88. *Employers Urged to Focus on Training to Increase Job Satisfaction*, Apr. 11, 2007, www.trainingfoundation.com/page/research/2913.html.

89. Andrew E. Clark et al., *Relative Income, Happiness and Utility: An Explanation for the Easterlin Paradox and Other Puzzles* 19, June 2007, http://papers.ssrn.com/sol3/papers.cfm?abstract_id=998225.

90. Elizabeth Goldberg, *Midlevel Blues*, 28 AM. LAW. 98 (Aug. 2006).

91. Kristin K. Stark & Blane Prescott, *Why Associates Leave: Research Shows That Attrition Has Very Little to Do With Money*, LEGAL TIMES, May 7, 2007, at 45.

92. Jon Lindsey & Chuck Fanning, *After the Handshake*, AM. LAW. Feb. 2007, *available at* http://www.law.com/jsp/tal/PubArticleTAL.jsp?id=900005472781.

93. Drew Combs, *The Revolutionaries*, 30 AM. LAW. 102 (Aug. 2008).

94. Clark et al., *supra* note 89, at 31.

95. PETER B. SLOAN, FROM CLASSES TO COMPETENCIES, LOCKSTEP TO LEVELS (Blackwell Sanders LLP 2007).

96. Faculty Colloquium, Oct. 10, 2008, UMKC School of Law.

97. *Gender or Childcare? Study Sheds Light on Career Roadblocks*, INDIANA L., Fall 2009, at 3 (quoting Marc Galanter).

98. MALCOLM GLADWELL, THE TIPPING POINT: HOW LITTLE THINGS CAN MAKE A BIG DIFFERENCE 187 (2002).

99. *Id.* at 179.

100. *Id.* at 180.

101. *Id.* at 190.

102. *Id.* at 184. Other researchers, while agreeing with Dunbar that relationships in organizations break down once the group reaches a certain size, have come up with slightly different numbers for what that tipping point is. For example, anthropologists such as H. Russell Bernard have come up with a median estimate of 231 for the number of significant ties that a person living in the contemporary world can have. See H. Russell Bernard & Christopher McCarty, The Network Scale-Up Method: Background and Theory 15 (Feb. 2009), *available at* http://nersp.nerdc.ufl.edu/~ufruss/scale-up/scale-up%20method%20theory%20and%20history%20with%20notes.pdf.

103. Douglas McCollam, *The End of Big Law*, Wall St. J., July 30, 2009, at A15.

104. Susan Saab Fortney, *Soul for Sale: An Empirical Study of Associate Satisfaction, Firm Culture, and the Effects of Billable Hour Requirements*, 69 UMKC L. Rev. 239, 283 (2000).

105. NALP Foundation for Research and Education, Keeping the Keepers: Strategies for Associate Retention in a Time of Attrition 14 (1998).

106. John Monahan & Jeffrey Swanson, *Lawyers at Mid-Career: A 20-Year Longitudinal Study of Job and Life Satisfaction*, 5 J. Empirical Legal Stud. 1, 41 (forthcoming 2009).

107. Sonja Lyubomirsky, The How of Happiness: A New Approach to Getting the Life You Want 130 (2007).

108. Adcock, *supra* note 59, at 24.

109. David Pollard, *Men Offer Appreciation; Woman Offer Attention*, How To Save the World, http://blogs.salon.com/0002007/2006/03/26.html#a1478 (Mar. 26, 2006).

110. Elizabeth A. Amos & Bart L. Weathington, *An Analysis of the Relation Between Employee-Organization Value Congruence and Employee Attitudes*, 142 J. Psychol. 615 (2008).

111. Ezra Tom Clark, Jr., *Characteristics of Successful Law Firms*, 33 Ariz. Att'y 16 (May 1997).

112. Peter Lattman, *Does "Thank You" Help Keep Associates?*, Wall St. J., Jan. 24, 2007, at B7.

113. The American Bar Association Standing Committee on Pro Bono and Public Service, Supporting Justice: A Report on the Pro Bono Work of America's Lawyers 5 (2005), *available at* http://www.abanet.org/legalservices/probono/report.pdf.

114. Ronit Dinovitzer et al., After the J.D.: First Results of a National Study of Legal Careers 49 (2004); American Bar Association, 2009 National Lawyer Population Survey, http://www.abanet.org/market-research/2009_NATL_LAWYER_by_State.pdf.

115. Linda Campillo, *A Dog's Best Friend*, 57 Or. St. B. Bull. 27 (Jan. 1997).

116. *25 Top-Paying Companies*, Fortune, Jan. 22, 2008, *available at* http://money.cnn.com/galleries/2008/fortune/0801/gallery.bestcos_toppay.fortune/25.html.

117. Michelle Conlin, *Out of a Fishbowl*, Forbes, Dec. 16, 1996, *available at* http://www.bartlit-beck.com/articles/detail.asp?whichid=1436407222004.

118. Huang & Swedloff, *supra* note 5, at 349.

119. Juliana B. Berry, *Motivating the Masses*, Legal Mgmt., 2007, *available at* http://www.alanet.org/publications/issue/octnov07/Motivation.pdf

120. Alain de Botton, The Architecture of Happiness 72 (2006).

121. Christopher Alexander et al., A Pattern Language: Towns, Buildings, Construction (1977).

122. Jamie Friddle, *Finding Our Happy Place*, Common Ground, Jan. 2008, http://commongroundmag.com/2008/01/happyplace0801.html.

123. Alexander et al., *supra* note 121, at 747.

124. *Id.*

125. *Id.* at 890.

126. Marni Barnes, Healing Gardens: Therapeutic Benefits and Design Recommendations 59 (1999).

127. Alexander et al., *supra* note 121, at 1165.

128. Thomas Merton, The Living Bread 126 (1980).

129. Alexander et al., *supra* note 121, at 702.

130. Sheila Muto, *Law Firms Give Thought to Office-Design Issues*, Wall St. J., July 8, 2003, *available at* http://www.realestatejournal.com/propertyreport/office/20030708-muto.html.

131. *Id.*

132. *Id.*

133. F.J. Roethlisberger & William J. Dickson, Management and the Worker 14–17 (1939) (describing the Hawthorne effect).

Chapter 7

1. Daniel Gilbert, Stumbling on Happiness 224 (2006).

2. Sue M. Halpern, *Are You Happy?*, 55 N.Y. Rev. Books, Apr. 3, 2008, *available at* http://www.nybooks.com/articles/21197.

3. The reports from lawyers in this chapter come from a variety of sources. Most stories come from about two hundred lawyers around the country who responded to a set of questions about career satisfaction that we sent by e-mail. In many cases respondents to the e-mail survey were contacted by phone and asked additional questions. Several other stories in this chapter come from student papers written for a short course we offered at the UMKC Law School. Students in the course were asked to report on interviews they conducted with experienced lawyers of their own choosing. A few additional stories, as indicated by footnotes, come from other publications.

4. Diane Curtis, *Billable Hours Intersect With the Profession's Woes*, CAL. B.J., Jan. 2008, *available at* http://www.calbar.ca.gov/state/calbar/calbar_cbj. jsp?sCategoryPath=/Home/Attorney%20Resources/California%20 Bar%20Journal/January2008&sCatHtmlPath=cbj/2008–01_TH_01_Bill-able-hours.html&sCatHtmlTitle=Top%20Headlines.

5. Melanie Lasoff Levs, *Best for the Business: "Top Workplace" Firms Garner Loyalty from Clients and Employees*, 94 A.B.A. J. 34 (May 2008).

6. John Monahan & Jeffrey Swanson, *Lawyers at Mid-Career: A 20-Year Longitudinal Study of Job and Life Satisfaction*, 5 J. EMPIRICAL LEGAL STUD. 1, 26–27 (forthcoming 2009).

7. *Depression Among Lawyers: Chicken or Egg*, http://www.thedisgruntledlawyer. com/law_school_advice/ (last visited June 19, 2009).

8. Alex Williams, *The Falling-Down Professions*, N.Y. TIMES, Jan. 6, 2008, at 91.

9. James Brosnahan, *"Nothing Compares to the Electricity of an Actual Trial, and It Is Magnified When It Is a Jury Trial,"* 95 A.B.A. J. 50, 52, 63 (Mar. 2009).

10. Beyond the Underground, *What Do You Like Best About Being a Lawyer?*, Feb. 14, 2005, http://www.legalunderground.com/2005/02/what_do_you_ lik.html (posted by NBT at 1:11 P.M.).

11. *Id.* (posted at 10:31 A.M.).

12. Monahan & Swanson, *supra* note 6, at 2.

13. Edward A. Adams, *Survey: Young Lawyers Glad They're Attorneys*, 95 A.B.A. J. 65, 65 (Mar. 2009).

14. Leslie A. Gordon, *Mid-Career Malaise*, 94 A.B.A. J. 38, 39 (Sept. 2008).

15. Leslie Gordon, *Beyond the Law: JDs in All Walks of Life*, STAN. LAW. 18, 21 (Spring 2008).

16. *Id.* at 22.

17. Dahlia Lithwick, *Legal Matters: The Importance of Being Irreverent*, STAN. LAW. 28, 30, 32 (Fall 2008).

18. *See* chapter 1, text at note 36.

19. *See* Martha Neil, *Which Lawyers Love Their Jobs?*, A.B.A.J. Law News Now, Jan. 22, 2008, http://www.abajournal.com/news/lawyers_who_love_the_law.

20. *See* chapter 5, text at note 11.

Chapter 8

1. Alice Park, *Wellness: A Primer for Pessimists*, Time, Apr. 6, 2009, at 2.

2. Eric Weiner, The Geography of Bliss 182 (2008).

3. Eduardo Punset, The Happiness Trip: A Scientific Journey 53 (2007).

4. David Ian Miller, *Eric Weiner, Author of "The Geography of Bliss," on What the Happiest Places on Earth Can Teach Us*, S.F. Gate, Feb. 11, 2008, http://www.sfgate.com/cgi-bin/article.cgi?f=/g/a/2008/02/11/findrelig.DTL&type=printable, quoting Eric Weiner.

5. Eric G. Wilson, Against Happiness: In Praise of Melancholy (2008).

6. Alan Wolfe, *Hedonic Man*, New Republic, July 9, 2008, *available at* http://www.tnr.com/booksarts/story.html?id=3bc0e959–3b4e-440d-9b99–69078429b82c&p=2. Happiness has drawn other naysayers. Barbara Ehrenreich argues that positive thinking is a collective form of "mass delusion." Barbara Ehrenreich, Bright-Sided: How the Relentless Promotion of Positive Thinking Has Undermined America 13 (2009). A national ideology of excessive optimism, she says, has fueled things like the subprime mortgage crisis and the invasion of Iraq. *Id.* at 11. On the personal level, certain positive thinking techniques, such as "self-hypnosis," promote "magical thinking" and require "deliberate self-deception, including a constant effort to repress or block out unpleasant possibilities and 'negative' thoughts." *Id.* at 46–47, 5. We won't attempt to tackle generalizations about America's collective mental state (although we agree that unthinking indulgence in positive thinking certainly has its downsides), but chapter 2 is a response to her wholesale dismissal of the science of happiness research.

7. Jonah Lehrer, *Depression's Upside*, N.Y. Times Mag., Feb. 28, 2010, at 38–44.

8. Joseph Brodsky, *Listening to Boredom*, Harper's Mag., Mar. 1995, at 11.

9. *Id.*

10. *Id.*

11. Conan O'Brien, Commencement Speech to the Harvard Class of 2000, Feb. 7, 2000, http://www.february-7.com/features/conan.htm.

12. Darrin M. McMahon, *The Pursuit of Happiness in Perspective*, Apr. 8, 2007, http://www.cato-unbound.org/2007/04/08/darrin-m-mcmahon/the-pursuit-of-happiness-in-perspective/ (quoting Thomas Jefferson's letter to John Page, July 15, 1763).

13. Weiner, *supra* note 2, at 74, quoting John Stuart Mill.

14. *Id.*

15. Daniel Nettle, Happiness: The Science Behind Your Smile 87 (2005).

15. Joshua Wolf Shenk, *What Makes Us Happy?*, Atlantic, June 2009, at 36, 46.

17. Penelope Trunk, *The Connection Between a Good Job and Happiness Is Overrated*, Brazen Careerist, http://blog.penelopetrunk.com/2007/01/16/the-connection-between-a-good-job-and-happiness-is-overrated (Jan. 16, 2007).

18. *Id.*, citing professor of urban studies and creativity, Richard Florida.

19. Nettle, *supra* note 15, at 180.

20. *Id.*

21. Weiner, *supra* note 2, at 54.

Index